DRIVING CHANGE

DRIVING CHANGE

Travel in the Twenty-First Century

DAVID METZ

agenda
publishing

First published in 2019 by Agenda Publishing

Agenda Publishing Limited
The Core
Bath Lane
Newcastle Helix
Newcastle upon Tyne
NE4 5TF
www.agendapub.com

ISBN 978-1-78821-120-8 (hardcover)
ISBN 978-1-78821-121-5 (paperback)

British Library Cataloguing-in-Publication Data
A catalogue record for this book is available from the British Library

Typeset by Deer Park Productions
Printed and bound in the UK by TJ International

CONTENTS

INTRODUCTION

Travel is central to our lives. The transport system is what makes travel possible. We have become dependent on its smooth functioning. Yet operational failures on the roads and railways, and at airports, cause personal inconvenience or worse and attract much media interest. In Britain, the benefits of substantial investment in improved rail services were delayed by a botched introduction of the new timetable in May 2018, leading to mass cancellations and long waits for travellers. In December of that year, hundreds of flights were cancelled at Gatwick Airport following reports of sightings of drones near the runway. In October 2012 Hurricane Sandy hit New York City, flooding subway and road tunnels and disrupting travel for many days. The scale of disruption is greatest when transport systems are operating at close to maximum capacity.

Even when systems are running smoothly, we experience crowding and congestion, the consequence of increasing numbers of us wanting to access the destinations that modern means of travel make possible. So we invest in the transport system to increase the capacity of roads, railways and airports; but the extra capacity seems to fill pretty quickly as more of us take advantage of the additions, and crowding and congestion reappear.

There is much wishful thinking about improvements from transport infrastructure investments. Politicians are keen to promote new roads and railways that they hope will benefit the voters by speeding travel and boosting the economy. Transport professionals naturally wish to provide better services for their users. Yet the adverse impacts of transport seem to persist – road vehicles damage health from both air pollution and crashes, while road traffic congestion is a ubiquitous and seemingly insoluble problem.

Until the early twenty-first century, investment in the transport system was very largely more of the same. But now we have new technologies that promise an improved travel experience – electric vehicles, digital navigation devices to help us find our way, digital platforms to match supply of mobility to our demand and autonomous vehicles that could transform the driving experience. The likely impact of these new technologies is the main theme of this book.

We want these innovative technologies to solve the problems that the traditional transport technologies have proved unable to fix. Naturally, there is much enthusiasm on the part of the innovators that their novel devices and business models are the answer. Wishful thinking is inevitable. My task is to scrutinize the evidence and assess likely impacts, both positive and negative.

To predict the contribution of new technologies, we need a clear understanding of how the very complex transport system works. The components are people, vehicles and infrastructure. The organizations comprise both public authorities and private companies. There are a number of modes of travel that we may use. For surface transport we can choose walking, cycling, bus, taxi, train, private car. The choices we make depend on distance travelled, cost, time and comfort. The introduction of an innovative service can have wide repercussions.

The transport system we have at present is the result of huge past investment in infrastructure assets that have very long lives. Indeed, most are subject to maintenance and renewal so that they have indefinite lives. While many parts of the consumer economy are subject to quite rapid turnover, so that the uptake of useful innovations can be quite quick, this is far less true for the main elements of the transport sector. To understand the prospects for the future, it is necessary to look back to see how we have reached where we are now.

The development of the modern transport system over the nineteenth and twentieth centuries has transformed our lives. If you lived in a village or town 200 years ago, your opportunities were limited to places you could reach on foot within the time that could be spared for travel. Modern transport in all its forms has allowed us to travel faster, allowing us much more choice of jobs, homes, shops, schools and the other services we regularly need, as well as longer business trips that make possible the global economy and leisure trips that enrich our lives. Our horizons stretch much farther than did those of our great-grandparents.

Yet I will present evidence that we have recently reached the end of an era of ever more growth of travel, in Britain and the developed countries generally. This growth was made possible by harnessing the energy of fossil fuels: first coal on the railways in the nineteenth century, then oil to power the mass-produced automobile of the twentieth century. But now we have run out of ways of travelling faster using established mechanical and civil engineering technologies, so that daily travel per person has stabilized. The total amount of travel now is driven by population growth and by decisions on where new homes are built.

An important question that I will discuss is how the new technologies may influence our travel behaviour. Will there be a further transformational change, with impact on the scale of that of the railway or the motorcar? Or can we expect only incremental improvement to the existing system? This book attempts to answer this question.

My perspective is as an analyst rather than an advocate. There are many who promote this or that form of transport, or argue against some particular means of mobility, usually the car. There are inventors and innovators who seek finance from investors to recruit good engineers and technologists to develop their inventions. And there are politicians who enthuse about particular investments that they hope will relieve bottlenecks and spread wealth.

To avoid wasting money on schemes with outcomes that disappoint, unbiased analysis is important, yet difficult to achieve. It is not straightforward to understand why the transport system has developed in the way it has. It is particularly difficult to anticipate the most important future determinants – behavioural, demographic, technological and political – all of which operate in a heavily regulated market involving both private and public providers. It is also necessary to attempt to cut through the complexity, to work out which factors are of first importance and which are secondary. Yet without attempting such analysis, we are likely to achieve outcomes that fall short of what may be possible and what we would prefer.

This book aims to help understand the working of the travel and transport system of developed economies, and to provide a basis for decisions about future developments. While each country's system has unique features reflecting the historic path taken – the past policy choices and investments previously made – my aim is to tease out the features common to the developed economies generally, and also to see if developing countries may be able to avoid some of the shortcomings of high-car-ownership societies. I outline, in Part I, the system we have inherited, the travel behaviour that has resulted and how this is changing. Part II deals with the impact of new technologies.

My own experience is relevant, in that I came into the transport sector in mid-career, without a prior education in the established principles or orthodox practices of that sector. My earlier education and employment was as a research scientist in biomedicine. Subsequently, I joined the British civil service for policy work in the energy sector. My next move took me to the Department for Transport as its Chief Scientist, responsible for oversight of the research programme. I arrived with an open mind, ready to be receptive to established knowledge. What I found was an approach to the economics of the transport system that seemed inconsistent with what was experienced by users, and which seemed misleading when informing investment decisions. My subsequent experience confirmed that initial judgement, as will become apparent in the following chapters.

After five years at the UK Department for Transport and 20 years in the civil service, I left to pursue my career in a variety of areas, including ageing, health and financial services, and also to pursue travel and transport issues from an academic base, as an honorary professor at the long-established Centre for

Transport Studies at University College London. I am grateful to colleagues there for hospitality, which has allowed me to develop my thinking, publishing in the peer-reviewed journals (a salutary check on quality) as well as in articles and books for a wider readership. This present book extends my analysis to the new transport technologies, attempting to chart the way forwards for both policymakers and investors.

It is commonplace nowadays for authors of new books to acknowledge the extensive support and encouragement they have received, often over much of their careers, from mentors, colleagues, friends and families. In my case, the omission of such a list reflects not a lack of grace, but rather because I have followed a rather independent path, outside the professional mainstream. I have nevertheless gained from participation in a number of valuable British organizations, including the Transport Planning Society, the Transport Economists' Group and the Transport Statistics Users' Group. I have also benefited from the critiques of the unsung anonymous peer reviewers that guard the gateway to journal publication. Specific acknowledgements and thanks to Kit Mitchell for kindly providing analysis of international data, to Diane Coyle for commenting on one chapter and to Alison Howson for constructive editing.

The manuscript of this book was completed early in 2019. Somewhat to my surprise, I have not found it necessary to mention the political topic of the day – Brexit. This is because most of the matters I discuss are either technologies that are potentially global in impact, or policies that are local to cities and regions. The European Union is an important source of initiatives for motor vehicle performance, to which British manufacturers will continue to have regard, but standards need to be set on at least a continent-wide basis, since vehicles travel across national frontiers.

PART I
TRANSPORT LEGACY

Our modern transport system has developed over the past 200 years. Enormous investment in infrastructure has changed the landscape, both the roads and railways themselves, and the growth of towns and cities they made possible. All these structures have long lives, and most of the corridors are effectively permanent. The transport system and the travel it permits have shaped our lives and enlarged our horizons.

Yet potentially substantial changes are underway in why and how we travel. These began at the end of the twentieth century and are destined to continue. We are seeing important developments in attitudes towards the car; in size, age and location of populations; and in new technologies, both transport and wider digital. So the future of travel and transport could be very different from the past.

I start Part 1 with a review of the transport system as it is at present and the travel behaviour that has resulted from it. I then discuss how the present situation has developed. The focus of the analysis will be on travel and transport in Britain, both because its travel and transport statistics are world-leading in scope and extent, and because interpretation of such data requires a deep understanding of the societal context, which is most readily gained by residence. The book will also address what is happening in other high-income countries, particularly in Europe and North America, and will note some developments elsewhere, mainly in China. While there are significant differences between countries as regards demography and governance, there are many underlying similarities in respect of travel behaviour and the influence of new technologies.

1

A SYSTEM UNDER STRESS

Travel is central to our lives: for our daily commute, getting children to school, shopping trips, social activities, holidays and the rest. For individuals, how we travel changes through our lives, becoming more varied as we reach adulthood, when we may learn to drive and as incomes increase. Decisions about where we live and work are important for how we travel. To understand how the aggregation of decisions by individuals leads to the observed behaviour of populations, our main sources are surveys of travel behaviour, of which the most important are those carried out by national governments.

The British Department for Transport first commissioned a National Travel Survey (NTS) in 1965. The survey became a regular event starting in the early 1970s, and is now carried out annually, involving 16,000 representative individuals (a different sample each year) completing travel diaries with full details of their movements for seven days. These have provided time series of travel data spanning 45 years in considerable detail. The NTS covers all modes of travel except international air, so in effect it largely records the pattern of our daily travel, the trips that take us away from home each day.

The United States Department of Transportation carries out its National Household Travel Survey less frequently. This started in 1969 and takes place at intervals of five to eight years, most recently in 2017 when 130,000 households participated, individuals logging travel for one day of the week only. Other countries that conduct national surveys include Germany, the Netherlands, Sweden, Denmark, New Zealand and South Africa. Such surveys allow us to understand how the transport system is used, as well as how uses change over time – the topic of the next chapter.

The broad picture we find for Britain is that in 2017 (the latest available data), on average people made 975 journeys a year, travelling 6,580 miles, spending 377 hours a year on the move, which is close to an hour a day.[1] These are averages for the whole population, so we expect quite wide variations to be found among individuals. Some people rarely leave home, for instance due to disability, while others commute heroic distances. Nevertheless, the average is useful for understanding the big picture, particularly because it has changed little over the past 20 years, as I will explain in the next chapter, so that the British population now has a fairly stable and settled pattern of travel.

In developed countries, the car is the dominant mode of transport, allowing convenient door-to-door travel where road space permits. In Britain in 2017, 61 per cent of all trips were made by car, accounting for 78 per cent of distance travelled (driver and passenger), with 76 per cent of households owning at least one car. Walking accounted for 26 per cent of trips (but only 3 per cent of distance); bus transport for 6 per cent of trips (5 per cent of distance); rail travel for 2 per cent of trips (8 per cent of distance); and cycling for 2 per cent of trips and 1 per cent of distance. These are national averages.

Other developed countries have different patterns of travel, reflecting different histories and geographies. The average distance travelled by car in Britain, France, Germany and Italy is similar at about 11,000 km a year, while for the US it is about 19,000 km, Canada 15,000 km and Japan 5,500 km.[2] Another big difference is the popularity of cycling, notably in the Netherlands, where more than a quarter of all trips are by bicycle,[3] and in Denmark where cycling accounts for 17 per cent of all trips.[4] Rail travel also varies widely between countries: within the European Union average rail usage exceeds 1,000 passenger-km per inhabitant in Germany, France, Austria, Sweden and Britain (and in Switzerland is more than twice that), whereas in other countries it is half that or less.[5]

The main purposes of travel in Britain are for shopping (19 per cent of all trips), followed by commuting (15 per cent) and education (including escorting children to school, 12 per cent). Travel on business accounts for only 3 per cent of trips, although 8 per cent of distance.[6] Trip lengths vary with purpose, commuting trips being longest (31 minutes on average) and escorting children to school the shortest (14 minutes).

The pattern of travel varies within countries. In dense urban areas, where road space is limited and traffic congestion is prevalent, public transport, walking and cycling are important alternatives for daily travel; so in London the car is responsible for a declining share of travel, in 2016 for only 36 per cent of trips, and there has been a corresponding growth in rail travel, which offers fast and reliable journeys compared with the car on congested roads.[7]

Densely populated towns and cities mean that large numbers of people want to travel at the same time, dictated in part by social norms for working and school hours. This puts the transport system under stress and generates a number of serious problems that we would like to tackle:

- carbon emissions from transport that contribute to climate change;
- air pollution and the damage to health this causes;
- deaths and injuries from road traffic crashes;

- road traffic congestion, and crowding on railways and at airports;
- severance of communities.

Much effort, both policy and practice, is devoted to mitigating these undesirable consequences of an era of mass mobility. I will discuss each of these in turn.

Climate change

The emissions from the internal combustion engine burning oil consists mainly of carbon dioxide, a greenhouse gas that contributes to climate change, together with the oxides of nitrogen (NO_x for short) and fine particulates (tiny particles of diameter a fraction that of a human hair), both of which are of concern on account of damage to health.

Transport is responsible for about 25 per cent of all man-made greenhouse gas emissions globally. In Britain, transport is responsible for 28 per cent, with cars contributing over half of this.[8] In the past transport has been seen as the most difficult sector in which to achieve the reductions needed to meet overall targets aimed at reducing global warming. Improved energy efficiency and switching to electricity from non-fossil fuel sources was thought to be easier for buildings and industry.

The most recent international targets for climate change were set out in the 2015 Paris Agreement: to hold the global temperature rise this century well below 2°C above pre-industrial levels and to pursue efforts to limit the temperature increase even further to 1.5°C.[9] This was the latest stage in a process that started with the 1992 United Nations Framework Convention on Climate Change. As yet, the voluntary national targets for reducing carbon emissions fall well short of what is required.

The main approach adopted by governments has been to set regulatory targets for the vehicle manufacturers to improve fuel economy and so reduce carbon emissions. This encouraged a switch from petrol to more efficient diesel engines, which had the unintended consequence of increasing NO_x emissions (see below). The most recent and most important response of the vehicle manufacturers is the development of electric vehicles, as I will discuss in Chapter 3. Switching to electric vehicles will eliminate the tailpipe emissions of internal combustion engines, both carbon and harmful pollutants.

Air pollution

Concerns about vehicle emissions first made an impact on public policy half a century ago in Los Angeles, prompted by the smog arising from ozone in exhaust fumes. Regulations led to the introduction of the catalytic converter, which effectively dealt with the ozone problem. It was also necessary to remove lead from petrol, a toxic material that had been included to improve engine performance but which poisoned the catalyst and was itself detrimental to health.

The success of the catalytic converter, as well as of technological innovations in other sectors that reduced environmental damage, encouraged regulatory authorities to persist with this approach in the transport sector. The general experience has been that the industry objects to proposed new regulations on grounds of technical feasibility and expense, as well as competitiveness and employment concerns, but in the event has been able to comply at acceptable cost. However, the limits of this approach have recently become evident in the case of emissions from small diesel engines.

Regulation of noxious vehicle emissions are driven by recommendations arising from assessments of health effects made under the auspices of the World Health Organization (WHO).[10] The European Union has adopted WHO recommendations as the basis for legal limits to the concentration in the atmosphere of NO_x and particulates. In practice, such limits have been exceeded in many cities in Europe, and the authorities, both city and national, are required to take action to reduce emissions or face legal action and possibly fines. The European Commission has referred six member states, including the UK, to the EU Court for failures to keep below limit levels for NO_x and particulates.[11]

The problem of air quality from transport sources has been exacerbated by the difficulty that many of the vehicle manufacturers have had in designing small diesel engines that meet regulatory requirements for NO_x emissions (bigger engines, as used in larger cars, buses and trucks, incorporate a device for injecting a chemical into the exhaust that converts NO_x to harmless nitrogen and water). A general problem has been that such engines were designed to comply with the narrow range of requirements of laboratory testing of emissions, but could far exceed the required limits when driven on the road under a wide range of conditions of engine power, temperature, speed, payload and rate of acceleration (Ligterink 2017).

While permitted emissions were reduced by 85 per cent between 2000 and 2014, on-road emissions decreased by only about 40 per cent. A particularly deplorable problem was cheating by Volkswagen, which programmed its vehicles to activate the emissions controls only under laboratory testing, and which emitted up to 40 times more NO_x on the road.[12] One consequence is that the regulatory authorities are now much more focused on real-world driving outcomes, where emissions for a range of vehicle types have been found to be over six times higher than under laboratory conditions, with substantial variations between car models.[13]

As a result of these shortcomings on the part of the manufacturers, city authorities need to introduce other measures to limit transport emissions, focusing on reducing the contribution from older diesel engines. These include the possibility of charging polluting vehicles to enter city centres, in order to encourage replacement by cleaner types.[14] London has introduced the T-charge (T for "toxicity"), which requires older vehicles driven in the central area to comply with minimum emission standards or pay an additional daily charge (effectively an addition to the congestion charge, see below). The T-charge will be replaced by an Ultra Low Emissions Zone that will apply from 2021 to much of London.[15] Such measures are stopgaps, aimed at reducing pollutant concentrations to below legal limits until the impact of electric vehicles is felt.

One possible approach to reducing emissions from older diesel vehicles, advocated by many, is a government-funded scrappage scheme, in the form of a cash incentive to remove such vehicles from the road. The challenge is targeting to get the best value for tax payers' money, since the most polluting vehicles are older and tend to be less used than newer vehicles. Moreover, there is limited benefit in scrapping vehicles used mainly in rural areas. One possible approach would be to take advantage of the T-charge and similar urban emission charging schemes, since the vehicles that pay the highest cumulative charges are those that make the largest contributions to poor air quality. A scrappage scheme could then take the form of a cash-back offer: for instance, £X00 refunded for every £1,000 paid in charges, if the polluting vehicle is scrapped.

Electric vehicles are the ultimate solution to the problem of poor air quality from road transport. Their quiet and smooth operation will also reduce noise pollution. Indeed, their noise reduction at low speeds is such that both the EU and US authorities have regulated a minimum noise level to alert pedestrians to their presence. However, at higher speeds tyre noise will persist. Tyre technology has in the past focused on improving adhesion to the road surface to improve safety, reducing rolling resistance to improve fuel economy and reducing wear to lessen replacement costs. For the future, we will seek noise abatement as well as further reduction in tyre wear to reduce the generation of particulates.

Electric vehicles will eliminate tailpipe emissions and reduce noise. But they will still take up road space, which leaves unchanged the environmental impact of streams of traffic, experienced as congestion and in the way that communities are divided by busy roads. And electric vehicles can be involved in crashes that result in injury and death.

Health impacts of vehicle emissions

Noxious emissions from transport are of particular concern on account of damage to health. NO_x and particulates are risk factors for a number of diseases, including cardiovascular disorders such as heart attacks and stroke, and respiratory conditions such as asthma and chronic obstructive pulmonary disease.

A much-quoted estimate is that some 40,000 deaths a year in Britain could be attributed to the two pollutants, through making existing illnesses worse and bringing forwards deaths by an average of seven months each (Holgate & Stokes-Lampard 2017).

This estimate was based on the advice of the official Committee on the Medical Effects of Air Pollutants. Recently, this Committee has reassessed the relationship between NO_x concentration and mortality risk, which has led to the conclusion that the health damage attributed to NO_x should be reduced by 60–80 per cent.[16] There is clearly much uncertainty about the magnitude of such effects, not least on account of the many factors other than air pollutants that contribute to illness and cause death.

The context is that life expectancy nearly everywhere has been increasing markedly in the decades of the late twentieth century and early twenty-first. In the 20 years between 1991 and 2011, life expectancy at birth for women in Britain grew by almost four years and for men by more than five years. In contrast, since 2011 this long-term improvement has tailed off, both in Britain and in other European countries, for reasons that are not yet clear.[17] Some commentators believe that cuts in health and social care expenditure have been causal. However, NO_x concentrations have been falling over this period, while particulate levels have been fairly static,[18] which does not suggest that air pollution is likely to be a cause of the slowdown in improvements in life expectancy. Increasing life expectancy has been due to better prevention and treatment of cardiovascular disease, better understanding of lifestyles conducive to longevity, as well as to cleaning up the environment. So eliminating transport emissions through electrification should help further extend life expectancy.

As well as concerns about the impact of transport air pollution on overall mortality, there is anxiety about potentially vulnerable population groups and communities, particularly children, for which evidence is accumulating from epidemiological studies. A large study of the possible relationship between air pollution in London and birth weight of newborn children found that long-term exposure during pregnancy to fine particulates was associated with an increased risk of low birth weight of 3 per cent for women exposed to more than the lowest levels (Smith *et al.* 2017). Another such study investigated the impact of average exposure of school children in inner London to NO_x, finding a loss of some 5 per cent of lung capacity, although this was not thought to be clinically significant in a healthy population (Mudway *et al.* 2018).

While the best evidence comes from such large population studies, individual cases attract attention, as, for instance, that of a nine-year-old girl living near a road pollution hotspot in London who suffered a fatal asthma attack, and whose past attacks coincided with spikes in pollutant levels near her home.[19]

Politicians and campaigners voice much concern about urban air quality in Britain, motivated in part by pollutant levels that exceed legal limits that in turn are based on health standards. While in the long term electric vehicles should largely eliminate transport-related pollutants, in the near term progress is not easy. Even the politically ambitious London Ultra Low Emissions Zone has been estimated to have only a small impact on hospital admissions associated with respiratory and cardiovascular diseases – 50 to 100 fewer a year.[20]

Other European countries are taking action to limit older diesel engines in urban areas. Municipalities in the Greater Paris region have agreed to ban diesel-fuelled cars built before 2000.[21] In Germany, Hamburg and Berlin are to ban older diesel vehicles on some streets, with other cities likely to follow.[22]

Yet the appetite of the public for stronger measures seems limited, given the generally low visibility of atmospheric pollution in the cities of developed countries – low in relation to both the situation in cities where coal is still widely used, such as those in China and India, and low in relation to what older people remember of past air pollution, whether the historic smogs of Los Angeles before catalytic converters or those in London before general use of natural gas for domestic heating. It is also relevant that road transport is only one of many sources of air pollution, responsible for 12 per cent of particulates and 34 per cent of NO_x, although contributions to roadside concentrations are greater.[23]

Lastly, on the topic of health impacts associated with vehicles, the prospect of eliminating particulate emissions resulting from combustion has focused attention on other sources of very small particles from the transport system – from the wear of brakes, tyres and road surfaces, which already account for half of the emissions from transport.[24] These sources have until recently been neglected and it is therefore likely that there is scope for technological development that would reduce released particulate matter, as well as prolonging the life of brakes, tyres and road surfaces. Electric vehicles employ regenerative braking, recovering kinetic energy to recharge the battery, which may largely reduce the need for friction braking and the particulates that are generated.[25]

Casualties from crashes

Another aspect of road transport where the appetite of the public for strong measures seems limited is the very direct impact on health and wellbeing when there are casualties resulting from crashes and collisions. Worldwide, the total number of road traffic deaths has plateaued at 1.25 million per year, with the highest road traffic fatality rates in low-income countries.[26]

Britain has a relatively good record, with 1,800 fatalities in 2016, down from 3,180 ten years before, although improvements have bottomed out. With fewer than 30 deaths annually per million inhabitants, Britain is one of the best-performing European countries. The US has over 100 deaths per million inhabitants, although the average distance driven per inhabitant is 13,500 miles a year, compared with about 5,000 miles in Britain. As well as deaths, some 24,000 people in Britain are seriously injured each year and 150,000 slightly injured.[27]

Public attitudes to deaths and injuries arising from road traffic are paradoxical. You might have supposed that 1,800 deaths a year would generate strong public demand for further reductions, similar to the widespread concern to reduce health harms from vehicle emissions, not least because those dying in crashes are real people who can be at any point in their life course, unlike the statistical deaths from vehicle emissions that are estimated from epidemiological data and very largely arise towards the end of life when general health is failing. Certainly, road safety professionals and some politicians are keen to improve outcomes. The new Transport Strategy of the London Mayor endorses "Vision Zero" – an international movement that aims for no one to be killed or seriously injured on the road system – in London by 2041.[28] Yet there is no comparable national objective in Britain, nor any evident public demand for this.

One reason for lack of public pressure for improvements is that we are habituated to a low level of crashes – low in relation to the total distance driven and to the frequency with which we observe them. We are comfortable with the motorcar: if this were a new innovation with the present fatality rate, it would surely be banned. We are also more concerned when larger numbers are killed in a single incident, or when we have handed responsibility for our safety to others, as on the railway or air travel. Such passing of responsibility is a feature of autonomous vehicles, for which safety performance will be crucial for public acceptability, as I will discuss in Chapter 6.

It may also be relevant that the death rate on the roads is relatively low in relation to other causes of mortality. On the one hand, in Britain, road crashes are responsible for only 0.3 per cent of all fatalities, in the US for 1.3 per cent, with most other high-income countries falling in between. On the other hand, road fatalities correspond to 5 per cent of deaths from stroke in Britain and 26 per cent in the US (Sivak & Schoettle 2017).

In short, although the public seems relatively relaxed about the current scale of deaths and injuries arising from road traffic crashes, there is plenty of scope for improvement through a combination of technological and policy measures. Many hope that autonomous vehicles will be safer than cars and trucks with human drivers.

Another well-recognized health impact of the car used for door-to-door travel is lack of physical exercise as a natural part of the travel experience. In 2016 26 per cent of adults in Britain were obese, compared with 15 per cent in 1993.

Countries vary widely, with 38 per cent obese in the US but only 4 per cent in Japan.[29] Obesity is caused by eating too much and moving too little. Making available alternatives to travel by car can help encourage regular exercise as part of the daily routine. So it is worthwhile for governments to improve the facilities for walking and cycling and invest in public transport, both to promote exercise and reduce vehicle emissions. This approach is central to the new transport strategy of the Mayor of London, which aims to increase walking, cycling and public transport to account for 80 per cent of all trips by 2041, driven by concerns to improve the health of Londoners.[30]

Congestion

Most road users would say that traffic congestion is the main problem of the transport system. It is a common and frustrating experience, which does not seem to improve over time. Our journeys are slower than they could be and we cannot rely on arriving when we plan. Trips take longer, we experience more stops and starts, more queuing at junctions and bottlenecks and more time spent stationary. Some journeys are predictably congested, particularly to and from work, while on others we experience erratic delays. All of which is very irritating.

Yet outside towns and cities the problem should not be overstated. When averaged across travel on England's strategic road network (motorways and other major routes), delays amount to just 9 seconds per mile yielding an average speed of 60 mph, which has been stable in recent years.[31]

A number of estimates have been made of the cost of urban congestion, based on the value of time lost. For instance, 13 per cent of total driving time in London has been estimated to be in congested traffic, with a total cost of some £9 billion a year, reflecting time wasted and extra fuel costs. For Los Angeles, the annual cost is put at $19 billion and, for New York, $34 billion.[32] Such estimates suggest a potential big economic benefit from measures to reduce congestion.

How much importance should we attach to these supposed costs of congestion? Not too much, according to Joe Cortright, a long-time commentator on US cities. He has estimated (tongue in cheek) the costs of waiting in line at coffee shops, which he puts at $4 billion a year for US consumers, who incur more delays per person than for traffic congestion.[33]

In the second half of the twentieth century, growth of car ownership prompted extensive road construction programmes in the developed economies generally. New urban motorways and freeways in many cities accommodated traffic growth, but without relieving congestion on account of the new trips made possible by the increased road capacity and car ownership. However, such high-capacity roads proved to be detrimental to the urban environment, obstructing social and business interactions between people, severing communities and generating air pollution, as well as incurring substantial construction costs. Building new roads in existing urban areas is therefore now far less common in developed economies. To tackle congestion, attention instead focuses on measures involving demand management: influencing the level of car use.

Parking control

Managing parking capacity has been used quite successfully in some medium-sized and larger cities, given the need to be able to park at both ends if a car trip is to be made. Steve Melia has reviewed the evidence and concluded that parking limitations are the most direct and probably the most effective way to reduce car ownership. He instances his own university (University of West of England in Bristol), which does not allow students living on campus to park there; one in five of these kept a car somewhere else in the area compared to three-quarters of students living off campus who had a car of their own (Melia 2015). However, restricting parking can be unpopular, and charges from permitted parking are an important source of revenue for local government. Local authorities in England had a total income from parking in 2017–18 of no less than £1.66 billion. Expenditure on administering the charges was £793 million, leaving a surplus of £867 million, which by law must be used for transport projects.[34]

Parking provision for new developments in London has long been limited, and the Mayor's transport strategy is to further restrict this to reduce car dependency, consistent with the aim to increase walking, cycling and public transport use noted above. Nevertheless, long-established provision of low-cost on-street parking for residents of London inhibits progress in the desired direction. Likewise, the practice of providing extensive free parking in US cities contributes to the attractions of car use in preference to bus transit, the more efficient use of road space (Shoup 2018).[35]

Road-user charging

The approach to tackling congestion most attractive to economists is road-user charging, also known as road pricing or congestion charging. This has been implemented in a few cities, the largest being London, Stockholm and Singapore.[36]

The essence of the argument for congestion charging is that since journey times increase with traffic volumes, an additional car on the road slows down all other cars, increasing time costs for all the occupants. The decision to travel made by the occupants of an additional car is based on their own travel costs, time and money (their private or internal costs). They ignore any increase in travel costs for all other car users (the external costs). It is economically inefficient when private costs are below the full social cost of the decision to travel. When decisions are made on the basis of underestimated costs, too much of a good (in this case, travel) will be consumed. A congestion charge is intended to confront users with costs imposed on other users, so as to align private costs with social costs. The charge would suppress some part of demand, reducing congestion and generating net revenues.

Congestion charging was implemented in a zone in Central London in February 2003. The initial charge of £5 per day was raised to £8 in July 2005, to £10 in January 2011 and, in June 2014 to the current charge of £11.50 per day for driving a vehicle within the designated zone between 07.00 and 18.00 hours, Monday to Friday. A range of discounts and exemptions are available for certain groups and in respect of certain vehicles, including exemptions for taxis, private hire vehicles and low carbon emission vehicles, and a 90 per cent discount for residents of the charging zone. Analysis of camera data indicated that in the charging zone around half of cars pay the full charge, some 30–40 per cent are exempt and around 10 per cent receive residents' discounts.

The impact of the congestion charge was monitored in detail for the first five years by Transport for London (TfL), the public body responsible for the transport system. The initial introduction of charges in 2003 led to a reduction of car traffic entering and leaving the zone of 33 per cent, following which entering/leaving traffic of all kinds remained broadly stable. The increase in the charge in 2005 had virtually no further impact on traffic levels, which suggests that those car users more sensitive to price had largely been deterred by the initial £5 charge and that the remaining car users were less sensitive to additional charges.

Congestion is measured by the "excess travel rate" in minutes per kilometre (min/km, the inverse of speed), subtracting travel rates in the early hours of the morning from those during charging hours, hence a measure of the delays due to congestion. Immediately prior to the introduction of charging, the mean excess travel rate was 2.3 min/km. With charging in place there was an initial 30 per cent reduction to 1.6 min/km. However, delays steadily increased in subsequent years, returning to 2.3 min/km by 2007, as shown in Figure 1.1. Thereafter, average traffic speeds in London were stable to 2012, although then declined somewhat, likely to be attributable to greater temporary disruption to the road network.[37]

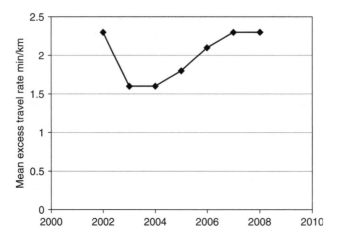

Figure 1.1 Mean excess travel time
Source: Metz (2018a).

So although the introduction of congestion charging led to a significant and sustained reduction in traffic entering the zone, the initial impact on congestion delays proved short-lived. Transport for London attributed this to increased allocation of road space for walking and cycling; improvements to public transport, urban realm and road safety; reduction in effective capacity of the road network due to street works and major building works; and changed timings of traffic signals for reasons of traffic management and pedestrian safety.

London congestion charging has been successful in many respects: its implementation was the result of skilful political leadership; there is good public acceptability, with no pressure to withdraw or reduce the charge; and the technology, which uses number plate recognition cameras to enforce compliance, has proved reliable. Moreover, there is a useful net financial surplus used to support public transport provision. However, the main purpose of the London congestion charging zone was to reduce congestion and journey times, and in this respect it has not succeeded.

The evidence available from Stockholm is consistent with a similar conclusion. The charging system involves a cordon around the inner city, with a toll charged for crossing in each direction according to time of day. Traffic across the cordon was reduced by about 20 per cent, a reduction that has remained stable over time. Introduction of the charging scheme was the result of effective political leadership; the technology based on number plate recognition has worked well; and useful revenues have been generated. But the impact on traffic congestion in the medium term has not been monitored and hence the long-term success of the scheme in reducing congestion delays is unproven.

In contrast, the experience of Singapore has been more favourable. The city-state introduced a congestion charge based on a paper licence in 1975, which was replaced in 1998 with electronic road pricing, utilizing a payment card inserted into an on-board unit that interacts with an exterior system of radio beacons mounted on gantries. The scheme covers a central restricted zone plus lower charges on four further zones. The aim is for vehicles to travel at a consistent speed in the restricted zone – between 20 and 30 km/hour on urban roads and between 45 and 65 km/hour on expressways. Accordingly, charges are reassessed quarterly by measuring average speeds: if speeds fall below a threshold, charges are increased to reduce the volume of traffic, whereas if speeds are above the threshold, charges are reduced. Charges also vary by vehicle class, time of day and location. Traffic is quite sensitive to price even though the charges are relatively low.

Traffic volumes in the central business district were reduced by about 10–15 per cent following the introduction of electronic road pricing. Data on traffic speeds published by the Singapore Land Transport Authority show that average speeds at peak hours on expressways have been consistently in excess of 60 km/hour in recent years, and for central arterial roads around 28 km/hour, in line with the objectives.

An important feature of Singapore, an urban city-state, is that private car ownership is limited through a licence bidding system aimed at restraining growth of the car stock to match planned increase in available road space. Vehicles are consequently expensive to purchase: a Certificate of Entitlement to own a car for ten years may cost S$80,000 (about £40,000), and car ownership is only about 100 cars per 1,000 population, compared, for instance, to 450 cars per 1,000 for the UK population and similar or higher figures for developed countries generally. The share of journeys by car in Singapore is declining, 33 per cent of all trips in 2012 reducing to 27 per cent in 2016.

In effect, road-user charging in Singapore comprises two elements: a high fixed charge for access to the network; and a low variable charge reflecting the use made as a function of congestion. This experience suggests that much higher charges would be needed in London, Stockholm and other prosperous cities to deter sufficient numbers of car drivers to relieve congestion significantly and sustainably.

Some cities in China, including Beijing, Shanghai and Guangzhou, have also limited car ownership by issuing annual quotas of new licence plates by lottery or auction, with vehicles with non-local plates banned for much of the day. In Shanghai, the recent price of a winning bid was ¥88,000 (£10,000).[38]

Other approaches to decongestion

Apart from congestion charging and parking management, a variety of other approaches are advocated to tackle road traffic congestion – for instance, encouraging people to walk, cycle or use the bus, rather than take their car, or to consolidate urban freight deliveries into a smaller number of vehicles for the "last mile". However, I would expect that drivers who preferred their car to the alternatives, but had been previously deterred by prospective delays, would take advantage of the road space that might be freed up by such interventions, negating the supposed congestion benefits. Evidence comes from a substantial and well-monitored British programme of sustainable transport initiatives costing about £1 billion. This included 12 large projects aimed at reducing car use, by introducing, for example, bus and cycle lanes along a major urban road corridor and by providing personalized advice on planning travel to work. On average car traffic per person fell by 2.6 per cent, compared with 0.3 per cent in comparator locations, a significant decrease. However, traffic speeds during the rush hour were slightly worse for the project group than for the comparators.[39]

Road traffic congestion arises from an excess of demand for road use that exceeds the available supply of road space in circumstances where that supply cannot be increased without damaging the environment. This excess of demand occurs because the roads are generally open to all users with suitable vehicles who are willing to pay the costs incurred. Congestion is difficult to mitigate because road space made available by some road users being deterred by charges, or deciding to use other modes, is taken up by others previously put off taking their cars by the prospect of delays.

For the same reason, congestion is largely self-regulating, in that if traffic volumes increase, delays increase and more potential car users are deterred from making trips in congested traffic. They may choose a different time of day, or a different mode of travel where available, or a different destination when there are options (shopping, for instance), or not to travel at all (working at home, for example). Gridlock is not the norm in well-managed cities with alternative modes of travel; rather, when it occurs it is generally the result of some unanticipated operational failure. I will consider further how we might tackle road traffic congestion in subsequent chapters, in the light of the development of new technologies.

Although congestion is difficult to mitigate, it is possible to change the volume and composition of traffic on a road network. Adding capacity, by widening existing roads or constructing new routes, increases the volume of traffic by initially reducing delays and so attracting previously suppressed trips. Conversely, removing road capacity available to cars results in less traffic. A study of 50 cases where road capacity had been reduced concluded that it is possible to reallocate road space to other modes or uses without prolonged gridlock or traffic chaos occurring because traffic effectively disappears (Cairns, Hass-Klau & Goodwin 1998).

In contrast to roads, rail and air travel are essentially closed systems: you can only operate with permission of the network controller, who ensures that capacity is available for those having permission. So for well-managed systems under normal operating conditions, traffic congestion is not a problem. Under abnormal conditions (of poor weather, for instance) congestion can arise, leading to delays. If maximum capacity is routinely used, resilience is reduced and relatively minor operational abnormalities can cause delays, as is found with commuter rail routes and airports operating at full capacity.

When buses are segregated from general traffic, they become a closed system, with speed and reliability nearer to urban rail than conventional buses. This is the principle of Bus Rapid Transit, which I will consider in Chapter 7. Even partial segregation using conventional bus lanes helps increase the attraction of buses at the expense of cars, which is justifiable by the far greater carrying capacity for a given amount of road space. Park and ride schemes allow car users to leave their vehicles on the edge of the city and take a bus or train into the centre where parking space may be very limited, as in historic cities like Oxford, Cambridge and York. Bus-based schemes can result in greater distances travelled by car from people driving for the first part of their journey, rather than taking a bus all the way, but there can still be an economic benefit if traffic in the city centre is reduced by providing an alternative to the car (Mills & White 2018).

While traffic congestion is not inherent to rail operations, crowding is common on many routes at times of peak demand, the consequence of the traditional practice of allowing standing passengers. Overcrowding is being tackled by means of longer trains and platforms where practicable, and by digital signalling technology that allows more frequent services on the existing track, as I will discuss in Chapter 7.

Crowding does not arise on aircraft, where fares are generally adjusted to match demand with supply, although the experience of excess numbers is often felt while waiting in line at airports. Runway capacity constraints can limit the services offered, which tends to limit competition between the airlines and results in higher fares. The scope for adding new capacity may be constrained by cost and environmental impact. A long-running debate about the case for building a third runway at London's Heathrow Airport has led to political agreement to go ahead, although legal challenges are expected based on environmental concerns, as well as questions about the private sector airport's ability to cover the financing costs from user charges.

Traffic and communities

The discussion has so far focused on the impact of road traffic congestion on the occupants of vehicles. Traffic also has important consequences for other road users, those who walk and cycle, and for residents of communities served by busy roads. The growth of motorized road transport has filled urban space with moving and parked vehicles, with decidedly mixed consequences for the quality of life.

Linear transport infrastructure, road and rail, can create barriers between communities known as *community severance*. Railways and controlled-access roads, such as motorways, have only limited locations for crossing. For other roads, the impact depends on the volume and speed of traffic. The types of crossings provided is important: a recent study in Britain found that participants rated footbridges and underpasses systematically below signalized crossings, especially in the case of women, older people and people with disabilities that limit walking (Anciaes & Jones 2018).

Severance increased as the growth of car ownership in the last century led to efforts to accommodate increased volumes of traffic in cities and towns. In many places, urban motor roads were constructed, some elevated above the existing road network. Commonly, existing streets were modified to cope with increased traffic flows by means of one-way systems and "gyratory" systems, the name given in Britain to large circular intersections, usually with buildings in the centre. For instance, the inner ring road of Coventry, England, built after most of the city centre was destroyed by bombing in the Second World War, comprises almost entirely grade-separated junctions located very close together. One local observer reported that he knew "one woman who hasn't been into the city centre for eight years. She doesn't like driving on the ring road and doesn't feel safe walking under it."[40]

In the event, such structures did not relieve traffic congestion and were felt to be damaging to the life of cities. Their removal could be beneficial – for instance, tearing down the elevated Embarcadero Freeway on the San Francisco waterfront that led to an urban renaissance. In London, a programme of reversion of a number of one-way gyratory schemes to two-way operations has proved popular, creating better facilities for pedestrians, as at Trafalgar Square where the north side was closed to traffic in 2003, allowing direct access to the National Gallery.

An influential report in 2013 by a Roads Task Force, appointed by the Mayor of London, recognized that roads both cater for *movement* by vehicles and pedestrians, and may also be *places* for shopping, leisure activities or local neighbourhoods. Accordingly, nine street types were proposed, reflecting three levels of importance for movement and three for place. For instance, an arterial road accommodates high volumes of traffic but is of limited significance as a place, while a city pedestrian space may largely exclude vehicular traffic.[41] Deciding the type of street provides a basis for actions to improve the way it functions.

Cities are constrained by their past when it comes to accommodating a growing population and meeting the needs of the inhabitants for mobility and access to desired destinations. Historic buildings, streets and neighbourhoods are generally valued. "Comprehensive redevelopment" of supposedly obsolete localities has often proved disappointing. Major new surface transport infrastructure tends to be resisted on account of the disturbance. When such projects are undertaken, the accompanying archaeological excavations may remind us of our civic history, as when skeletons dating from the fourteenth-century's Black Death were discovered during construction of Crossrail, London's new underground route.[42] New housing developments provide additional accommodation for population growth, but most people live in established stock, which largely determines daily travel patterns. So the scope for changing travel behaviour is limited by the huge historic investment in the built environment.

Transport inequalities

The structure of cities and the distribution of their inhabitants both reflects and contributes to societal inequalities. Transport resources are unequally distributed and so contribute to inequality. For instance, not everyone who would like to own a car can afford one and may be disadvantaged in their ability to access employment opportunities. The availability of good public transport could alleviate this disadvantage. David Banister has thoroughly discussed the complexities of the relation between transport and inequality in a new book (Banister 2018). While there are good arguments for seeking to lessen societal inequalities when reaching decisions on new transport investments and policies, the diversity of travel needs and wants makes such an aim difficult both to measure and achieve. In this respect transport differs from services such as education and health, where public provision funded from taxation can aspire to meet the needs of the whole population, subject to ability to benefit.

There may be conflicts between reducing inequalities in transport and other objectives. High taxes on petrol and diesel fuels promote energy efficiency and reduce carbon emissions but can be a burden on low-income motorists, who may spend a fifth of their income on buying and running a vehicle.[43] Public subsidies for buses are a common means to help those who do not have access to a car to make essential journeys, but subsidies have an opportunity cost – the alternative expenditures forgone. The standard economic case for congestion pricing outlined above emphasizes efficiency but places little emphasis on equity aspects – that the charge is less affordable for those on low incomes. Road traffic congestion is equitable in that all vehicle users share the common experience of delays.

An example of a transport policy aimed at tackling inequalities is the entitlement of older people in Britain to free off-peak travel on local buses, aimed at increasing their mobility, which could be constrained by low pension income. The introduction of the policy was a political decision with the stated objectives of increasing public transport usage by older people, improving their access to services and increasing social inclusion. The government compensates the bus operators. Clearly, the usefulness of this entitlement depends on the availability of bus services, which in rural areas may be very limited. Roger Mackett has reviewed the evidence and has concluded that the policy objectives have largely been met (Mackett 2014). A recent evaluation has found that households with access to no cars made three times more trips by bus on average compared to those with access to one car, consistent with the policy aim. However, a quarter of those eligible to hold a pass entitling them to free travel had not taken it up, raising questions about the effectiveness of targeting. A question about cost-effectiveness arises from the eligibility of well-off older people who could readily afford to pay for bus travel. The scheme is expensive, costing around £1 billion a year, with benefits to passengers estimated to be worth a similar value, so having a benefit-to-cost ratio of about one. This represents relatively low value for money, compared with other uses to which such funds could be put.[44]

Conclusion

The very success of the modern transport system in meeting our need for mobility has been accompanied by a number of detrimental consequences. It has been a struggle to clean up vehicle emissions and to improve road safety, although we can see how this might be achieved. In contrast, the benefits of travel stimulate demand that negates measures to reduce congestion and crowding. In particular, road traffic congestion is ubiquitous and resistant to remedies, and so is arguably the main and most intractable problem of the transport sector.

Policy measures aimed at mitigating harmful consequences have lacked coherence, prompting many to demand a national "integrated transport policy", which has not in practice been delivered. The reasons include the involvement of many players, both public and private sector, with continuing argument about the boundary between the two; debate about the benefits of integrated transport networks versus the benefits of competition in the market for transport services; and the lack of clear boundaries between the transport sector and the economy at large, prompting questions about the objectives of transport policy and, in particular, about the role of transport investment in making land accessible for new property development. All these policy conundrums persist as we ask what it is we can hope for from the new technologies – digital and electric – that are entering the market.

To understand what new technologies may offer, we need to understand the developments in travel behaviour and population that have been occurring in recent decades, and think through how these might play out in the coming years. So having reviewed the present situation, the next step is to understand the key developments that have taken us to where we are now, which is the subject of the following chapter.

2

TWENTIETH-CENTURY TRAVEL

I mentioned in the previous chapter the national travel surveys that provide detailed information on how, why and where we travel. They also show trends over time, which both allow us to see how our travel patterns have changed and help assess possible future developments.

The British NTS, first administered over half a century ago, offers a 45-year time series of fairly continuous data. Figure 2.1 shows outcomes per person for annual distance travelled, time spent on the move and number of journeys made, by all modes of travel (except international air travel). This very largely reflects our pattern of daily travel – the journeys to work, school, shops, to visit friends and family, for leisure activities and so forth. What is evident is that two aspects of individual travel have changed relatively little over 45 years: average travel time has remained close to 360 hours a year, or an hour a day, and the average number of trips has been about 1,000 a year.[1] There has been some small decline in annual trips in recent years – by 9 per cent between 2002 and 2017, almost all of which is due to a reduction in walking trips of less than one mile, mainly for shopping, personal business and visiting friends.[2]

In contrast, the average distance travelled has changed substantially over this near half a century, from 4,500 miles per person per year in the early 1970s to reach 7,000 miles by the mid-1990s, since when growth has ceased; indeed, there has been some reduction. Travelling further over the same amount of time has been possible by increased speed of travel, the result of investment in the transport system: mainly private investment in more and better cars and public investment in more capacity on the road network. However, as we transitioned to the twenty-first century, growth ceased in the average distance travelled. In Britain, about three-quarters of the total distance travelled by road and rail is by car, so it is no surprise that the average distance travelled by car has also stopped growing.[3]

Data from the 2017 US National Travel Survey also shows that average miles travelled per person grew from 1969 to the mid-1990s, but then growth ceased.

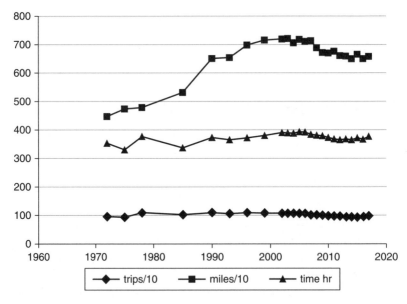

Figure 2.1 National Travel Survey
Source: NTS Table 0101.

The average distance travelled by vehicle increased from 8,700 miles in 1969 to reach 13,500 miles in 1995, after which growth stopped and, indeed, distance fell to 11,600 in 2017. Average travel time is not recorded, but average time spent in a vehicle as driver or passenger is about an hour a day. The average time spent driving in a private vehicle by all drivers increased somewhat, from 50 minutes a day in 1990 to 56 minutes in 2017. Overall, the latest US travel survey finds that per capita growth in travel experienced over the past four decades may be changing, in that of ten major indicators of personal or household travel behaviour, seven are lower than the 2001 estimates while the remainder are unchanged.[4]

An hour a day

The hour a day of average travel time found in the British National Travel Survey is not unique. Similar findings emerge from other such travel surveys, both at national and city levels.[5] On the one hand, average travel time does not depend on the average income of the population, although how people travel depends on what mode they can afford. On the other hand, when we look at travel behaviour within populations, we observe variations according to age, income and geographical location. For instance, in Britain, people in the age range 40–60 years travel twice as far as children or people over the age of 70. People in the highest income quintile travel twice as far as those in the lowest. And people living in rural villages travel twice as far as those in urban conurbations.[6] Travel time similarly varies: people in their 40s and 50s spend some 60 per cent more time travelling than children or people over 70. People in the highest income quintile spend 50 per cent more time on the move than those in the lowest, a likely reflection of more active lifestyles in respect of both business and leisure travel (Metz 2010). In contrast, there is relatively little variation of travel time according to geographic location.[7]

Some researchers within the transport studies community have advocated a concept known as a "travel time budget", implying that individuals allocate a fixed amount of daily or weekly time to travel. By analogy with money budgets, travel time budgets are supposed to act as control over the expenditure of time spent on the move. However, the variation in average travel time observed in relation to age and income does not suggest any fixed budget. Rather, what we observe is time expenditure that reflects individuals' need for travel according to their circumstances. There is, nevertheless, some evidence that individual travel time expenditure may be stable over periods of up to eight years, consistent with the existence of steady employment and regular habits (Stopher, Ahmed & Liu 2017).

The hour or so a day of travel time expenditure observed on average for a population is constrained by the unvarying 24 hours of the day for all the daily activities that must be undertaken – sleeping, eating, working and the rest – which limits time available for travel. Those who commute over long distances trade the advantages of their residential neighbourhood against the travel time commitment. The invariance of travel time observed over many years reflects the constant 24 hours of the day that limits the scope for upside growth.

What also needs to be explained is why average travel time has not declined over the years, as investments have been made in the transport system to enable faster travel, which logically could have led to people spending less time travelling to reach the same destinations. This has not happened.

The main reason for this is that faster travel opens up more destinations, opportunities and choices that are further away. Another factor may be certain intrinsic benefits of travel, irrespective of destination, including the psychological boost from being out and about, physical exercise when walking or cycling, and engaging with the community beyond the home. There is evidence that people may travel further than the minimum to reach a particular destination, taking the scenic route, for instance (Mokhtarian & Chen 2004; Metz 2008; Mokhtarian, Salomon & Singer 2015). For leisure travel, the journey may be as or more important than the destination.

The observed stability of travel time averaged across a population is at odds with a fundamental concept of orthodox transport economics, namely that the main benefit of investment in the transport system is that it allows faster travel and so saves time. Such postulated time savings are valued since they would allow more productive work or desired leisure activities. There has been very considerable effort by transport economists to attribute monetary values to time savings, so that the benefits can be assessed against the cost of investment in money terms – known as cost-benefit analysis (see Small 2012).

When the modern sub-discipline of transport economics was initially developed half a century ago, a simplifying assumption was made – that origins and destinations of journeys could be regarded as fixed. It followed that investments that increased the speed of travel, a general feature of transport improvements, would result in time savings. Although this simplifying assumption was subsequently relaxed, recognizing that the pattern of travel demand might change as a result of an investment, time savings continue to be the main economic benefit identified in the appraisal of possible transport improvements.

This focus on time savings is hard to reconcile with the stability of average travel time, as observed in the UK National Travel Survey, and similar national surveys, over nearly half a century during which many £ billions of public money have been invested in the transport system, justified by the value of the time saved. The National Travel Survey provides a long-term perspective, which means that the possibility of short-term time savings is not precluded, but it is the nature of the benefits in the long term that is relevant to investment in long-lived infrastructure such as roads and railways.

Rather than save time, the real outcome of investments that allow faster travel is that people go further in the amount of time they allow themselves for travel (the hour a day on average), to gain access to more opportunities and to have more choices – for work, shopping, leisure, education, homes and so forth. For someone who lives in a village not served by public transport and who does not drive a car, opportunities and choices are quite limited. This is how some people in developed countries live today, and how most lived two centuries ago. Modern transport in all its forms has served to expand horizons, as people have taken advantage of faster means of travel to venture further, to better satisfy their wants and needs.

Real consequences of transport investment

To understand the consequences of investment, we need the right data. While UK transport statistics are generally world class in their extent and timeliness, there are regrettable gaps in coverage, in particular a lack of data for origins, destinations and purposes of journeys on the road network and the impact of investments on travel behaviour (much more is known about the use made of the rail system from ticket sales data). It is this lack of appropriate data that has encouraged economists to persist in their assumption that time savings are the main benefit of investment. However, the evidence that is available is consistent with road users taking advantage of faster travel: initially to save time on established regular trips; then to make longer journeys to optional destinations such as for leisure and shopping, to gain more choice of price and quality; and subsequently to exercise more choice within personal time constraints as people change jobs or move house.

An illuminating example of the short-term unintended consequences of increasing road capacity is provided by a scheme to create a *smart motorway* on a heavily used section of the M25 orbital motorway to the north of London; this involved converting the hard shoulder to a running lane, so increasing capacity, plus setting variable speed limits aimed at smoothing the flow of heavy traffic. The result was traffic growth of 16 per cent by the third year after opening, far higher than motorway traffic growth in the region over the same period, with the largest growth at weekends – of up to 23 per cent, compared with 6–9 per cent on other days.[8] While the nature of this additional weekend traffic was not reported, it is unlikely to be commuting or commercial purposes. It most probably reflects lengthier leisure trips, for which the considerable choice of possible destinations allows road users to take advantage of the extra road capacity and initially faster travel to make longer journeys to new locations. This in turn increases the volume of traffic, with the outcome that journey times and reliability are effectively unchanged, as was observed in practice. These findings lend no support to the notion that time savings are the main benefit of an investment, in this case costing £180 million to provide an additional 33 lane-miles of capacity.[9]

To illustrate the longer-term impact of new road construction, consider a study by transport researchers Lynn Sloman and colleagues, commissioned by the Campaign to Protect Rural England, which monitored the impact of a number of road schemes that had been initially evaluated five years after opening by Highways England, the public body responsible for funding construction. This study of a sample of 13 road projects found that average increases in traffic over the short run (three to seven years; seven schemes) were 7 per cent, whereas average increases over the long run (eight to 20 years; six schemes) were 47 per cent, over and above background traffic growth in the relevant region. Four case studies of projects completed 13–20 years ago found that road building was associated with a car-dependent pattern of land development such that increased road capacity was "consumed" in the form of housing developments in the countryside and business and retail parks, all of which generated traffic.[10] For those concerned to protect the countryside, such development is bad news. For my present argument, the evidence for substantial traffic growth over the long run, and for concomitant land development, is consistent with the proposition that people take the benefit of increased road capacity that allows faster travel to travel further for more choice of homes, jobs and services, rather than to save time for other activities.

With the benefit of hindsight, a better simplifying assumption on which to have based the development of transport economics would have been to hold average travel time constant. The outcome of investments that allowed faster travel would then have been changes in origins and destinations of trips as people travelled further, with consequential changes in how land is used and in the value of land and property. This would be consistent with the National Travel Survey findings that average travel time is stable at an hour a day, but that the average distance travelled increased from 4,500 miles in the early 1970s to 7,000 in the mid-1990s, as mentioned earlier. (I will discuss below why this growth then ceased.)

The further it is possible to travel in the time available to individuals, the more access that is possible to desired destinations, choices and opportunities. Access increases approximately with the square of the speed of travel – since the locations that are accessible are located within a circle, the radius of which is proportional to the speed of travel, and the area of which is proportional to the square of the radius (recall from school maths: area of a circle equals π times the radius squared). So, for instance, if acquiring a car permits travel at an average speed of, say, 20 mph, seven-fold faster than walking pace (say 3 mph), this would increase access by a factor of 50. The average speed of travel by all modes (except air) is currently about 17 mph in Britain, some six-fold faster than walking.

An important question is whether the improvements in access can best be valued using notional time savings, as in orthodox economic appraisal methodology, or using changes in land value as a proxy, or indeed whether we could put a value on access to different classes of destinations. There is a divergence of view among professionals. The economists have developed an elaborate and comprehensive theoretical approach to investment appraisal based on time savings as the main benefit. They employ transport models that largely disregard changes in land use, so that the outputs are changes in travel time that can be used as inputs to the appraisal methodology. Transport economists are generally the intellectually dominant professional group in national transport ministries, not least in the British Department for Transport.

The transport planners, a less influential profession, are critical of the economists' focus on time savings. A survey of members of the UK Transport Planning Society found that a third wanted to replace time savings by land use or employment changes to capture long-term impacts, and 60 per cent wanted such changes to be appraised alongside time savings. Only 12 per cent wanted to continue to use time savings alone.[11]

What may seem a rather arcane debate among professionals in fact has important implications for investment and policy decisions. Transport planners operate in the real world and have to address the actual consequences of transport investments. Transport economists are more concerned to build computable models that conform to a theoretical framework, the relevance to observed behaviour often being of secondary importance. The economists focus on efficiency and are less concerned with equity – how the benefits of investment are distributed between different kinds of people – a question that is important for decisions on investments. In my view, the planners have the correct attitude. I will suggest in Chapter 7 that we need to change our approach if we want to make investments in the transport system that are of real benefit to the community, as opposed to being defensible in conventional cost-benefit analysis (see Metz 2017; Mackie, Batley & Worsley 2018).

Peak or plateau?

I have already noted that in Britain and the US, the average distance travelled by all modes of travel within the country has not increased over the past 20 years. Similar data are found for other developed countries. Given the dominance of the car in the transport system of developed economies, it is inescapable that car use per person also ceased to grow, as illustrated for Britain in Figure 2.2; indeed, there has been a modest decline. Figure 2.3 shows a compilation of data

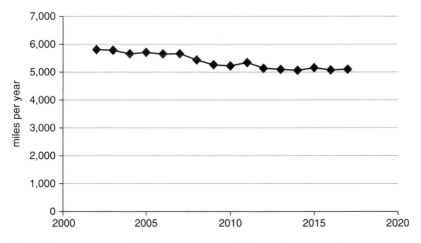

Figure 2.2 Distance travelled by car per person (driver and passenger)
Source: NTS Table 0303.

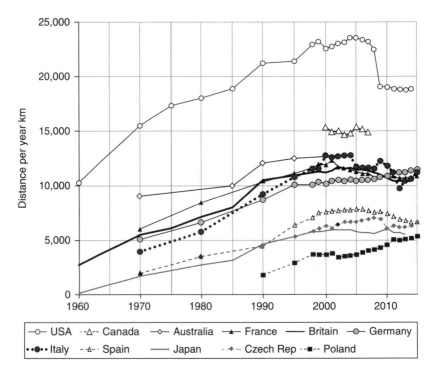

Figure 2.3 Distance travelled by car (and similar) per person
Source: Kit Mitchell, from UN ECE Transport Statistics for total distance travelled by car and official population statistics for total population.

from 11 developed countries, all but Poland showing cessation of growth or even decline. In the US, distance driven per person and per household peaked in 2004 and subsequently fell (Sivak 2018).

This cessation of growth of car use per person was termed "peak car" by a number of researchers, notably by Phil Goodwin. An analogy was made with "peak oil" – the prediction that world output of oil, a depleting resource, would reach a peak and then decline – a concept overtaken for the time being at least by the discovery of shale oil (Goodwin 2012; Goodwin & Van Dender 2013; Millard-Ball & Schipper 2011; Newman & Kenworthy 2011). In the case of car use, arguably a better term would be "plateau car", since what we see most obviously at present is a stagnation of growth, rather than an evident peak followed by decline (Millard-Ball & Schipper 2011). What seems fairly clear is that the steady growth of personal car use, characteristic of the twentieth century, has come to an end in the developed economies. There has been an important transition in car use as we moved from the previous to the present century. Why has growth of personal car use come to an end? There is evidence for a number of contributing factors – technological, behavioural, economic, as well as the consequence of changing demography (Metz 2013a).

The most basic impediment to travelling further is the difficulty of going faster. As I explained earlier, the main reason for the steady increase in average distance travelled in the last century was private investment in cars and public investment in improvements to roads. The main reason why growth of distance travelled has ceased is that household car ownership has stopped increasing. As shown in Figure 2.4, the proportion of households in Britain owning one or more cars steadily grew in the last century, from 14 per cent in 1951 to 75 per cent as we entered the present century, since when it has been stable, with a small increase in households owning two or more cars and a corresponding small decline in those owning just one.[12]

Car ownership in developed economies generally is high, exceeding 450 cars per 1,000 population for most high-income countries, and the US exceeding 800. Growth of ownership in many countries has ceased, including the US, Germany, France, Italy, Spain and Sweden.[13] In the US, ownership of light-duty vehicles (cars and light trucks) peaked in 2006 and then fell back slightly (Sivak 2018).

So the era has now ended in which the average speed of travel increased as people switched from public transport (mass transit) to the personal vehicle. Furthermore, it is not feasible to travel safely at significantly higher speeds on uncongested roads. Road traffic congestion, which in practice constrains speeds in and near populated areas, has proved difficult to mitigate, as I discussed in the previous chapter. And road construction is very costly. Although Britain has a major investment programme underway to improve the strategic road network

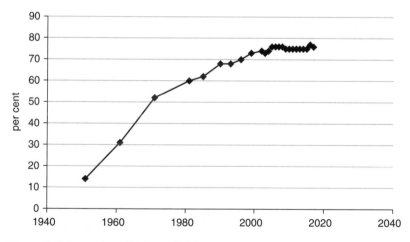

Figure 2.4 Proportion of UK households owning one or more cars
Source: NTS Table 0205.

(comprising the motorways and major trunk roads), the average rate of addition over the past ten years has been only 115 lane-km a year, or some 0.5 per cent increase in lane length per annum, which amounts to only two-thirds of the annual rate of population growth.[14]

There is scope for faster travel by rail. Many countries, are investing in high-speed rail routes, China most notably, as will be discussed in Chapter 7, where possible new rail-type technologies will also be considered. However, rail is responsible for only a minority of trips, and high-speed rail therefore for a minority of a minority. So little impact is to be expected on overall average travel speed.

Demographic change

Beyond the technological constraints on travelling faster, there are significant demographic and behavioural developments that impinge on travel patterns in the developed economies, in particular changes in travel behaviour of young people, demand saturation, urbanization and population ageing. There have been changes in where we live and how we live, which affect travel behaviour, as we moved from the twentieth to the twenty-first century.

There has been a long-term trend over the past two centuries, since the Industrial Revolution, for people to move from the countryside to towns and cities in search of employment and a better life. However, in many developed countries there was a reverse "counter-urbanization" movement in the second half of the twentieth century, during which people left overcrowded, polluted cities with obsolete housing for a superior quality of life in new suburbs and towns beyond, taking advantage of the motorcar for mobility in low-density settlements (Headicar 2009). However, this tendency has recently reversed in many places, as cities have improved their environments and amenities, and as the balance within economies has shifted from manufacturing to business services and the "knowledge economy" that prefers to locate in city centres. Globally, 55 per cent of the world's population at present live in urban areas, a proportion that is expected to increase to 68 per cent by 2050, according to UN projections.[15] In Britain, the major cities were losing population in the 1980s, but then began to gain inhabitants in the following decade and showed strong growth in the present century, a break in the previous counter-urbanization trend (Champion 2014).

Contributing to urbanization is the process that economists term "agglomeration", which advantages many business service sectors. Concentrations of firms in one geographic area benefit from learning, sharing and matching.[16] Firms acquire new knowledge by exchanging ideas and information, both formally and informally. They share inputs via common supply chains and infrastructure. And they benefit by matching jobs to workers from a deep pool of labour with relevant skills. Examples are the concentration of financial services in the City of London and Wall Street, and the technology clusters in Silicon Valley and the two cities of Cambridge, in Massachusetts and in England. Agglomeration also operates in media, entertainment and other cultural industries, and a similar process facilitates more extensive personal interactions, both networking for business and to cultivate social relationships (dating apps provide more choice of new friends at high population densities).

The shift in the structure of developed economies away from manufacturing has led to the growth of service businesses in city centres, fostered by agglomeration effects, which has driven urban development and population growth at higher densities, despite the high land prices, rents and other costs. This growth has increased congestion on the urban road network, but at the same time has improved the economic viability of public transport.

The growth of the economy in cities, as well as the expansion of city centre universities, has attracted young people to move to vibrant cities to study, work and live. This has contributed to a significant change in travel behaviour among young people in developed economies. A recent comprehensive review of the research evidence and survey data by Kiron Chatterjee, Phil Goodwin, Tim Schwanen and colleagues noted a trend that began some 25 years ago for young people (ages 17–29) to drive less than previous generations. This contrasts with the baby boomers, born from 1946 to 1964, who led a rapid, prolonged and persistent growth in car ownership and use. In Britain, driving licence holding among young people peaked in 1992–4 with 75 per cent of those aged 21–29 holding a licence, falling to 63 per cent by 2014. All trips per person by young people fell by 36 per cent between 1995–9 and 2010–14, as shown in Figure 2.5. The general trend has been for each cohort of young people since the early 1990s to travel less and to own and use cars less than the previous cohort, not just in Britain but also in other developed countries (Chatterjee *et al.* 2018).

Factors contributing to this trend away from car use include the cost of car ownership (not least, high insurance charges for younger drivers), problems of parking in cities and on campuses, and the viability of alternatives such as bicycles, public transport, shared car use, and smartphone apps to summon a taxi. However, the main causes lie largely beyond the transport system and include increased participation in higher education, for which the car is not part of the lifestyle; the use of digital communications and social media; and more generally a delayed transition to what was traditionally seen as adulthood – commitment to a career, getting married, home ownership, starting a family. Chatterjee and colleagues found that stable employment was a strong determinant of being a car driver.

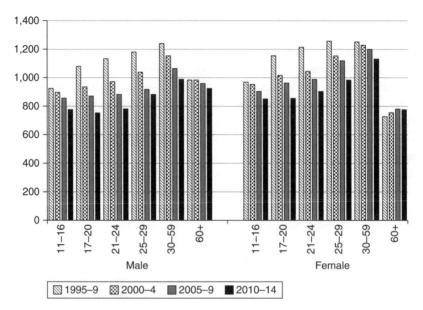

Figure 2.5 Trips per person per year by age group
Source: NTS data from Chatterjee *et al.* (2018) (used with permission).

An important question is how this shift away from car use by young people will affect the way they travel as they get older. Gordon Stokes has shown that those who start to drive later drive less when they do start; for instance, for those now in their 30s in Britain, if they learnt to drive when age 17, now drive 10,000 miles a year on average, while if they learnt at age 30, they are likely to drive around 6,500 miles a year (Stokes 2013). This reduced mileage seems likely to reflect greater experience of alternative modes to the car gained before learning to drive, as well as living in places where such alternatives are viable for journeys such as those to work. Chatterjee and colleagues concluded that while there are many uncertainties about the travel behaviour of future cohorts of young people, as well as about how this may change as they get older, it is nevertheless hard to envisage realistic scenarios in which all these uncertainties combine to re-establish earlier levels of car use.

While the urban young are driving less, the car remains important for older people (as Figure 2.5 indicates) and continues to be the dominant mode of travel in lower density suburbs and rural areas. Twice as many miles are travelled by car in rural areas of Britain compared with urban areas. Although there has been a shift in the population in recent years from rural to urban, Peter Headicar has concluded that these changes in the composition and distribution of the population have made only a small contribution to changes in per capita travel, largely because such population changes are at the margin, most people con-tinuing to live in their established neighbourhoods (Headicar 2013; Headicar & Stokes 2016).

However, econometric modelling by Tim Schwanen and colleagues led to the conclusion that urbanization *has* been important in explaining the plateauing of car use: a 1 per cent increase in the proportion of the population living in the five largest UK cities being associated with an estimated 1.7 per cent decrease in dis-tance travelled over the period 1970–2012 (Stapleton, Sorrell & Schwanen 2017).

Far enough

The motorcar is popular because it is convenient for door-to-door travel to get to places that meet our needs. I have proposed that one factor that has contributed to the cessation of growth of car use is the high level of choice available arising from wide car ownership. A study of access to supermarkets by the urban popu-lation of Britain showed that 80 per cent of households had three or more large stores within 15 minutes' drive, and 60 per cent had four or more (Metz 2010). You could ask yourself whether you would bother to drive further to have the choice of a fourth or fifth. If not, your demand for travel for the purpose of shopping at supermarkets would be said to have been "saturated". Economists would describe the effect as evidence of diminishing returns (or benefits) to add-itional choice. In short, we need not travel further if our needs are meet.

Demand saturation is a general phenomenon. Household ownership of con-sumer durables has reached high levels in developed economies, over 90 per cent for many classes of goods. New products are adopted first by those keen on innovation (the so-called early adopters), following which market growth accelerates during the initial part of the main phase of uptake, and subsequently decelerates as saturation is approached. It is not unexpected therefore to find demand saturation for daily travel (Metz 2013a). As noted above, car ownership in Britain and other developed economies has ceased to grow in recent years, an instance of demand saturation of central importance for the stagnation of the average distance travelled.

Demand saturation for daily travel is a likely general situation for people with use of a car or good public transport in or near urban areas where services are well developed. As I explained earlier, access and choice increase with the square of the speed of travel. So if there are diminishing returns to choice, demand satur-ation is to be expected. This has come about over the years through the growth of car ownership and road construction, and, in the case of supermarkets, through more stores being opened to meet the new demand. However, in most developed economies, these processes are increasingly played out, resulting in good levels of choice for consumers, who need travel no further. And, of course, online shopping increases choice yet more, as will be discussed in Chapter 5.

Travel demand saturation is not limited to supermarkets. The British Department for Transport compiles statistics on accessibility, linking where people live – from national census data – to the services they use by means of a geographical information system: a digital map calibrated for speed of travel by car, bicycle, public transport and walking. This allows estimation of numbers of sites accessible within specified journey times by the different modes of travel. Such sites include primary and secondary schools, family doctors, hospitals, food stores, town centres and employment locations. A general conclusion that can be drawn is that people living in urban areas with access to a car or adequate public transport have good levels of choice of the services offered. The inference is that there is generally a limited need to travel further for more choices (Metz 2013b).

One important exception to this generalization concerns housing in circumstances where demand exceeds supply, often because constraints of various kinds prevent construction of new homes at a rate that meets needs of a growing population. In this situation, people will look further afield for accommodation they can afford, which may involve longer distances for travel to work. New transport services can make housing more accessible, whether newly built or existing stock, the prices of the latter rising to reflect the greater demand. Some of the biggest percentage house price increases in London in recent years occurred as the result of the modernization of old rail routes to form an inner orbital and suburban line, renamed the Overground. This has experienced a large growth in passenger numbers due in substantial part to the improved access of previously relatively low-cost nineteenth-century housing to the main centres of employment.[17]

Economic factors influencing travel demand

As well as the technological, demographic and behavioural factors discussed above, economic considerations need to be taken into account in explaining the cessation of growth of car use per person. Factors such as the growth of incomes and national economic output (GDP), and fluctuations in oil prices, have been important in the past in predicting future car use. Some economists think the cessation of growth can be explained largely by a weakening of GDP growth over the past two decades, together with increases in oil prices (Bastian, Borjesson & Eliasson 2016).[18] There is on-going debate, not yet resolved, as to the relative importance of these economic factors and the wider range of possible influences on car use per capita. The UK Department for Transport believes that traditional economic factors remain the key determinants of car use, which are the dominant inputs to forecasts of road traffic growth, along with population growth.[19] A recent review commissioned by the Department endorsed the view that economic factors remain of vital importance.[20] The implication is that per capita car use will grow in the future as economic growth resumes, a conclusion that justifies a continuing programme of publicly funded road construction.

One shortcoming of conventional travel and transport modelling used to project future trends is the failure to recognize the breaks in trend as we moved from the previous into the present century. The assumption is that the future will be quite like the past, so that historic relationships between factors such as personal income and distance travelled will continue to apply in the future. However, the breaks in trend that are evident from National Travel Survey data for both distance travelled and car ownership (Figures 2.1, 2.3 and 2.4, with further instances later) tells us that relationships between key parameters (known as "elasticities") changed significantly. For example, in the last century growing income was an important driver of the increase in car ownership, whereas in the present century this relationship has been much weaker, a change that happened well before the 2008 economic recession. Use of historic data for such relationships leads to misleading projections of future developments, for instance the amount of road traffic.

My own view is that the wider range of factors discussed above are both relevant and operate in a way that is unlikely to result in a resumption of per capita growth of travel by all surface modes or by car alone.[21] Most important are the constraints that limit our ability to travel faster, both technological and saturation of demand of car ownership. Given the unvarying average hour a day of travel time, the scope for travelling further is quite constrained.

Accordingly, to think about future policies, investments and the impact of new technologies, we might most usefully envisage a business-as-usual scenario in which personal travel remains stable in respect of average distance travelled, trips made and time taken. We can then consider alternative scenarios in which emerging technological and other developments impact on our travel patterns, as I will address in subsequent chapters. When planning for the future, we should not assume that per capita travel is still on the growth path that it was in the previous two centuries.

Changes in where we live

The discussion so far has focused on individual travel, per capita or per head. Where populations are growing, total demand for travel will increase. The global population is growing, mainly in the urban areas of low-income countries. In contrast, in many developed countries the fertility rate is below the level required to keep the population stable, so that population growth may arise from inward migration to fill vacancies in the labour market, as well as to achieve a better life for the migrants (Metz 2016). Yet the combination of low fertility and population movement within a country can lead to a fall in numbers in economically less active cities, often the consequence of industrial decline.[22] For instance, the population of the port city of Liverpool peaked at 850,000 in the 1930s, declining to 435,000 in the 2001 census. Such cities often seek support from central governments to invest in the transport system, hoping to attract inward investment (discussed further in Chapter 7).

The UK population has been growing at around 0.75 per cent a year over the past decade and is projected to increase by some 5 per cent over the next ten years, about half of this growth resulting from more births than deaths, and half from net migration.[23] This increase adds to the total amount of travel, but the pattern, both geographically and between modes of travel, depends on where the additional inhabitants will live and work, which in turn depends on where the planners allow housing to be developed and where the developers judge it attractive to build.

To the extent that people are accommodated in new homes built on greenfield sites, they will find cars attractive, or even essential, to get around, and more road capacity may be needed. But for city living at higher densities, road travel is limited by traffic congestion and alternatives to the car would be required. Where people are willing to live depends on where they are employed, bearing in mind the constraints on travel time discussed earlier. So where a growing population is housed will depend on where the new jobs are located. A study of 20 new housing developments in England found that most were on greenfield sites, based on car use, with extensive space for parking and limited possibilities for public transport walking and cycling. A main cause was a planning system which attached much weight to building new homes and little to transport provision.[24]

In contrast, the recent experience of London illustrates the consequences for travel of increasing urban population density and employment. The population of the city grew steadily through the nineteenth century and the early decades of the twentieth to reach 8.6 million in 1940. There followed a 50-year period of decline in numbers as people left war-damaged, poor-quality and overcrowded housing for better living in new towns, garden suburbs and other attractive locations beyond the city boundaries – the counter-urbanization trend mentioned above. By the 1981 census, London's population had fallen to 6.6 million. However, this decline reversed around 1990 as people began to see the attractions of higher-density city living and working in improving environments, where agglomeration economics increased the productivity of the business service sector, allowing higher pay to be offered. Since then London's population has been increasing quite rapidly, recently passing the previous peak and on course to reach about 11 million by 2041, on recent official projections.

Despite this population growth, road vehicle traffic in London as a whole, about 80 per cent of which is car traffic, has not increased over the past 20 years (Metz 2015). This is due mainly to the limited capacity of the road network. Plans were made in the 1960s to build more roads to accommodate the expected growth in car use. An initial section of elevated motor road was constructed westwards from central London, but this was seen as damaging to the urban fabric and plans for similar new roads around central London were largely abandoned. So London has essentially retained its historic road network, which has constrained the growth of traffic. Indeed, there has been a reduction in the capacity of the road network, defined by the amount of traffic that can be accommodated for a given speed, particularly for cars in central London (down by 30 per cent), the result of reallocation of road space to bus and cycle lanes and pedestrian uses.[25]

If London's population has been increasing but car traffic has not, it follows that the share of journeys by car must have fallen, as is indeed observed. In 1993, when the relevant data series starts, 50 per cent of all trips in London were by car (driver and passenger), but this steadily declined to 36 per cent in 2017. Over the same period, the share of walking trips held steady at 24 per cent, while cycling grew from a low base to reach about 2 per cent of all journeys. The decline in car trips was compensated for by the growth in use of public transport, both buses and rail, which between them currently account for 37 per cent of all journeys.[26]

Figure 2.6 shows my estimate of the share of journeys by car in London in the century 1950–2050, based on historic data, Transport for London's recent data mentioned in the previous paragraph and my future extrapolation that

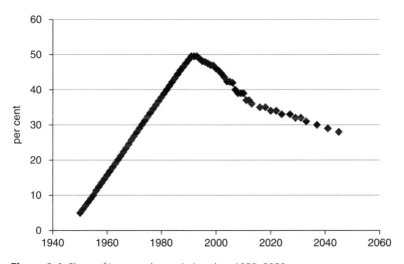

Figure 2.6 Share of journeys by car in London, 1950–2050
Source: Author's estimates and Transport for London.

takes account of projected population growth and assumes no addition to road capacity but continued investment in rail. The story it tells is this: in 1950 car ownership was low, but subsequently, as incomes grew, car ownership and use increased while at the same time the population was falling. Car use peaked at 50 per cent of all journeys at around 1990, the time when the decline in population had bottomed out. As the population subsequently grew, the historic road network acted as a capacity constraint, which meant that the share of trips by car had to fall, a trend projected to continue out to 2050, when some 27 per cent of trips would be by car, on the stated assumptions. The Mayor of London has more ambitious plans, aiming to reduce car use to only 20 per cent by 2041, driven by concerns about health impacts, as I discussed in the previous chapter.

What we see in Figure 2.6 is the clearest illustration of the concept of "peak car", a peak followed by decline in the *share* of trips by car. I term this "peak car in the big city", to distinguish it from peak or plateau car, referring to the distance travelled per person as discussed above (Metz 2015). It should be noted, however, that car trips on average are longer than trips by other modes, so that although the car is responsible for 36 per cent of trips in London currently, these trips amount to 50 per cent of distance travelled.[27]

While London provides the best data sources, there is evidence for a peaking in share of car journeys for other large cities. A substantial study, led by Peter Jones, identified a peaking of car use in terms of car trips per day for Paris, Berlin, Vienna and Copenhagen, as well as London. However, data from US cities indicates a continuing very high level of car use.[28] There is supporting evidence of a decline in car traffic in a number of UK cities, particularly in their centres, including Manchester and Birmingham (Metz 2013a),[29] as well as in the major Australian cities (Newman & Kenworthy 2011). In Beijing, the share of all journeys that are made by car has been stable since 2005, with public transport's share growing through investment in urban rail and the decline of bicycle use (Gao & Newman 2018).

Cities vary widely in their travel and transport characteristics. Peter Newman and Jeffrey Kenworthy have compiled extensive data from 44 cities in developed countries to 2005. They found a large spread in dependence on the automobile, measured by a variety of parameters. Based on a stringent criterion of person-km for each mode of travel, US cities were mostly more than 90 per cent car dependent, Australian and Canadian more than 80 per cent, while most European cities fell in the range 55–75 per cent. Singapore was 45 per cent and Hong Kong 15 per cent car dependent. Newman and Kenworthy take the view that cities with less than 75 per cent of person-km travelled by car can be considered as not "auto dependent" in that there are alternatives to the car for daily travel (Newman & Kenworthy 2015).

We might make a broad distinction between cities with historic central areas where the street pattern limits car use and the population density makes public transport economically viable, and more recent cities built at low density with the car in mind as the main means of mobility. This distinction is broadly between European and North American cities, although with central parts of some of the latter having high density, and suburbs of most generally being of low density.

There is evidence then for a general phenomenon whereby successful cities with well-established centres attract people to work, study and live; both the total population and population density increase, particularly in the centre; the authorities recognize that the road network cannot be expanded to accommodate more car use without damaging the urban environment; hence decisions are made to invest in public transport, particularly rail, which provides speedy and reliable travel compared with cars, buses and taxis on congested roads, as well as to improve facilities for walking and cycling. A common characteristic is the existence of a historic city centre that people find attractive for work and leisure, where declining car use increases the attraction. In the absence of an appealing downtown district, population growth may lead to continued low-density development.

In contrast, cities that expanded in the era of the motorcar and that lack a centre of particular attractiveness find it difficult to effect a shift from car dependency, a common situation in the US. There has been some growth of light rail systems there, with passenger numbers tripling between 1993 and 2011, although from a low base (Newman, Kenworthy & Glazebrook 2013). However, the impact on car use is quite small and the high cost of new rail schemes means that it can be hard to gain the support of the local electorate for the issue of bonds to finance the development, not least because a number of metros that opened in the 1980s failed to boost transit use.[30]

In the twentieth century, increasing prosperity was associated with increasing car ownership and use. In the twenty-first century, increasing prosperity is associated with *decreasing* car use in big cities with growing populations that can afford to invest in an extensive network of high-quality public transport.

Encouraging this shift away from the car is the approach adopted by the Corporation of the City of London, responsible for the historic "Square Mile" financial district, with a working population of nearly half a million, at the very centre of the metropolitan area. Given expected substantial population growth and a fixed amount of street space, the proposed policy is to put the needs of people walking first, which will proactively constrain motor traffic to achieve a 25 per cent reduction by 2030, eliminate deaths and serious injuries, and create a safe cycle network.[31]

For smaller cities and larger towns, rail investments are often seen as too expensive an alternative to conventional buses, the attractiveness of which is limited by their immersion in congested traffic. Nevertheless, there has been an impressive programme of tram development in France, involving schemes initiated by some 30 cities, where tram routes are the backbone of public transport (with buses serving as feeders) and the preferred location for regeneration and development (Boquet 2017). There is scope for innovative approaches, such as the single-track bi-directional tram route in Valenciennes that minimizes land take and reduces costs. Advantage can be taken of existing infrastructure to allow urban trams to extend over national rail tracks to serve wider city regions.[32]

Buses operating on road space protected from general traffic can be fast and reliable and are known as bus rapid transit (BRT). This mode of travel depends on making such space available, as was possible in those cities of South America that pioneered BRT by segregating a carriageway on their wide boulevards, but tends to be difficult in historic European cities. More generally, we inherit our built environments from our predecessors, which for the most part we are not willing to knock down and build afresh. So we find we are constrained when contemplating innovative transport technologies that could be beneficial in the absence of such constraints. A question for subsequent chapters is how new transport technologies might benefit towns and smaller cities faced with traffic congestion from high levels of car use.

Travel for work and shopping

Coping with higher population density in successful cities depends not only on growing numbers of inhabitants, but also on where they work, go shopping and reach the other services they need. From an economic perspective, a city is a labour market, and the larger the market, the more productive and innovative the city will be. Maintaining mobility is therefore essential to the success of cities.[33]

The transport system is used most intensely during the morning and evening hours when people are travelling to and from work, including places of education. Crowding and congestion encourage people to explore alternatives, where feasible. Working at home becomes more practicable with the advent of broadband connection. Remote meetings are increasingly possible as an alternative to travel for face-to-face gatherings. Conceptually, information and telecommunications technologies make achievable what has been termed the "death of distance", allowing people to work remotely from colleagues. Yet at the same time, we see the agglomeration phenomenon whereby people congregate in vibrant cities for face-to-face engagement, for both work and leisure.

Data from the British National Travel Survey show a downward trend in the number of commuting journeys, from 7.1 per worker per week around 1990 to 5.7 in 2014. This is attributed to people working fewer days a week, more working from home and more self-employment. There has also been a growth in "trip chaining" – for instance, dropping off children at school on the way to work – as well as more people without a fixed usual workplace, neither of which count as home-to-work commuting in the statistics.[34] The statistical decline in commuting is due to changes in work patterns rather than less work being carried out and, in part, may be prompted by difficulties in commuting, unwelcome time taken in crowded or congestion conditions.

Shopping trips have also been on a downward trend in Britain – 15 per cent decline in numbers of trips and 19 per cent in distance – between 2002 and 2017. A likely contributing factor is the growth of online shopping and delivery of goods at home, with 80 per cent of households ordering goods for delivery, and next-day supply increasingly offered. Shopping trips replaced may be offset in part by new trips to collect the goods.[35] Online sales currently amount to 17 per cent of all retail sales and have been growing at 13 per cent year-on-year.[36] There has been a widespread perception that Britain's high streets are in crisis and while factors such as squeezed incomes may be temporary, the shift to online shopping probably is not. Online sales are also contributing to the declining numbers of US shopping malls.[37]

The growth in home deliveries adds to road freight traffic, which competes for road space with passenger traffic. Van traffic in Britain has increased by 20 per cent in the years 2007–17, whereas car traffic grew by only 3 per cent, while heavy goods vehicles (trucks) fell by 6 per cent. Information on van use is rather limited. A survey in 2008 indicated that about half of van mileage was used to carry equipment and a quarter to carry goods. Factors contributing to the increase in van traffic include growth of home deliveries, changes to tax rules that encouraged a switch from company cars to vans, and substitution of vans for lorries, prompted by less strict regulation: for instance, a van can be driven by a person with a standard UK driving licence, whereas a lorry driver needs additional qualifications.[38] A recent study of "last mile" parcel deliveries in central London highlighted the importance of walking by the driver, which took 60 per cent of total vehicle round time, leading to conflicts with other road users for kerbside parking (Allen *et al.* 2018).

Population ageing

I have discussed the implications for travel of changes in both the location of the population and the declining use made of cars by younger people. A further aspect of demographic change is the ageing of the population.

The populations of both high- and low-income countries are ageing. Life expectancy in the leading countries has been increasing linearly for a century and a half. Moreover, the baby-boom generations, born in a number of countries following the Second World War, are now ageing. The resulting increase in the proportion of older people has wide-ranging implications for society, although much depends on how the health of those in later life develops. The balance of evidence suggests that as people live longer, deterioration in health is postponed, so that levels of health that used to be prevalent at age 70 are now found at age 80 (Metz 2016; Musselwhite 2018). One consequence is that people continue to drive until a greater age.

Growth in the numbers and health of older people leads to more travel by this group. Car use in later life also reflects the increasing proportion of women holding driving licences in successive cohorts. In Britain, 80 per cent of men age 70 and above hold a driving licence, whereas only 50 per cent women do. However, for the 50–59 age group, the gap is much narrower, at 90 and 80 per cent respectively.[39] The convenience and security of the personal car are attractive in later life. Yet car dependency is not without its problems as the population ages. Although older drivers generally are not a greater risk to other road users than are younger drivers, they are at risk themselves because of the increase in fragility with age, so if involved in an accident they are more likely to be injured (Mitchell 2018). Perhaps for this reason, insurance costs tend to increase with age.

Car dependency also contributes to the lack of walking exercise to counter obesity. And, when driving must be given up on account of frailty, there is loss of independence, in part the consequence of the lack of prior experience of alternative ways of travelling. I discussed in the previous chapter how free use of local buses contributes to the quality of life for older people in Britain, where nearly 80 per cent of those eligible hold passes, albeit more in urban areas than in rural areas where services are more limited.[40]

There is good evidence that mobility is important for our quality of life and that loss of mobility as we age is deleterious in that it deprives us of the opportunities and choices of places and people to which we have become accustomed. I shall discuss later how advances in technology may help mitigate the consequences of encroaching disability in later life.

Four eras of travel

The cessation of growth of personal travel, discussed above, took place as we moved from the twentieth century to the twenty-first. Taken together with prospective developments in transport technologies, I propose that we have entered a new era of travel. Looking back, we can discern three previous eras of travel in human history (Metz 2014: chapter 1).

The *first* era began some 60,000 years ago when modern humans journeyed out of Africa to begin to populate the remainder of the habitable globe. These ancestors were hunter-gathers, foraging for their daily food. Studies of remaining hunter-gatherer societies indicate that they typically spend around three or four hours a day on the move, covering 3,000–4,000 miles a year at walking pace.

Human societies changed with the Neolithic Revolution, starting some 12,000 years ago, a transition from hunting and gathering to agriculture and settlement. The early farmers worked long hours because they could secure increasing returns from their efforts, and as well accumulate stores of grain to survive poor harvests and sell to the towns that could accordingly develop. Once people had settled in communities, the need to travel was much less. Time for travel had to compete with time for work and all the domestic activities. Evidence from the size of historic settlements and of contemporary low-income rural communities indicates that it rarely took more than an hour to walk out and back to the limit of the land holdings of the village or the boundaries of the city.

So it seems likely that the hour a day average travel time discussed above, which is found generally for settled human populations, was established at the time that humans began to dwell in villages, towns and cities. In an hour a day at walking speed, the average distance travelled is about 1,000 miles a year. Horse-drawn carts and carriages on poor roads moved only modestly faster than walking pace, and the proportion of the population who benefited was small. So in this *second* era, which lasted until 1830, the average distance travelled was about 1,000 miles a year, taking about an hour a day.

The first passenger railway opened in 1830, between Manchester and Liverpool in the north of England. Thus commenced the *third* era of travel, in which the energy of fossil fuels was harnessed to permit faster travel. The nineteenth century was the great age of the railways, which spread across Europe, the Americas, India and beyond, with coal as the fuel. The improved transport provided by the railways, both lower cost and higher speed compared with water or roads, was crucial to the growth of economies and incomes that allowed an increasing proportion of the population to benefit. Railway passenger numbers reached their peak early in the twentieth century, as shown in Figure 2.7 for Britain, thereafter declining as the motorcar, fuelled by oil, grew in popularity. But note the major revival of rail travel that began around 1990, the result of investment in the railways, increasing congestion on the roads and a shift in the composition of the economy from manufacturing to services, which are increasing located in vibrant city centres served by rail.

The third era of travel spans the nineteenth and twentieth centuries, during which the efficiency of engines increased substantially: by a factor of ten for coal-fired steam engines and by 100 for oil-fired internal combustion engines, in terms of power-to-weight. This allowed faster travel by more of the population, so that the average distance travelled steadily increased from the walking-pace 1,000 miles per person per year to a level many-fold higher, differing between

Figure 2.7 Rail passenger numbers in Britain 1830–2015
Source: Wikipedia https://commons.wikimedia.org/wiki/File:GBR_rail_passengers_by_year_1830-2015.png

countries mainly because of differences in the scale of the road network in relation to population density. The considerable range of average distances travelled by car in the developed countries is shown in Figure 2.3, notably a three- to four-fold difference between the US and Japan, reflecting very different geographies.

The bicycle was an important means of travelling faster than walking pace on roads, in the middle of the third era, before widespread ownership of cars. The modern bicycle, with rear-wheel chain drive was introduced in the 1880s. While using human muscle power, it nevertheless required materials and manufacturing techniques that only became possible following the Industrial Revolution.

The main feature of the latter part of the third era is widespread individual car ownership. Motorized two-wheelers have been important in many countries before cars became affordable. Car ownership is more than merely an efficient means of travel since the particular models people choose may be meaningful, reflecting their self-esteem, their wish to display status and a means to have stimulating and pleasurable adventures. They may drive for enjoyment, as well as for practical purposes (Steg 2005). The popularity of the sports utility vehicle (SUV) may reflect associated feelings of strength and security more than purely practical qualities.

The third era of travel ended towards the end of the last century. Growth of travel per person in the developed countries has ceased, for the reasons discussed, and seems unlikely to resume. We have now entered the *fourth* era, where the new technologies to be described in Part II could have a significant impact on how we travel. However, demography is also important: where the population of countries is growing, so too will overall travel demand. Population growth puts pressure on transport systems in countries such as the US, Britain and many others where such growth is significant.

Conclusion

Looking at trends in daily travel in Britain and other developed countries during the twentieth century, we have seen that:

- average travel time remained unchanged at about 360 hours a year or an hour a day and average number of trips at about a thousand a year;
- faster travel, mainly the result of increasing car ownership, led to increased distance travelled as people benefited from more opportunities and choices of jobs, homes, shops, schools, etc. By the end of the century, the car dominated personal travel;
- car-based mobility meets many needs but leads to substantial problems that need to be mitigated, of which road traffic congestion is the most challenging.

As we entered the present century, a number of breaks in past trends have been observed:

- per person car ownership, car use and travel by all modes in Britain and other developed economies ceased to grow;
- car use as a share of all travel peaked in some successful cities and then declined, a consequence of more people moving into cities where road infrastructure cannot be increased to accommodate additional road traffic;
- car use by urban young people began to decline;
- railway passenger numbers in Britain began to grow rapidly;
- as will be discussed in Chapter 7, some well-established air travel market segments ceased to grow.

These breaks in trend are the consequence of significant changes in individual travel behaviour. In addition, there are important demographic developments underway: the population is growing, ageing and urbanizing, which increases and alters demand for travel.

External developments interact with changes in personal circumstances to modify habitual travel patterns. The future need not be like the past. A study of the travel behaviour of Londoners found that in a 12-month period half had experienced a major lifestyle change such as a new job or moving house (Marsden & Docherty 2013). So there is churn in travel behaviour, which facilitates adoption of new modes. We cannot simply extrapolate into the future assuming the persistence of behaviour as in the past. This complicates forecasting, but also means that travel behaviour may be more open to modification through intervention than usually supposed, whether by means of policy measures or investment.

Nevertheless, despite all these changes in behaviour, a key feature of our lives is that the 24 hours in the day limits the time available for travel. In general, we find that for settled human populations average travel time is about an hour a day. Innovations that make faster travel possible allow people to travel further, thus generating more traffic. The growth of average distance travelled during the last century was due very largely to increased car ownership plus road construction, a progression that has largely ended in developed economies. Higher speeds on roads are less safe. Congestion limits speed. Growth of cities at higher densities increases the prevalence of congestion, which lessens the attractiveness of the car, particularly for the urban young. Higher urban densities promote more choice of local services – public transport, shopping, leisure activities and the rest – which reduce distances travelled.

So we have reached a position in which on average daily travel per person is fairly stable. A key question for subsequent chapters is whether new or traditional transport technologies are likely to permit us to go farther in the time we allow ourselves for travel, so breaking out of this stable pattern and transforming our lives, as happened with the coming of the railway and the motorcar.

PART II
TWENTY-FIRST CENTURY TECHNOLOGIES

New technologies may provide solutions to the negative consequences of travel. Four major technologies under development offer promise of a better transport system if managed well:

* electric propulsion
* digital navigation
* digital platforms
* autonomous vehicles.

The following chapters will discuss how these new technologies could improve the present transport system, including how they might influence our travel planning and behaviour. These new technologies will themselves create problems that governments may need to anticipate, not least the longer-term implications of choices that are made today. An important question is whether to adopt a reactive or a proactive approach to regulation of the new technologies to achieve societal benefit while mitigating potentially harmful outcomes. Should governments allow new technologies space to develop creative approaches with minimal regulation, or should they regulate to head off undesirable investments?

There are many examples of innovative technologies currently being developed and deployed. My aim is to elicit the key features, both technological and economic. To this end I will focus on the leading exemplars of each kind of innovation, but will also indicate the range and variety of competitors.

3
ELECTRIC VEHICLES

In an effort to curb tailpipe emissions of standard petrol and diesel vehicles, governments have introduced increasingly stringent regulations of noxious emissions for vehicle manufacturers to meet. The tests involve running the engine in a laboratory setting under defined conditions, including speed, load and temperature. All new cars sold must comply with the emission requirements.

The vehicle manufacturers have generally resisted tighter standards, on grounds of technical feasibility and production cost. Nevertheless, they have developed new technologies, most importantly the catalytic converter for petrol (gasoline) engines, now standard, which converts noxious exhaust gases into less harmful species, in particular converting toxic NO_x to inert nitrogen. Because the catalyst is poisoned by the lead additive that used to be included in petrol to improve combustion, lead was eliminated from petrol. This was doubly desirable because lead is a toxic substance.

The context for electric vehicle development

Following regulation to tackle health impacts, the need to reduce transport carbon emissions, to counter the risk of global warming, has led to regulatory action to improve fuel economy. Transport is responsible for a quarter of Britain's greenhouse gas emissions, and road transport accounts for 90 per cent of this. Voluntary CO_2 emission standards were introduced in the European Union in 1998 and became mandatory in 2009. The 2015 target of 130g CO_2 per km for new passenger cars was met in advance in the UK. By 2021, the requirement will be 95g, averaged across manufacturers' new fleets of vehicles. This in effect requires manufacturers to market zero, or ultra-low, emission vehicles to offset the carbon of conventional vehicles.

Concerns about both urban air quality and carbon emissions prompted the British government to commit to a "mission" for all new cars and vans to be effectively zero emissions by 2040, which involves ending the sale of new petrol and diesel cars and vans by that date and ensuring that at least 50 per cent of new car sales are ultra-low emission by 2030.[1] Other European governments have also adopted target dates to phase out oil fuels for road transport: for instance, France by 2040, the Netherlands, Austria and Ireland by 2030 and Norway by 2025.[2] Target dates 20 or more years ahead cannot be more than aspirational, given the likelihood of unanticipated developments in the meantime. But they do send a signal about the direction of travel that vehicle manufacturers are not ignoring.

In the US, the impetus to introduce ultra-low emission vehicles has come from California, prompted by unhealthy air pollution in Los Angeles and other parts of the interior of the state. The California Air Resources Board in 1990 adopted a rule that would require manufacturers to start phasing in zero-emission vehicles by 1998, to reach 10 per cent of sales by 2003. This stimulated investment in electric vehicles (EVs) and batteries. Initially, the rate of technological progress was insufficient to meet this optimistic regulatory timetable, but subsequent advances allowed a target to be agreed with the industry of about 15 per cent of auto sales to be EVs by 2025 (Sperling 2018a).

National corporate average fuel economy (CAFE) standards were introduced in the US in 1975, prompted by fears about energy security. However, fuel economy worsened in the 1990s and early 2000s due to a shift to larger vehicles. Concern about climate change led President Obama's administration to announce in 2009 more stringent requirements to reduce average CO_2 emissions per km by 26 per cent by 2016, and subsequently by 35 per cent in 2025 compared with 2016.[3]

President Trump withdrew the US from the Paris Agreement on climate change and there are plans to revise fuel economy requirements, which are likely to be scaled back. However, California has the authority to set emission standards that are more stringent than federal standards, and other US states are able to adopt California's standards: a dozen have. Vehicle manufacturers are unlikely to want to apply different standards within the US, so the more stringent requirement may in practice apply, unless the right of California to set its own standards were to be revoked. This may be less likely following the congressional elections of November 2018 that gave the Democrats control of the House of Representatives.

While the US is reconsidering the incentives for electric propulsion, concerns about China's urban air pollution are driving growth of demand for EVs, a large market in which the major vehicle manufacturers are keen to participate. Half the global sales of over a million EVs in 2017 were in China.[4]

Despite regulatory efforts, progress has been relatively slow, with annual improvement in fuel efficiency of cars and other light vehicles in the developed economies of less than 2 per cent a year in the period 2005–15. This reflects in part the increasing popularity of larger vehicles such as SUVs, particularly in the US. Progress is sensitive to the bite of the regulatory regime; for instance, fuel economy in Japan worsened by 4.5 per cent between 2014 and 2015, a reversal of trend, the result of a decline in hybrid vehicle sales and an increase in average engine size at a time when average fuel consumption was below the policy target.[5]

An important response of European vehicle manufacturers to carbon reduction regulation was to switch from petrol to diesel engines, which are 15–20 per cent more fuel-efficient on account of the higher combustion temperature, although the incentive to switch depends on the relative levels of tax for the two fuels. This led to a substantial increase in the share of new cars sold in Western Europe powered by diesel engines, from 20 per cent in 1993 to 55 per cent in 2012.[6] However, it has proved difficult for some car manufacturers to reduce NO_2 emissions from mass-market diesel cars, which were tweaked to comply with laboratory tests while emitting much more on the road (and notoriously Volkswagen went so far as to cheat in the lab testing).

This experience points up the challenges of modifying behaviour through technical regulation, which is often preferred because it tends to be less contentious than taxation. Long-established technologies like the internal combustion engine may be approaching the limits of further refinement. The proprietary knowledge of the technologies may limit insight by regulators as to what advances are feasible. And the huge existing investment in manufacturing and its labour force generates push-back to fresh regulation. However, there may still be scope for useful innovative regulation, in particular to reduce the fine particles generated from tyres, road surfaces and brakes as particles from tailpipes are eliminated.

Development of electric propulsion

The persistent regulatory pressure to reduce carbon emissions has proved easier to accommodate for smaller cars, less so for larger, heavier, higher-value vehicles. Accordingly, all the major car manufacturers are increasingly focused on reducing carbon emissions of their fleets by developing and marketing low- or zero-emission vehicles in which the internal combustion engine is supplemented or replaced with an electric motor and battery.[7]

The initial approach was the hybrid, exemplified by the Toyota Prius, which entered service in 1997. The main source of power is a petrol engine, supplemented by an electric motor and battery, which has the effect of improving the fuel economy of the main engine, in part by use of regenerative braking that recovers energy that would otherwise have been dissipated as heat. Only short distances can be travelled in pure electric mode, most usefully for stop-start urban driving.

In contrast, the pure EV relies solely on electric propulsion, the batteries used for storage being charged by plugging in to the mains electricity supply. The pace for EV development has been set by Tesla, founded in 2003 and led by the entrepreneur and evangelist Elon Musk who was convinced of the need to eliminate road transport carbon emissions to counter climate change. The initial models were up-market, elegant in design, capable of high performance on the road, had adequate range between charging (greater than 200 miles) and gained a strong and enthusiastic following. The latest Model 3 is aimed at the mass market and, despite early production difficulties, is the best-selling EV in the US.

Most other car manufacturers are now marketing EVs, many still with limited range between charges, but some offering 200 miles or more, including General Motors' Chevrolet Bolt. The top selling EV, Nissan's Leaf, achieves 140 miles under ideal conditions, but, as for all EVs, the range is less in stop-go traffic, at high speeds or in winter conditions. However, most daily use can be managed within such a range, with overnight recharging.

A solution to "range anxiety" is the plug-in hybrid (PHEV), in effect an EV that is routinely plugged in to recharge, but which also has a petrol or diesel engine that can be used to drive the wheels when the battery is low, or to power an alternator to recharge the battery – a range extender – when plug-in recharging is not available. This adds to the cost of the vehicle but offers assurance that the journey can be completed.

Electric motors are inherently efficient, converting up to 95 per cent of stored energy into kinetic energy, compared with a maximum of 40 per cent for internal combustion engines. Moreover, while the internal combustion engine is a mature technology, there remains substantial scope for further development of batteries and electric motors. Annual global sales of electric cars exceeded 1 million in 2017, although this represents only about 1 per cent of global vehicle output, indicating the opportunities for growth of market share as EV technology advances.

Battery technology

Batteries comprise an anode (negative pole) and a cathode (positive pole), immersed in a liquid electrolyte. The familiar lead-acid car battery has a lead anode and a lead oxide cathode, with sulphuric acid as the electrolyte. This battery has relatively low capacity to store energy, but it is able to deliver the high surge current required to start a conventional car.

A key requirement for an EV battery is energy density – the electrical energy stored per unit of weight. The motorcar with internal combustion engine technology has been made possible by the high energy density of oil-derived fuels, which batteries at present fall well short of emulating. The current best battery technology is lithium-ion (Li-ion) in which lithium ions flowing from anode to cathode discharge a current that powers the vehicle. Lithium ions flow back when the battery is recharged. There are a variety of lithium-based composite materials used for the cathode, which include the elements cobalt, nickel, aluminium and manganese. Generally, the anode is made of graphite. Lithium ions are held in tiny voids within the crystals of the electrode material.

As well as energy density, other important battery characteristics are the rate of charge and discharge, battery life and safety, and weight (a typical battery for an electric car can weigh 600 kg). There are trade-offs between production costs and performance, dependent on the chemistry. For instance, increasing nickel content reduces reliance on expensive cobalt and increases energy density, which reduces the production cost per unit of energy stored, but at the price of decreased thermal stability of the battery cells, which must be mitigated (Jones *et al.* 2017). Battery life is improving; Nissan will replace a Leaf battery if it fails before 100,000 miles or eight years, whichever comes first.

Production of batteries is quite complex, involving manufacture to stringent quality standards of small cylindrical cells (typically 65mm in length, 18mm diameter) containing anode, cathode and electrolyte, which are assembled into larger battery packs designed to fit the vehicle type, and which are accompanied by a battery management system to regulate charging and discharging, and a thermal management system to prevent overheating.[8] There is extensive experience of manufacture of Li-ion battery technology as used in mobile phones and laptop computers. Costs of Li-ion battery packs for EVs have been falling steadily as experience is gained, as for instance Tesla's collaboration with Panasonic – a battery manufacturer – to fabricate Li-ion batteries as used in laptops on a very large scale for use in cars; the Gigafactory, as it is called, has a planned annual output of 35 gigawatt-hours, necessary for the production of mass-market EVs.

At present the total cost of ownership of an electric car is greater than that of a conventional car, the higher purchase price more than offsetting the lower operating and maintenance costs. The gap reduces as annual mileage increases and as the cost of batteries falls, and is less at higher levels of fuel tax. There is therefore a strong incentive to advance battery performance and reduce costs. Li-ion battery prices fell by 80 per cent between 2010 and 2017, according to one authoritative estimate, average energy density increasing at 5–7 per cent a year, with the prospect of upfront cost of EVs becoming competitive without subsidy by the mid-2020s.[9]

It is not clear whether Li-ion technology will eventually be displaced by another chemistry with superior properties. Two possibilities with substantially higher energy densities than Li-ion are Li-sulphur, which uses a sulphur-carbon cathode, and Li-air (Service 2018a). Another option is the solid-state battery, which replaces the liquid electrolyte with solid components, and which opens up use of a wider range of anode and cathode materials, as well as improving safety (Little 2018). There are also proposals for electrodes based on cheap abundant materials such as iron, copper and silicon (Turcheniuk *et al.* 2018). The theoretical limit to battery energy density is unclear, unlike the energy extractable by an internal combustion engine from oil-based fuel, the maximum of which is determined by the second law of thermodynamics. Battery technology advances incrementally and the eventual outcome remains to be seen.

There are concerns about the availability of key materials to support the growth of EV numbers, particularly of lithium and cobalt. Lithium is relatively abundant and comes mainly from Chile, Argentina and China, with major new mines recently opened in Australia.[10] Cobalt is extracted mainly in the Democratic Republic of Congo where political instability, environmental degradation and poor labour conditions are concerns. Generally, increased demand for any mineral drives up market prices, as has happened with cobalt, which in turn prompts exploration and development of new sources by mining businesses. Alternative chemistries using less scarce materials may become attractive.

Unlike fossil fuels, the materials used in batteries are not consumed and so may be recycled, which would ease demand in the long term. As with every technology, reliability and whole-life costs will be important, including the use made of vehicle batteries as performance declines, such as for domestic storage of electricity generated by roof-top solar power.

The range of an EV that is possible depends on factors other than the battery: principally the efficiency of the electric motor, the weight and design of the vehicle and the style of the driver. While the principles of design of the various types of electric motors are long established, there is active development to improve performance. For example, Tesla utilize a "switched reluctance motor" for their latest Model 3, made possible by recent progress in the design of such motors.[11] A heavier vehicle requires a larger, more expensive battery, so that reduction of weight, aerodynamic drag and rolling resistance all improve range. Quick acceleration and high speeds cause energy drain, while aggressive braking lessens the benefit of regenerative braking.

Vehicle manufacturing

Major vehicle manufacturers have ambitious plans for EVs. General Motors intends to develop 20 all-electric vehicle models over the next five years. Volvo has announced that every new model it launches from 2019 will have an electric motor.[12] And the other major auto businesses have similar intentions.

China is currently the world's leading manufacturer of EVs, motivated by poor urban air quality and emission reduction targets, although it is not leading in technology. Sales are mainly to city-owned taxi fleets and transportation companies, and in major cities that limit purchase of conventional vehicles by private buyers, such as Shanghai (Dunne 2018).

Initial sales of EVs have been supported by governments by means of subsidies, aimed at encouraging uptake while vehicle purchase costs are well above those of conventional vehicles, and in anticipation of cost reduction as battery performance improves and manufacturing experience is gained. Such subsidies may also help overcome other barriers to uptake such as range anxiety, the availability of public charging points and re-sale values.

In Britain, financial support for plug-in vehicles depends on their CO_2 emissions and the distance they can travel with zero emissions. Nineteen best-performing car models are currently eligible for grants worth 35 per cent of the purchase price up to a maximum of £3,500 (cut from the previous £4,500 following a surge in orders). EVs are also exempt from the annual vehicle tax. In the US, there is a federal income tax credit of up to $7,500, which individual states may supplement.

Some European countries support sales of new EVs: in particular Norway, which exempts new EVs from purchase tax and value added tax, cutting the purchase price roughly in half, and has a much-reduced annual road tax plus free access to toll roads, ferries and parking. The result was that 40 per cent of new car sales in Norway in 2017 were battery EVs or plug-in hybrids.[13] The Chinese government also subsidizes vehicle sales and plans to set steadily increasing quotas that will reward manufacturers for producing more battery EVs, driven by concerns about serious urban air pollution and high oil imports. Vehicle licences for internal combustion engine vehicles are limited in some major cities. China, as the world's largest maker of EVs, is currently responsible for 45 per cent of global output.[14]

Government support will not continue long-term, which means that EV costs must be driven down if sales are to grow as planned. Battery technology is crucial to EV cost and performance. The major vehicle manufacturers have not themselves developed batteries – electrochemistry has not been their core competence. So they have formed partnerships with battery manufacturers, which introduce a major risk of not choosing the partner with what turns out to be the most competitive technology, a risk that also arises if they commit themselves to electrochemical innovation. However, flexibility to buy in the best battery technology could be beneficial if a competitive market in battery supply emerges. There is also the question of geographical source, with 80 per cent of the world's existing and planned battery production in Asia, and very little in Europe, which has prompted the European Union to establish a Battery Alliance, to support research and innovation, materials sourcing and production. The British government is also supporting battery development through the multi-university Faraday Institution, named after Michael Faraday, the British pioneer of the application of electricity and magnetism.

Vehicle manufacturers are facing turbulent times. Their traditional competences are internal combustion engine technology, vehicle design, mass production on the assembly line, and marketing and distribution. Many components are bought in – including electricals, brakes and tyres. The manufacturers have mastered production of complex high-performance internal combustion engines that are the culmination of a century of development and perfection of what is fundamentally nineteenth-century technology involving pistons, cylinders, crankshaft, gearbox and clutch. Electric propulsion takes them into a new era (as does autonomous vehicle technology, discussed later).

EV technology is much simpler than the standard petrol or diesel car, with less heat generation and no emissions. An analysis of GM's Chevy Bolt, the first mass-market EV, found only 24 moving and wearing parts in the powertrain, compared with 149 in a conventional VW Golf, and that 56 per cent by value of the Bolt's content came from outside the traditional auto supply chain.[15] This simplicity reduces the cost of both manufacture and maintenance (the Bolt requires virtually no maintenance for the first 150,000 miles or five years), which have implications for employment – companies that make gearboxes are not going to make batteries. However, dependence on bought-in batteries and electric motors for EVs would be a significant change to the auto industry business model, involving new risks. A strategic issue for an EV maker is whether to embrace battery development and manufacture as a core competence, given that battery properties influence other aspects of vehicle design. The development of new battery designs is continual and complex, involving many trade-offs in performance characteristics, so there is risk both in own development and in buying in from specialists (Beuse, Schmidt & Wood 2018).

The major manufacturers must consider whether to emulate Tesla's vertically integrated approach by developing their own innovative electric motors and batteries. At the same time, they will face competition from further new entrants to the market that can rethink vehicle design, unencumbered by the heritage of the established auto manufacture. James Dyson, the British inventor of the bagless vacuum cleaner and other innovative domestic devices, plans to manufacture an electric car in Singapore, taking advantage of his company's expertise in electric motors, batteries, aerodynamics and manufacturing. In China, there are reported to be more than 300 registered EV start-up businesses.[16] New entrants are motivated to build wholly new businesses based on innovative EV technologies, whereas existing car manufacturers are defensive, needing to avoid loss of market share and profit while complying with increasingly demanding emission requirements.

As well as these questions of the approach to EV development, the manufacturers are faced with the issue of whether to develop or purchase the wherewithal for automated vehicles (AVs), as will be considered in Chapter 6. Evidently, the vehicle manufacturers are now operating in a much more uncertain world than in the past, not just in relation to the new technologies but also the changes in people's behaviour that are emerging, in particular the possible shift away from individual car ownership to sharing in one form or another, as will be discussed in subsequent chapters. After a century of incremental improvement to the technology, they are now faced with step changes in respect of vehicle propulsion and operation. Yet while there is much uncertainty about the prospects for AVs, the imperative for electric propulsion is clear. It is likely that further developments of the internal combustion engine will be quite modest.

Electric charging

An important constraint on sales of EVs is the availability of charging points to top up the battery.[17] The most convenient and lowest cost option for cars is overnight off-street charging at home. This suffices for most commuting trips, especially when workplace charging is also possible. Similarly, overnight charging at the depot is suitable for local delivery vans and trucks. For housing that lacks off-street parking (the situation of more than 40 per cent of Britain's car owners), public charging points are needed. A number of innovative technologies are being tested, including retrofitting lamp posts with charging points, cable gullies to allow residents to charge their cars parked at the kerb and an app-operated pop-up charge point that retracts underground when not in use.

For longer-distance journeys, the assurance of en route recharging is important, which needs to be at a much faster rate than for home charging. Public charging points are mainly of three types, depending on power output: slow, taking six to 12 hours to charge a battery EV; fast, three to four hours; and rapid, around 30 minutes. Clearly, for longer-distance trips by EV, rapid charging points are necessary. Some 1,200 may be needed near the UK major roads network by 2030, two and a half times the number available in 2016.[18] For the UK as a whole, a smartphone app identified 1,350 locations with publicly available rapid charging points in January 2019, included within the 6,800 locations with publicly available charging points of all kinds.[19]

The oil companies that serve the retail market are adding charging points to their petrol stations, and BP has acquired the operator of the UK's largest public network of EV charging points.[20] Car parks at shopping and leisure centres, hotels and other destinations where people spend time are also likely locations. However, a high standard of reliability of charging points is required, which when not achieved can leave EV users stranded. In part for this reason, Tesla guides owners of its cars to the nearest Supercharger, dedicated rapid chargers for its vehicles located along well-used corridors.

Electricity sources

The intention of the UK and other governments is that conventional cars and vans should no longer be sold by a specified date, to tackle road transport's contribution to climate change and air pollution. Accordingly, governments need to ensure both that electricity supply systems are developed to allow charging of EVs at and away from home, and that electricity generation from fossil fuels is phased out. The British government has committed itself by law to reducing greenhouse gas emissions by 80 per cent by 2050 compared with 1990, which will require the full decarbonization of electricity generation, replacing coal and gas with renewable sources and nuclear power. Coal's share of UK electricity generation is rapidly declining, from 22 per cent in 2015 to 9 per cent in 2016, with gas (having a lower carbon content) taking its place; renewables contributed 25 per cent and nuclear 20 per cent.[21] For the future, coal and gas are projected to decline gradually, replaced by renewables and nuclear.[22]

The share of electricity generated in other countries from fossil fuels varies widely: for France it is 9 per cent, reflecting the large investment in nuclear power, whereas for the US it is 67 per cent and for China 73 per cent.[23] While urban air quality will be improved as EV uptake increases, the carbon reduction dividend will not be achieved until electricity supply systems are substantially decarbonized.

As well as shifting from fossil fuel generation, the electric supply system will need to be reinforced locally for EV charging. Typical current domestic electricity supplies (with mains fuse of 60–80 amps) would limit home EV charging to the lowest rate, so there would be a case to uprate the supply to 100 amps. There will also be a need to reinforce local electricity distribution networks, as EV ownership increases.[24]

The daily timing of EV charging would need to be regulated to avoid excessive demand for electricity in the early evening, when people have returned home. Smart metering should incentivize deferment of EV charging until demand reduces later in the evening, with lower-priced electricity as the reward. There is also scope for parked and plugged EVs returning power to the electricity grid to help meet peak demand, again for reward.[25] The overall increase in UK electricity demand arising from the general adoption of EVs seems manageable: around an

8 per cent increase in current UK peak demand with smart charging, if no new non-electric cars are sold after 2040.[26] A study of the expected impact of EVs in London suggested that this would contribute only 0.7 per cent of total expected demand growth by 2050, with just one to two years advancing of investment in the local distribution network.[27]

Government support for EV charging infrastructure is necessary at the early stages of deployment, including grants for domestic charging points and to support private investment in publicly available charging points. To tackle the inhibiting effect of "range anxiety" it may be desirable to ensure more access to public charging points in the near term than would be needed in the longer term as battery technology improves and range increases.

Electric propulsion for cars is the main opportunity for manufacturers. Small vans and taxis have similar characteristics. Electric delivery trucks operating in urban environments, with availability of overnight charging at the depot, would benefit from lower operating costs compared to diesel. For instance, United Parcel Service plans to switch its entire central London fleet to electric, taking advantage of "smart grid" technology that allows the recharging of a large number of vehicles without expensive upgrade to the power supply.[28] For long-distance trucking, the weight of the battery limits the load that can be carried. Nevertheless, Tesla is developing a large electric truck with an expected range close to 600 miles. Electric buses are currently available; London is planning to have 240 electric buses in 2019, but this is modest compared to Shenzhen in China where the whole fleet of 16,000 buses are electric, driven by the urgent need to reduce urban air pollution.[29] Indeed, 99 per cent of all electric buses are located in China.[30] But there can be problems with ensuring sufficient battery capacity to operate all day, prompting development of various forms of en route charging, including wireless charging at bus stops.

Hydrogen

An alternative to electric propulsion for large trucks and buses is the hydrogen fuel cell. A fuel cell is an electrochemical technology, not unlike a battery, but which uses hydrogen as input. This reacts with the oxygen in air to generate electrical energy and water as the chemical output. Ballard, a Canadian company, pioneered fuel cell technology for buses. London operates one bus route using this technology, which offers a similar range and refuelling time to conventional diesel fuel. Demand for fuel cell vehicles is at an early stage; the technology is still costly. Moreover, hydrogen refuelling stations are limited, which limits more general application despite the attractions of range and rapid refuelling for zero-emission cars and vans. Nevertheless, both Hyundai and Toyota are marketing hydrogen fuel cell passenger cars.

Just as the environmental impact of a battery EV depends on the source of electricity, that of the fuel cell depends on the source of the hydrogen. Most hydrogen is generated from methane (natural gas), which liberates carbon dioxide; in principle this carbon could be captured and stored, which would be costly but would eliminate any contribution to greenhouse gas emissions.

Hydrogen can also be made from electrolysis of water, also a costly route; if the electricity were generated from renewable sources or nuclear, then there would be zero-carbon emissions.[31] A further possibility, still at an early stage of development, involves a fuel cell that uses nitrogen gas, the main component of air, and water, plus electricity from a renewable source, to generate ammonia, a gas readily liquefied for transport; and then breaking up ammonia to yield hydrogen (Service 2018b).

Natural gas is the main fuel for domestic heating in most developed economies. The greenhouse gas reductions required to meet climate change targets will require replacement by a non-carbon source. Electricity is possible, although the very seasonal nature of domestic heating requirements would necessitate substantial investment in both generation and distribution. An alternative might be to retain the existing gas supply network, which allows storage to meet both daily and seasonal variation in demand, but to replace natural gas with hydrogen. This would in part be a reversion to the era of gas generated from coal, which had a hydrogen content of about 50 per cent. A gas distribution system for hydrogen would facilitate the use of this fuel for vehicles.

Loss of tax revenues

Petrol and diesel fuel for road vehicles is taxed to varying degrees, according to country. An eventual complete switch to electric propulsion for cars and vans would lead to loss of most revenue from fuel duty, in Britain currently about £28 billion a year, offset to a small degree by value added tax (VAT) of 5 per cent on electricity. Vehicle excise duty (VED), an annual charge on vehicle ownership, raises some £6 billion a year, rather less than the annual capital and current expenditure on national and local roads of £8 billion in total. So VED could be raised to cover the full cost of the road system. But that would leave a major gap in public revenues and would, in the long run, imply much cheaper motoring – welcome to motorists but problematic in respect of the detrimental impacts of the car.

To ensure that EVs contributed to the cost of the road network and to fill the revenue gap, it would be reasonable to levy a charge on the use of EVs. This would be related to distance travelled, weight of vehicle (which determines damage to the road surface), location and time of day (reflecting congestion that imposes costs on other road users). It would also be possible to relate charges to the cost of the vehicle when new, so that the better-off road users paid more than those who could only afford a reasonably priced family car.

In 2015 the US State of Oregon successfully introduced a pilot voluntary road usage charge programme, to test this means of raising revenue to fund transport projects as an alternative to the taxation of fuel, revenues from which had been diminishing. Those participating paid 1.5 cents per mile travelled and received offsetting credits for the fuel tax they paid at the pump.[32]

In the US, individual states set their own gasoline and diesel taxes, and there is also a federal tax. In European countries there is a single national tax on road fuel, paid by the suppliers and passed on to users. A charge for road use by EVs would allow local road authorities to set an element of the charge to raise revenues to fund highway maintenance and local transport improvements. The other element would raise revenue for national government. This is in effect the position in central London when motorists pay tax on fuel which goes to the national government, and pay the congestion charge which is levied by London's local government (see Chapter 1).

Climate change and sustainable transport

Concerns about damage to the environment in the 1970s led to formulation of the concept of "sustainable development", defined as development that meets the needs of the present without compromising the ability of future generations to meet their own needs. Anxiety about depletion of non-renewable oil and gas resources was an important motivation, coupled with nervousness about energy security in countries largely dependent on oil and gas imports.

In Britain, this general disquiet coincided with anxieties about plans in the late 1980s for a major new inter-urban road construction programme to meet projected increases in demand for road travel. Subsequent concerns about climate change have reinforced unease about the growth of carbon-emitting road traffic and proposed investments to accommodate this growth (Headicar 2009: chapter 7; Givoni & Banister 2013).

Transport accounts for about one quarter of energy-related CO_2 emissions and had been seen as the most problematic sector of the economy as regards reducing greenhouse gas emissions, given the growth of car ownership and the high dependence on oil fuels. In contrast, the scope for reducing carbon emissions from buildings and from industry was regarded as much more promising, given the scope for carbon and cost savings from more efficient use of energy. Zero-carbon domestic buildings are feasible and have been constructed.

For the transport sector, reducing dependence on the car was seen as the main means of achieving sustainability. Transport planners recognized this imperative and promoted walking and cycling as healthy alternatives, public transport in the form of buses as a more efficient mode of road transport and rail in all its forms as an electrified (or electrifiable) alternative to road use. The move away from car use, seen in successful cities like London as discussed in Chapter 2, shows that a shift towards more sustainable travel behaviour is possible in urban areas where most of the population resides (Metz 2015).

However, we need to rethink transport sustainability in the light of plans for electrification of cars and vans, and decarbonization of electricity generation, which will go a long way to eliminate carbon emissions. Diesel engines on the railway can be replaced by track electrification, batteries or hydrogen. Although heavy duty transport – trucks, aviation, shipping – are more challenging, there is scope for significant efficiency improvements to existing technologies, together with the development of electric propulsion for short haul, and biofuels, hydrogen or synthetic fuels for long haul.[33] However, while the ultimate objective of zero-carbon electrified land transport can be envisaged, there is a question as to whether the rate of progress is sufficient to meet climate change objectives.

Britain has enacted legislation that mandates a reduction in greenhouse gas emissions by 80 per cent by 2050 compared with a 1990 baseline. An independent Committee on Climate Change was created to monitor progress. In its most recent report to Parliament, the Committee notes that as emissions from other sectors have reduced, transport is now the largest emitting sector of the economy, responsible for 28 per cent of the UK's greenhouse gas emissions. The Committee is concerned that demand for travel by car and van continues to grow while efficiency improvements have slowed, so that the sector is off-track from a cost-effective reduction pathway. Action from the government is sought to tighten emission standards for conventional vehicles, achieve higher uptake of EVs, strengthen incentives to purchase cleaner vehicles, and promote walking, cycling and public transport.[34] The Committee has recognized that the UK government's Road to Zero strategy[35] goes some way to what is needed, but wants a faster pace in the transition to electric propulsion. Given the timescale to 2050, as well as the possibility that the carbon reduction target may need to be made more ambitious, the Committee seeks more energetic action, in particular to bring forwards to 2035 the end of sales of internal combustion engine vehicles, more rigorous enforcement of emission standards for conventional vehicles to prevent manufacturers cheating and more effort to install electric charging infrastructure.[36]

The UK Department for Transport has issued new road traffic forecasts based on a number of scenario assumptions, one of which supposes 100 per cent of sales of cars and vans are zero emission by 2040, in line with government policy. However, no additional tax is assumed to replace the lost tax on oil fuels, so that the fuel cost for cars declines by 63 per cent by 2050. The result is a

50 per cent increase in traffic by 2050, compared with 2015, the largest growth of all scenarios considered and the one that results in the biggest increase in traffic congestion. But this scenario shows the greatest decrease in carbon emissions, of 80 per cent, and a 95 per cent fall in NO_x emissions, both by 2050.[37] This zero-emission scenario demonstrates the impact of a switch to electric propulsion on tailpipe emissions and indicates the implications for traffic congestion of a substantial reduction in fuel cost.

For the issue of sustainability, there is also the question of the source of raw materials used in vehicle and infrastructure construction, in particular those of concern as regards secure and sustainable supply, such as cobalt and other minerals used in batteries. In principle, these materials could be recovered and recycled for economic benefit, although in practice current technologies do not permit all components to be reclaimed at economic cost. Given the harmful environmental impact of discarded motor vehicles and components such as batteries, the economic incentive to recycle may be reinforced by legislation to mandate safe disposal, as is the case in the European Union. At present, some 35 per cent of cobalt used in the EU is derived from recycling. More than 90 per cent of the cobalt in a battery can be recovered.[38] Energy is, of course, required for vehicle production and recovery of materials, which would need to be derived from non-carbon sources if full sustainability is to be achieved.[39]

A further helpful trend as regards resource utilization would be increased vehicle life, for which there is some evidence. The bodies of modern cars are much less liable to corrosion than those of previous generations. In Britain the average age of cars has increased from 6.7 years in 1994 to 8.1 in 2017.[40] The life of EVs remains to be seen, but could be longer, given fewer moving parts and lower operating temperatures compared with conventional vehicles, subject to the possibility of battery replacement.

"Sustainable transport" has become an important concept in transport policy. For some, the thinking has extended beyond the original concern, of avoiding compromising the ability of future generations to meet their own needs, to cover a wide range of desirable aims, including increasing social inclusion, reducing inequalities, improving health and safety and engaging with communities (Greaves & Stanley 2018). While these wider matters are undoubtedly of concern, their impact on subsequent generations is limited, and indeed there may be conflicts between inter-generational impacts and others. For example, in 1993 the British government introduced a "fuel price escalator", a policy by which road fuel tax was to increase by 3 per cent faster than inflation, to cut emissions and reduce the need for road construction. However, following protests about the high cost of fuel in 2000, the policy was effectively abandoned. Holding down the cost of fuel is of particular benefit to those on low incomes who depend on a car to get to work, which is beneficial therefore in respect of inequalities but not for sustainability, as originally defined.

In my view, it is better to conceive sustainability narrowly, as avoiding reducing the welfare of future generations by our actions, whether to consume a non-renewable resource or to raise global temperatures to unacceptable levels. For land transport, sustainability can be achieved in principle by technological means – electric propulsion of road and rail travel using electricity generated from non-fossil fuel sources. In practice, much technical development remains to be undertaken, and policies need to be developed to ensure uptake.

The contemporary critique of "car dependence" has been a key element of thinking about sustainability, with much effort aimed at promoting behavioural changes to encourage use of alternative modes – public transport, and the active modes of walking and cycling. However, the planned switch to electric propulsion lessens the case for reducing car use principally on the grounds of sustainability.

While there are important detrimental consequences of car travel that need to be tackled, particularly deaths and injuries from vehicles crashes, lack of exercise associated with car use, and road traffic congestion, these are not problems of sustainability. There was traffic congestion in ancient Rome, which led Julius Caesar to ban most vehicles from streets in the centre between 6am and 4pm, later extended to all towns in the Roman Empire (Lay 1992: 176). Although the Roman Empire eventually declined and fell, congestion was not a contributory factor. Indeed, congestion reflects economic success that is generally welcomed by those who chose to live in cities, despite the density of people and traffic. I consider possible remedies for traffic congestion in the next chapter.

Conclusion

Electric road vehicles offer the prospect of zero emissions from tailpipes and zero-carbon emissions if coupled with electricity generated from non-fossil fuel sources. This is the aim of policy in Europe and China (although the position in the US is less clear), to which the established motor manufacturers, new entrants and component suppliers are responding by developing EV technology, batteries most importantly. While there remains uncertainty about the pace of change, the direction seems clear.

Electric propulsion for road vehicles is a decisive step towards achieving sustainable transport that minimizes depletion of non-renewable resources and avoids both polluting the atmosphere and contributing to global warming. Improving urban air quality would be an early win if rapid uptake could be achieved through incentives for EV purchase and provision of charging infrastructure.

But electric vehicles will travel no faster than conventional counterparts, so their deployment will not transform our travel behaviour. In this respect, electric propulsion is very different from the coal-fired steam trains and oil-fuelled motorcars, both of which had large transformative impacts on how and where we lived. Nor will electric propulsion as such reduce traffic congestion or improve road safety.

Electric propulsion will reduce tax revenues from road fuel, which would either have to be replaced from other sources or by introducing road-user charging for EVs.

4

DIGITAL NAVIGATION

There have been a number of important recent advances in digital technologies that impact on travel. This chapter considers the by now generally familiar navigation devices, which we acquire as apps for our smartphones or find in our new cars. These offer direct benefits to individuals but also have the potential to benefit all road users by improving the operations of the network.

The key technology is satellite navigation (satnav), which uses satellites to provide spatial positioning by means of small receivers that determine location to high precision. The Global Positioning System (GPS) is the US version. Russia, China and the European Union have developed similar systems.

Digital mapping has essentially digitized traditional paper maps, in the same way that digital documents have digitized their paper versions. However, digital maps have the capacity to accommodate vast amounts of data, including from satellite images and street level information, data that can be readily updated, including traffic information in real time. The combination of satnav location and digital mapping provides a navigation service. For ships and planes, this takes the form of a recommended course between waypoints. For road vehicles, turn-by-turn route guidance is provided.

Satnav location allows the progress of vehicles to be monitored and congested conditions to be detected. Real-time traffic information is included in the most useful route guidance, pioneered notably by Waze, an Israeli tech start-up, an approach now widely adopted. This collects crowd-sourced data about traffic conditions from users' satnav devices, including slow going in congested traffic, and feeds back suggestions for routes with least travel time, taking account of traffic conditions. Also provided are estimated journey times in advance of setting out. In 2013 Waze became a subsidiary of Google, which employs the Waze technology for route guidance for Google Maps. These smartphone apps are free to use and are funded from advertisers who pay to have their locations indicated on the map by small icons.

Optimizing the road network

A challenge for road authorities is to optimize traffic flows on their networks, to minimize delays and improve reliability. An approach adopted on Britain's strategic road network is known as "smart motorways". This involves increasing capacity by utilizing the hard shoulder for moving traffic and employing variable speed limits to smooth traffic flow by avoiding stop-start driving. Monitoring of the first such scheme, on the M42 near Birmingham, found that 73 per cent of road users rated their experience as good or very good (van Vuren *et al.* 2012). However, the cost of such schemes limits their application to major motor roads.

The development of digital navigation is the best means we have to tackle the problem of road traffic congestion generally. Congestion arises in or near areas of high population density, where the capacity of the road network is insufficient to cope with all the trips that might be made. Drivers are deterred by the prospect of time delays and so make other decisions – to travel at a different time, by a different mode, to a different destination (where there are options, as for shopping), or not to travel at all (by shopping online, for instance). Adding road capacity initially reduces delays, which attracts some of the previously deterred drivers, so that more car journeys are made, but the resulting additional traffic restores congestion to what it had been. This additional traffic arising from increasing road capacity is known as "induced traffic", and is the consequence of road users taking the benefit of investment that permits faster travel by travelling further to gain access to more destinations, opportunities and choices within the fixed travel time constraint of an hour a day on average. Induced traffic is the basis of the maxim that you cannot build your way out of congestion, which we know from experience to be generally true; it is why, for instance, the successive addition of extra lanes to the M25, the major orbital motorway around London, failed to offer more than short-term relief of congestion.

Digital route guidance technology that takes account of congestion in real time can offer less congested routes, so making better use of the existing road network and reducing road users' exposure to congestion. One problem that may arise is that traffic may be diverted onto unsuitable roads, where local environments and neighbourhoods may be adversely affected, or even where large vehicles can get stuck. Some satnav systems are designed specifically for heavy goods vehicles and avoid use of unsuitable routes, taking account of size, weight and load. However, it is not clear how many truck drivers use a bespoke system, which can be expensive, and how many rely on more popular satnav devices designed for cars or free-to-use options like Google Maps on a smartphone. Google Maps is considering how to minimize urban rat-running through residential roads.[1] Diversion onto unsuitable routes is a problem that could be mitigated through collaboration between digital navigation providers and road authorities.

A related issue is whether diversion onto alternative routes is optimal for the road network as a whole. The route guidance apps use proprietary algorithms whose performance is difficult to assess externally. An algorithm might respond to build-up of congestion by diverting all traffic to a single alternative route until that became congested, repeating the process to spread traffic across available routes until congestion abated. Or the algorithm might spread traffic across all available routes at the outset. And the algorithm might anticipate the build-up of congestion based on historic experience.

There is little published information on the design and performance of route guidance devices: an exception is a paper by Microsoft staff that describes a method for predicting the probability distribution of travel time for specified routes at chosen times, which is reported to perform well on the Seattle road network (Woodard *et al.* 2017). Google Maps say that each route is calculated on an individual basis, resulting in the fastest route across the network at the particular instant of request; the route is reassessed at regular intervals during the journey to see if a faster route now exists and a new route may be offered.[2]

When only a few people used digital navigation that took account of congestion, there were benefits for those diverted onto less congested routes as well as for those that did not divert, who experienced rather less traffic. But as more drivers use route guidance as it exists, the net benefit to society is less clear.[3] Nevertheless, there is potential for digital navigation technologies to make a significant impact on how the road network functions, with implications for users beyond those equipped with the technology – a further good reason for collaboration to achieve the best outcomes for all road users and for those exposed to traffic in their environment. There is therefore a case for a regulatory regime for digital navigation services.

The road system is already regulated for reasons of safety and efficiency. Vehicles must be certified as safe and are tested annually; drivers must be licensed and are penalized for traffic offences; and new road infrastructure is built to prescribed standards. Given the potential scale of impact of digital navigation devices on network operations, there is a good argument for the regulation of navigation providers, with the aim of improving the experience of road users and those suffering from excessive traffic through their neighbourhoods. It is likely that harnessing digital navigation technology would be a more cost-effective approach to improving efficiency and productivity than costly civil engineering investments.

A licensing regime for digital navigation providers might require information to be exchanged with road authorities, guidance to be accepted to avoid adverse environmental and social impacts, and mutual collaboration to optimize the operational efficiency of the network as a whole. This need not adversely affect the providers' business models based on advertising from retail outlets.

In Britain, there is in fact legislation, dating from 1989, which requires dynamic route guidance systems that take account of traffic conditions to be licensed by the government.[4] The intention was to facilitate the introduction of a pilot route guidance system that had been developed by the government's Transport and Road Research Laboratory, although in the event this was not taken forward. The licence could include conditions concerning the roads that should not be included in route guidance and provision to road authorities of information on traffic conditions. However, in practice this legislation has been disregarded since no licences have been issued.[5] The government's response to a consultation in 2011 concluded that further regulation would be counterproductive and that the most practicable approach is voluntary data sharing between road authorities and mapping providers.[6] The consultation was part of a "red tape challenge", aimed at reducing unnecessary regulation generally; it seems unlikely that serious consideration was given at that time to the case for regulating navigation devices, although the legislation was not repealed and could be used in the future.

Examples of voluntary data sharing exist. In London, Transport for London makes data freely available to app developers and is a partner with Waze's Connected Citizens Programme, which provides real-time data on traffic disruptions.[7] Uber, the ride-hailing provider, also provides anonymized data on traffic movement for many cities, based on data from its fleet of vehicles.

Many city authorities operate urban traffic management systems aimed at optimizing traffic flows by varying the timing of traffic signals. They may be able to take advantage of data from digital navigation providers. In London, where three-quarters of congestion is the result of excess demand and one quarter from planned events or unplanned incidents, 75 per cent of the 6,000 sets of traffic signals vary their timing continuously to optimize flow across both individual junctions and the network as a whole, reducing delays at junctions by about 13 per cent.[8] The benefits from such dynamic traffic signal technology were shown during the 2012 London Olympic Games when major changes in flow were managed successfully (Emmerson 2014). TfL is planning improvements to its urban traffic management system, including a new predictive signalling system that will automatically detect and deal with the many smaller incidents, plus better capability to manage the location of traffic congestion to where and when it has least impact.[9]

An important question concerns the scope for improving traffic flows by means of the algorithms for digital navigation used by individual drivers. A study using data collected before and during the 2016 Rio de Janeiro Olympics, including data from Waze, compared the expected journey times for three scenarios, according to whether drivers followed their usual routes, chose routes with the shortest time for the individual, or were directed to routes that were best for travellers as a whole. This modelling study found that sticking to the usual habits involved up to 7 per cent longer journey times during the Games compared with both the "selfish" and "altruistic" approaches (Xu & Gonzalez 2017). This suggests some modest benefits for users of digital navigation, although the advantage of attempting to optimize use of the network for all users is unclear.

We can regard encouraging drivers to modify their behaviour to get better outcomes for all road users as an example of a "nudge", an intervention that structures the choices available to help individuals to make better choices for the benefit of all, without restricting their freedom to choose. Indeed, Richard Thaler, winner of the Nobel Prize for economics and proposer of the nudge concept, cites GPS technology on smartphones as an example: you decide where you want to go, the app offers possible routes and you are free to decline the advice if you decide to take a detour (Thaler 2018).

Nudging to improve the operation of a transport system has considerable potential. Providing real-time information about travel conditions to targeted groups of travellers may allow more choices to individuals and at the same time achieve better collective outcomes by steering people away from road congestion or rail hold-ups. This would require collaboration between transport authorities and navigation providers, exemplified by TfL's making its travel data freely available to those developing new apps and services for its customers, generating economic benefits and savings estimated at up to £130 million a year.[10]

Data sharing with road authorities generally would enhance operational efficiency and make better use of the road network. However, route guidance technologies would not be expected to have much impact on congestion in well-populated areas on account of the previously deterred trips that might now be made. Using digital navigation to make better use of the network is similar to adding physical capacity in that delays are initially reduced, giving rise to induced traffic that restores congestion to what it had been.

Mitigating the impact of congestion

While it is ineffectual to tackle congestion head-on, we need not be without hope of mitigating its impact. To see a way forward, we need to enquire why congestion is a problem in practice. We can ask road users about their experience of congestion, both in surveys and in discussion. The available evidence from their responses is that the uncertainty of journey time is more important than slower speed. One survey of road users in England asked about priorities for increased expenditure on motorways: almost half of respondents ranked improved flow and reduced congestion as a priority, compared with less than a quarter wanting reduced journey times.[11]

On the one hand, people get anxious if their journey is taking longer than anticipated, particularly if they need to be at their destination at a particular time. On the other hand, they do not want to rush out early and then find themselves at the destination with too much time to spare. This is where the route guidance apps provide their main benefit. They estimate the time of arrival in the light of prevailing traffic conditions on the selected route, in this way substantially reducing journey time uncertainty. There is a lack of publicly available data on performance, but my personal experience of urban car travel indicates that estimated times of arrival can be reasonably reliable.

Estimation of journey times before setting out may also increase the operational efficiency of the road network. To a first approximation, there are two kinds of road users. There are those who need to be at their destination at a particular time, whether to get to work or a meeting or to deliver time-critical goods; they can use predictive journey time information to decide when best to set out. Alternatively, there are those who are more flexible in timing their trips, for instance for shopping, leisure activities, or delivering goods in wide time slots; this group can use estimate journey times to minimize their exposure to congested traffic. This is potentially win–win, in that the more the flexible road users can avoid peak traffic, the less traffic at peak times experienced by those not flexible.

So the digital navigation technologies offer the best prospects for mitigating the adverse experience of road traffic congestion. They are not limited to cars and trucks. For public transport, information on the real-time progress of buses can be provided, both at visual displays at bus stops and on smartphone apps. The pioneer is the Citymapper app that provides detailed journey information in the cities served for public transport, walking and cycling, including cost and time for each mode, with real-time information for buses and trains where available and a map showing present location and route to destination. Citymapper also links to taxi apps such as Uber. Such route guidance apps encourage the use of public transport and the active modes of travel.

Road freight

Road freight businesses, whether short-distance urban delivery or long-distance road haulage, need to meet their customers' needs for timely service while minimizing costs. This involves choosing routes that minimize the overall distance travelled and time taken, allowing for the impact of traffic congestion on reliability. Digital routing and scheduling systems exist, although take-up has tended to be low, particularly for small businesses. For large businesses, logistics is a core capability to maintain competitive advantage. Congestion is a major concern as this affects costs and service, and route optimization under congestion is an aspect that needs development (Rincon-Garcia, Waterson & Cherrett 2017).

The major road freight businesses already manage their fleets to achieve just-in-time delivery at their customers' premises. A haulage business under contract with a supermarket chain to distribute from central warehouses to stores typically has to deliver within 30-minute time slots or face a penalty. This they can achieve by controlling the progress of each vehicle and understanding traffic congestion. I once had the opportunity to ask a senior executive of a well-known freight haulier to what extent unanticipated congestion detracted from performance. I was impressed by his response that unanticipated congestion had less impact than unanticipated delays at customers' premises. This illustrates the potential of digital navigation to reduce journey time uncertainty for all road users.

Innovative digital technologies seem likely to make a significant impact on the use of the road network for deliveries. For example, DriveNet, a British business started in 2016, offers a smartphone app that provides a live link between drivers and customers, to guide to precise destinations for unloading on arrival and avoid needless delays at sites and stores. But such efficiency gains are likely to be offset by the growth of online retailing and the consequential home deliveries. People and goods will continue to compete for road space.

Digital or civil solutions to congestion?

As noted above, urban authorities are beginning to exploit digital technologies for traffic management. However, this thinking seems to have had only limited impact on those responsible for inter-urban road construction, who remain largely wedded to traditional civil engineering to attempt to solve the problem of road traffic congestion.

The UK government is funding a large inter-urban road-building programme, as part of a general enthusiasm for investing in infrastructure to boost economic growth. The road investment strategy for the period 2015–20 involves expenditure of £15 billion on the motorways and main trunk roads in England, with one aim being a free-flow core network with a mile a minute speeds increasingly typical.[12] A draft strategy for the subsequent five-year period proposes expenditure of £25 billion.[13]

The economic rationale for road building is based on the idea that reducing congestion allows the saving of travel time, the value of which is based on the extra work or leisure that would be gained, together with economic gains from enhanced connectivity between cities and from "agglomeration" effects arising from higher density of economic activity. However, this is misleading because, as noted in Chapter 2, travel time is not reduced – average travel time has remained unchanged for the past 45 years. In fact, people take the benefit of faster travel to go further, the economic benefit being the additional opportunities and choices gained, while the extra traffic (induced traffic) restores congestion to what it had been. I discussed in Chapter 2 the example of the widening of part of the M25 orbital motorway to the north of London, where the increase in traffic volumes resulted in no improvement in travel time. So the case for huge expenditure on civil engineering road infrastructure is misleading and overstated (Metz 2017).

Civil engineering involves traditional techniques to shift earth, pour concrete and roll tarmac. This approach is very costly. For example, an improvement to a single, albeit important, junction on an existing motorway is estimated to cost £282 million, and widening three miles of single-lane carriageway to cost £250–500 million.[14] Substantial productivity improvements in civil engineering seem hard to achieve.

In contrast, the productivity of digital technologies advances in leaps and bounds, as computing power and bandwidth soar and costs plummet. Digital technologies are making a big impact on the railways, as I will discuss in Chapter 7. They also offer great promise for achieving a more efficient use of the existing road system. For instance, improvements to London's urban traffic management system mentioned above are intended to reduce planned and unplanned delays and improve journey time reliability, yielding a benefit-to-cost ratio of 7.8, which means an economic benefit of £7.8 for every £1 spent.[15] This is high compared with typical civil engineering investments for which recent estimates are benefit-to-cost ratios of four for junction improvements and road widening, and two for new roads, albeit these values overstate the benefits since they are based on modelled time savings that underestimate induced traffic.[16]

What is needed is a shift in mind-set on the part of both highways professionals and the politicians responsible for allocating funding for roads. Common to both is the simplistic but mistaken idea that more road capacity is always a "good thing", resulting in less congestion, faster travel and economic stimulus. We also need a rethink of the economic models and investment appraisal methods used to justify road construction. Existing approaches underestimate the amount of induced traffic and so overestimate the reduction in congestion. Existing methods also attach greatest weight to the theoretical saving in travel time and play down the value of journey time reliability, whereas road users take the opposite view, as noted above.

So public authorities responsible for road systems need to focus much more on the scope for digital technologies to improve their networks, an approach that seems very likely to be highly cost-effective and publicly acceptable, compared with traditional civil engineering.

Conclusion

Digital navigation technologies help us find our way around the world by providing the quickest routes and estimating how long our trip will take. This is the best approach we have to mitigating the impact of road traffic congestion, particularly if there can be collaboration between the providers of route guidance and the road authorities with the aim of optimizing the performance of the road network and improving the experience of users. Digital navigation can also make more accessible modes of travel other than the car, by providing real-time information for public transport and suitable routes for walking and cycling.

The ubiquity of free-to-download digital navigation apps on our smartphones is an important addition to the existing spatial infrastructure of signs and signals. Routes can be selected according to mode of travel and the environment through which we move, as, for example, the choice of fast, regular or quiet cycle routes available on Citymapper. Regular journeys, such as commutes, can be recognized and problems on particular days forewarned. There is scope for further development, such as better guidance for walking. All this meets our need for instantly available spatial information, to complement the most recent news of political, economic, cultural and social developments.

Yet while they will improve the quality of our journeys, digital navigation technologies will have at best quite limited impact on the overall speed of travel, and so will not importantly affect how and why we travel. Speedier availability of more spatial information does not imply faster movement.

5

DIGITAL PLATFORMS

The digital revolution is making a big impact on transport, from smart bus stops with real-time tracking, to satnavs, to apps for taxis and train times and tickets. The interconnectivity offered by the internet and mobile phone technology has radically altered the information available for us when we travel. These developments have not been without controversy or disruption. This chapter will explore some of the major innovations that are transforming urban travel by harnessing the power of the internet to match demand to supply by means of "digital platforms". These are revolutionizing many areas of our lives, most notably by making possible online shopping. I focus here on the way that this innovative technology has disrupted and transformed the taxi market in many cities.

Taxis and apps

The best-known example of a digital platform for transport is the Uber smartphone app, which has stimulated considerable controversy. The app connects users and taxi drivers transparently. Users know in advance the approximate price of the journey, see the progress of the taxi as it approaches the rendezvous, know the name of the driver and the number of the vehicle, pay through the app, rate the driver after the trip and receive a follow-up email recording trip details. The success of the company is mainly because the app provides a more efficient and effective way of matching the demand from travellers with the supply of vehicles: more effective than trying to wave down a regular taxi in the street or summoning a vehicle by a phone call.

A word about terminology. I use the term "taxi" broadly to cover all types of car with a driver where each trip is paid for individually, while recognizing that a range of more restricted usages is also in use. A traditional distinction is between licensed taxis equipped with a meter that regulates the fares charged and private hire vehicles without a meter where charges are agreed for each trip. In London, for instance, the iconic black cab equipped with meter can be waved down in the street; in contrast private hire vehicles without meters, commonly known as "minicabs", cannot legally be hailed but must be summoned by phone.

Uber-type services, often known as "ride-hailing", have been controversial, not least because they do not fit these traditional categories and so have been able to evade key aspects of taxi regulation. In 2015 a London court ruled that the smartphone app was not a taximeter, as defined in legislation, and so Uber was not constrained by the rules applying to black cab drivers.[1] Ride-hailing operators (sometimes known as transportation network companies) position themselves as intermediaries between passengers and self-employed drivers, earning a fee for service that amounts typically to between a quarter and a third of the fare.

As well as managing that immediate match of vehicle with user, the Uber and similar ride-hailing platforms help achieve an overall balance of supply and demand by means of "surge pricing", whereby charges for users are raised when demand exceeds supply. This serves to deter some users while at the same time attracting more drivers onto the road. The platform is two-sided in that it must be attractive both to users and drivers, meeting and balancing the needs of both.

While Uber pioneered the digital platform for taxi services, there are now many competitors with very similar offerings, including Lyft in the US, Didi Chuxing in China, Grab in eight countries across South East Asia, Ola in India and Gett, an app for licensed black cabs in London and other UK cities that also functions in cities in Russia and Israel. What is not clear at present is whether ride-hailing in individual city markets is naturally competitive, or whether there is a tendency to monopoly, as I shall discuss later.

The digital matching of demand and supply is a development of an older approach known generally as demand-responsive travel, mainly employed to meet the needs of older people and those with disabilities that prevent them using public transport. This is often still known as "dial-a-ride", reflecting its origin in the days when telephones had dials. Booking this service in London requires emailing a request the day before travel. The smartphone app is vastly more streamlined and accordingly has become enormously popular.

Impact of ride-hailing

Ride-hailing may have important consequences for public transport use and for road traffic congestion. It could complement by catering for the "last mile" from fixed-route public transport to home, but also substitute for public transport for some trips. The growth of ride-hailing could add to congestion, or might substitute for private vehicles. Relevant evidence is still accumulating and the eventual outcomes are far from settled.

Generally, ride-hailing in the US is currently concentrated in large, densely populated metropolitan areas. A study of the impact of ride-hailing services in six US cities in 2016 found that heaviest use was during evening hours and weekends, in part to meet the needs of people who want to drink and not drive. Most trips were short and concentrated in downtown neighbourhoods where the cost of parking is high, with journeys to airports the main exception. No clear relationship was found between peak-hour ride-hailing and transit (public transport) use; commuting involves routine use of car or transit, whereas ride-hailing use is more occasional. Where ride-hailing was preferred to transit, reasons given by survey respondents were fast travel and shorter waiting times. Frequent ride-hailing users were less likely to own a car.[2] Another study of seven US cities confirmed parking and drinking alcohol as top motivations to prefer ride-hailing.[3] A study in San Francisco found the main attraction of ride-hailing to be ease of payment, short wait time and speed of travel (Rayle *et al.* 2016).

Comparison of travel times in Washington, DC, found that for longer trips between the downtown area and the suburbs the Metro (light rail) tended to be quicker than Uber. But for trips within the city that require a Metro transfer, Uber was often quicker, especially when Metro wait times are long, as on weekends. While Uber's regular service tended to be much more expensive than the Metro, some UberPOOL shared trips were nearly as affordable as the Metro.[4]

A study in New York City found that ride-hailing had not driven the growth of congestion in the central business district since this had substituted for licensed yellow taxi trips.[5] A subsequent detailed analysis showed that although ride-hailing has been growing rapidly, it had contributed to a growth of traffic in the city of only 3.5 per cent between 2013 and 2016. Most trips were in the Manhattan core.[6]

An analysis of data from US metropolitan areas concluded that Uber complemented public transit on average, increasing ridership on the latter by 5 per cent after two years. Substitution was not found to be significant, given the differences in fares between Uber and transit (Hall, Palsson & Price 2018). However, a study of transit data in major US cities over the period 2002–18 found bus ridership could be expected to decrease by 1.7 per cent a year after ride-hailing entered the market.[7]

The impact of ride-hailing in London seems similar to that in the US in that analysis indicates an inverse relationship between Uber usage times and congestion peak periods, with only some 30 per cent of Uber travel occurring between 7am and 6pm.[8] This suggests that the impact of ride-hailing on peak hours congestion is limited. Analysis of changes to the traffic composition in the central London congestion charging zone led Transport for London to conclude that the substantial increase in private hire vehicles (essentially Uber) has largely been a matter of substitution for other vehicles and has not therefore contributed directly to increased congestion.[9]

Sharing

Public transport naturally involves sharing space within a vehicle with others. Historically, shared taxis were common before widespread ownership of private cars (Dienel & Vahrenkamp 2018). Digital platforms now facilitate sharing a vehicle with others travelling in the same direction, the incentive being lower fares through sharing the cost of the trip.

The UberPOOL option on this app allows cheaper travel for those willing to share. Lyft, another ride-hailing service in the US, offers a similar option, costing up to 60 per cent less than an unshared ride. However, the appeal of cost saving may be offset by the extra time involved in dropping off passengers en route.

The main cost of a taxi service is the pay of the driver. This can be avoided if the person making the trip drives the vehicle. Car sharing in the form of car clubs has been made possible by digital platform technology that allows people to make trips by car without owning their own. Cars for sharing can be booked in advance, located via smartphone apps at designated points in the street, to which they are returned, and paid for direct from the user's account, with charges based on time and distance. This mode of car sharing is exemplified by Zipcar, founded by Robin Chase in Boston, Massachusetts, in 2000, which is in effect a local version of traditional car hire that offers rental by the hour as well as by the day, and indeed Zipcar was purchased by the Avis car rental business in 2013. Other car clubs operate as cooperatives or social enterprises.

An alternative approach to car sharing is the floating car club, in which vehicles have no fixed location but are found within a broad area using an app. DriveNow, owned by BMW, offers car sharing in 13 cities in Europe. car2go, owned by Daimler, operates in a number of US and European cities but withdrew from the UK in 2014, as well as from cities elsewhere, raising a question about the commercial viability of this approach. In March 2018, BMW and Daimler announced they were to merge their car sharing and ride-hailing services.[10]

Another kind of sharing involves the owner of a car finding people willing to share the cost of the journey via an app, in effect an extension of car sharing among friends or colleagues. BlaBlaCar, a carpooling platform started in France in 2003, claims 60 million members in 22 countries; passengers book and pay for city to city trips via the app, and drivers receive payment after the ride. The British Liftshare business, with the slogan "cut the cost of your journey and meet amazing people", facilitates car sharing for both regular commutes and occasional longer-distance trips. Waze Carpool is similar.

Shared mobility is seen by many proponents as central to taking advantage of vehicle electrification and automation by making more efficient use of underused capital assets. Daniel Sperling sees filling empty seats on all vehicles as the way to ameliorate congestion and reduce climate change. Shared use of ride-hailing allows fares to be reduced and so could attract more passengers (Sperling 2018b). Such sharing fits with the more general move towards the "sharing economy", in which assets owned by individuals but not used full time can be made available to others via a digital platform, as I will discuss later. Yet there are uncertainties about people's willingness to share with others in smaller vehicles, both on account of personal comfort and safety, and because shared trips take longer than a solo journey, whether between a single origin and destination or the more complex multi-purpose journeys that are common.[11]

More importantly, although it might be supposed that sharing of vehicles would reduce the amount of traffic on the roads and so lessen congestion, this is too simplistic a conclusion. As discussed in Chapter 1, congestion arises in areas of high population density and high car ownership, such that many potential car trips are suppressed by the prospect of unacceptable time delays. So traffic reduction through sharing that reduced delays would be expected to induce more trips by those previously deterred, consistent with the experience that it is very difficult to reduce traffic congestion.

Bicycle hire

Digital platforms make possible matching demand to supply in other areas of travel, giving rise to innovative services. The popularity of cycling, in wide use before car-based mass mobility, is undergoing a revival in urban areas, reflecting relative reliability of journey times on congested roads, low cost and the health benefits of exercise. Bicycle hire allows those without their own bikes to have a go, whether to try the experience or for regular trips. City bike hire schemes were pioneered in France – Lyon in 2005 and Paris in 2007 – using fixed docks where bikes are found and returned, with charges based on a subscription. Many other cities have adopted such authorised cycle hire schemes.

A disadvantage with these schemes is the lack of information in advance as to whether a bike will be available at the nearest dock and whether there is a vacant space when it needs to be returned. An answer is dockless bicycle hire, which involves bikes equipped with satellite positioning. This allows users to identify an available nearby bike on a smartphone app, unlock it and pay via the app. Docks are not needed, avoiding their cost. Chinese innovators have been prominent in establishing global businesses. Ofo was founded by members of the Peking University cycling club in 2014 and at its peak served 50 cities, although it subsequently withdrew from international markets. Mobike, also originating in Beijing, currently operates in over 200 cities.

Because no physical installation of docking stations is required, it has been possible for dockless bicycle businesses to enter the market without agreement of city authorities. A consequence has been improperly parked bikes that block and clutter pavements. There are striking photographs of huge piles of discarded bikes in Chinese cities.[12] In consequence, many cities have attempted to regulate the dockless businesses. London, where both ofo and Mobike have been active, has introduced a code of practice that requires cycle providers to engage with the authorities to avoid negative impacts.[13]

Although substantial finance has been raised by dockless bike start-ups, the ultimate value of such investment is unclear. Significant labour costs are involved to recover abandoned bikes, service them and move them to where they will be used.[14] Competition between bike providers constrains charges and profits. Investors who supported very rapid growth of the companies may be disappointed.[15]

An attractive alternative to the regular bicycle is one equipped with an electric motor and battery, to supplement the rider's effort. Ebikes are now available for hire via apps in many cities, which allows prospective purchasers to try them out. A trial of shared ebikes sponsored by the UK Department for Transport indicated that they could attract new riders to cycling and enable longer and hilly trips to be made.[16]

Cycling is generally seen as a desirable transport mode – good for health through exercise and good for the environment by getting people out of their cars. Cities like Copenhagen and Amsterdam that are very friendly to cyclists are regarded as exemplars of what can be achieved. In Copenhagen, 62 per cent of residents' trips to work or education were by bike in 2016. For all trips in the city, 29 per cent were by bike, 34 per cent by car and 18 per cent by public transport.[17] It is interesting to compare this with London, where only 2 per cent of trips were by bike, 37 per cent by car and 37 per cent by public transport.[18] So car use in these two cities is substantial and similar, whereas public transport use in Copenhagen is half that of London. It seems that it is hard to get people out of their cars onto bikes, but easier to divert them from crowded trains and buses. In a city like London, where it is difficult to invest in public transport to keep pace with a growing population, promoting cycling to relieve overcrowding is good policy. However, in cities where bus use is in decline, encouraging cycling is more problematic.

More platforms: scooters, minibuses, parking

Electric scooters (a scaled-up version of the child's toy) have recently been introduced in many US cities, and also in Paris and some German cities (although they are not legal in Britain). They travel at up to 15 mph. Venture capital seems keen to invest in this latest transport innovation, regarded hopefully as a short-distance alternative to the car or ride-hailing on congested streets.[19] Unlike dockless bikes, these dockless scooters can be cleared from streets overnight by local people for charging in their home garages for a fee.[20] However, the eventual scale, public acceptability and impact of electric scooters remain to be seen. To address these questions, the City of Santa Monica, California, is operating a 16-month pilot programme that started in September 2018, in which four shared mobility companies provide initially up to 2,000 scooters for use on public rights of way.[21]

The digital platform with driver is being extended to a variety of vehicle types. Uber offers a motorbike service in India and Pakistan, as does Grab in Vietnam and Indonesia.

Meeting suburban and rural demand for transport is different from the inner city, and demand-responsive options are more limited. Minibuses, sometimes known as "microtransit", offer the possibility of cheaper and attractive alternatives to regular buses in suburban and rural areas. Microtransit can operate in various modes, depending on whether both the route and the timetable are fixed or flexible. The common element is the app to summon the service. However, the economics of this mode depend on usage, which in turn depends on the precise service on offer. Recent trials in the US provide varied experience (Polzin & Sperling 2018).[22]

The Ford Motor Company purchased Chariot, which operated minibuses on defined routes booked through a smartphone app in a number of US cities and in London, where four routes were trialled. Rather than halting at regular stops, these minibuses would take up and put down passengers at any convenient location on the route, the passenger making known their wishes in advance on the app. However, this effort of Ford to invest in modes of mobility other than the car proved a commercial failure and the service was withdrawn early in 2019.

Via, which offers a similar demand-responsive minibus service in New York, Chicago and Washington, DC, makes its digital platform available to other operators. This is used by Arriva, a UK bus operator, for services around the Kent Science Park and in Liverpool, with plans to roll out to other areas, a rational initiative by a traditional bus company in response to an innovation that permits services on routes with too little demand for a timetabled bus and that could be applied to regular bus services more generally. Zeelo is a British platform that matches passengers with long-distance coaches, for both regular commuting and attendance at sporting and social events.

Parking is another service where demand and supply can be effectively managed on a digital platform. A variety of smartphone apps indicate the location, real-time availability and cost of on- and off-street parking spaces in cities, and the ability to pay via the app. Some apps allow householders to rent out their off-street parking spaces. A complementary approach operates in San Francisco where the price of kerb parking at meters varies by location and time of day, with the aim of better matching demand with supply and achieving occupancy rates of 60–80 per cent, so that cruising to find a space is minimized (Pierce & Shoup 2013).

For travel by rail and air, online reservation and payment via digital platforms is routine. The budget airlines pioneered flexible pricing to achieve high seat occupancy, allowing travellers willing to commit well in advance to travel at low cost, while keeping seats available at higher prices for those booking near the time of departure. Such flexible pricing to match supply and demand maximizes revenues for the operator and, in a competitive market, lowers costs to travellers.

Mobility-as-a-Service

All the digital platforms discussed so far have made available a single means of travel for a single trip. To accommodate more complex journeys requiring different modes of transportation, there is an aspiration to extend the approach to allow a journey comprising more than one mode to be planned, booked and paid for on a single digital platform. This concept is known as Mobility-as-a-Service (MaaS). It would allow the traveller to use conventional public transport, taxis of all types – including ride-hailing – and bike rental, and is seen by many as the next big thing in transport.

MaaS has been pioneered in Helsinki, Finland, where travel by public transport, taxi, rental bike and self-drive hire car are available on a commercial platform via a single app named Whim. Payment can be either per trip or by means of a subscription for a monthly package of travel. A low-cost package covers public transport and bicycle hire; a high cost package includes as well unlimited urban taxi and car hire. Other trials and implementations of MaaS are underway in Vienna, Hannover, the West Midlands of the UK and Antwerp. The public policy aim of MaaS is to offer a cost-effective and convenient alternative to the private car, thereby reducing urban car ownership and, it is hoped, road traffic congestion.

The coordination of information for the MaaS offering is quite demanding: journey options, route guidance, ticketing and payment for linked travel by different modes. City public transport undertakings can achieve this in part. For instance, Transport for London offers an online journey planner that includes options for bus, rail and the active modes of walking and cycling (but not taxi), with cashless payment during the trip by the Oyster card or standard bank or credit card.

In some 70 cities of developed countries, the app of tech company Citymapper offers public transport and active modes, plus a number of taxi options, but no means for payment via the app. Nevertheless, where other convenient means of payment are available, Citymapper can effectively function as MaaS, as I found on a recent trip to Berlin. I purchased a three-day travel card at the airport that covered all public transport use, navigated using Citymapper and, when I wanted a taxi for a late ride back to my hotel, Uber was available via the app, using my account opened in the UK. Following Citymapper's example, Google Maps also offers routes by different modes of travel, both urban and between cities.

There are two broad approaches to developing MaaS: leadership by a public body, whether the local government of a city or its public transport organization; or through a private sector initiative, for instance Whim in Helsinki. Another private sector initiative is that Uber is to expand its offering with dockless bike rental and car sharing, and has announced partnership with Masabi, a British company that has developed mobile ticketing for public transport, to add that facility to the Uber app.[23] Uber is offering a transit option on its app in Denver, Colorado, an initiative that is significant, given Uber's reach and ambition. Lyft offers a transit option on its app in Santa Monica, California.[24]

It is not clear at present whether one approach is likely to be better than the other. Indeed, partnership between city transport undertakings and private providers could be optimal. Yet this may not be easy to achieve, given conflicting priorities. Public transport agencies may be keen to maintain public recognition of their brand, which could be weakened by a MaaS intermediary. Moreover, the requirements for a seamless and reliable travel offering are quite demanding. Linking different modes to form a complete journey would depend a lot on the reliability of the components, a particular problem for travel on congested roads. Alternative options in the event of delay would need to be part of the offering but could prove difficult to achieve on the scale required if MaaS is to be more than a niche market and make a significant impact on urban mobility, as its protagonists seek.

The issues associated with the development of MaaS are also those that are challenging for urban travel generally: the need to operate reliable transport services, but at the same time to encourage innovations that meet the desires of travellers; the relationships between public and private sector providers; the role of public authorities in both regulating the transport system and operating part of it, and possible conflicts of interest; and the extent to which services may be funded by fares or by public funds. I will return to these issues in the final chapter.

Digital innovations beyond transport

Beyond transport services, other digital platforms are impacting on travel behaviour. Airbnb matches those wanting short-term lodging with those wishing to rent out spare rooms and other accommodation. This has boosted tourism by adding to the supply of hotel rooms in popular destinations, sometimes to the point of generating a backlash from local people concerned about unsocial behaviour by visitors. The authorities in Barcelona, a city hugely popular with visitors, operates and enforces a licensing system for vacation apartments, with which Airbnb cooperates by sharing data.[25]

Online shopping, pioneered by Amazon and the supermarkets, is leading to the decline of the high street and shopping malls. Our individual need for shopping trips has dropped. In 2016, 77 per cent of all adults in Britain bought goods or services online; 73 per cent of young adults bought clothes and 35 per cent bought food or groceries.[26] Of people shopping for Christmas in 2015, 85 per cent reported doing so online for at least some of their needs.[27] This growth of online purchases doubtless contributes to the declining trend in shopping trips observed in the UK National Travel Survey; individuals made around three shopping trips a week in 2015, compared to around four in 2002.

Two-thirds of shopping trips are made by car, so the decline in such trips would reduce car traffic, although the growth of online shopping means more vans delivering to homes. However, optimized routing allows the efficiency of home deliveries to increase as the number of deliveries per mile grows, and the economics of same- or next-day delivery improve as volumes grow. Light goods vehicle numbers in Britain have been increasing rapidly in recent years, with van traffic up by 23 per cent over the past decade and accounting at present for 15 per cent of all traffic.[28]

Digital technologies, in the form of information and telecommunication technologies, have enabled working remotely, whether at home or at places other than the usual workplace. This has doubtless made possible the steady decline in commuting trips in Britain, from 7.1 journeys per worker per week in 1990 to 5.7 in 2014, as discussed in Chapter 2. Digital technologies also allow meeting online rather than face-to-face, which could reduce the need to travel; but ease of communication allows people to develop wider networks of colleagues, prompting more travel to consolidate relationships through informal get-togethers. On the whole, the available evidence indicates no great net effect on travel of the information and telecommunication technologies (Aguilera, Guillot & Rallet 2012).

However, the effect of the recent rapid growth of social media has yet to be fully appreciated. On the one hand, a recent study of young adults in Australia suggested that more frequent "virtual" interaction was associated with more frequent face-to-face interaction, not less (Delbosc & Mokhtarian 2018). On the other hand, travel survey data in Britain show young people aged 17–29 making fewer trips and spending much more time at home: for men 80 minutes a day more from 1995 to 2014, and 40 minutes for women (Chatterjee *et al.* 2018). Although there is no information on the additional activities carried out at home, one might speculate that 40 minutes on social media might substitute for face-to-face contact, with men taking a further 40 minutes to play online games. A study of how time is used by young men aged 21–30 in the US found a decline in the hours worked of 2.5 hours a week between 2004–07 and 2012–15, and an increase of 2.0 hours in recreational computer time, of which 1.4 hours were used for video games (Aguiar *et al.* 2018).

Economics of platforms

Digital platforms are having an undeniable impact on the transport system and how we use it by matching users with services more effectively than before. This can attract users away from traditional services where there are options, as when ride-hailing competes with conventional taxis, or where online booking displaces travel agents. Traditional businesses are being disrupted by digital platforms, although the future impact of all these innovations is far from clear. Much will depend on the underlying economics. A key question is the importance of "network effects".

Network effects have long been recognized in circumstances when services become more valuable to each user as more people use them. The telephone is the historic example; the social media are recent instances. Network effects reflect demand-side economies of scale, where benefits to users, the source of demand, grow as the scale increases (contrasted with supply-side economies of scale where costs fall as scale increases). Networks may naturally tend to monopoly supply since competing providers may segment the market and so limit connections between users on different networks, unless a regulator requires connection, as with the mobile phone networks of different providers. In contrast, an unregulated network such as Facebook can become effectively a global monopoly.

The digital platforms of interest in transport are two-sided in order to match supply with demand. They have separate interfaces for users and providers. In the case of Uber, for instance, there are separate apps for those who want a taxi and for the drivers who provide the trips. Network effects arise because the more users there are, the more providers benefit, and vice-versa. The efficiency of platforms in matching supply to demand can ensure drivers get more rides and experience less unoccupied time, thus permitting fares that are more attractive than less efficient competitors. An analysis of vehicle utilization in five large US cities found that Uber drivers on average had a passenger for about half the time their app was turned on, whereas regular taxi drivers had a passenger for 30–50 per cent of the time they were working. On average the capacity utilization rate, the fraction of miles driven with a passenger, was 50 per cent higher for Uber drivers than for taxi drivers. This is attributed to Uber's more efficient technology for matching of supply and demand, its larger scale, flexible labour supply and surge pricing (Cramer & Krueger 2016).

It is this enhanced efficiency that would be the basis of the long-run success of a ride-hailing operator, enabling it to offer competitive fares to customers and better earnings for drivers. The question is to what extent new entrants to the market might emulate the success of the initial incumbent.

The most successful platforms take advantage of network effects to become powerful aggregators of both supply and demand. They are early to the business space and pay a great deal of attention to user interfaces and experience, since users may be unwilling to employ more than one or two competing platforms.[29] New entrants to the market may find it hard to achieve critical mass in the face of a dominant incumbent.

In the transport sector, we are concerned with platforms that function "online to offline": digital access to physical mobility (as distinct from online to online for downloads of digital music or e-books). As well as matching users with services, the platforms employ algorithms to optimize operations, such as selecting the fastest routes and predicting the location of future demand. The negligible cost of digital scaling means that these platforms can handle huge volumes of information about user preferences, availability and price of services, and payments. In the past such data handling would have been limited to large organizations. Now, the availability of cloud computing with unlimited amounts of capacity helps innovators enter the market, scale rapidly and compete aggressively. This accumulation of data about customers' preferences and behaviour is a new factor that tends to reinforce network effects.

On the demand side – the customers – economies of scale can increase much faster than cost, which prompts innovators to raise venture capital in order to grow market share as quickly as possible and gain what is termed "first mover advantage". Large amounts of capital can be made available to promising technologies by investors hoping for high returns from establishing a dominant position in the market. However, the main challenge for transport digital platforms arises because the supply side involves physical plant and infrastructure whose capacity is finite, and where economies of scale may be limited or absent. Accordingly, capacity must be carefully managed.

An important tool is revenue management, pioneered by the budget airlines, where varying price is used to match supply with demand. This needs lots of data and lots of supply and demand to run well. Surge pricing employed by Uber involves applying a multiplier to standard fares, announced prior to booking a journey, when demand exceeds the supply of drivers. Surge pricing both attracts more drivers at times of high demand and deters some potential users, thus bringing supply and demand into better balance. This illustrates how two-sided digital platforms can make possible a wide but non-localized market, in contrast to a traditional market in which buyers and sellers congregate in one physical location: the marketplace.

As well as benefiting from network effects, digital platforms can reduce information asymmetries that inhibit transactions, such as whether you can trust your taxi driver, particularly in an unfamiliar city. Uber asks both customers and drivers to rate each other after each journey, which allows poor performers to be dropped and increases confidence in quality of service. Another question of trust concerns those with whom you might share a journey, motivated by lower fares. Confidence in shared use of small vehicles could be enhanced by the routine rating of the journey experience via a peer review process.

A key item of information for a taxi journey is the fare. Traditional regulated taxis charge according to distance and time: the meter provides assurance that the customer is charged correctly, but no advance estimate is offered. In contrast, the operator of a ride-hailing app can flex the charging structure to bring supply and demand into balance, but the customer is given an estimate of the charge in advance. There is a clear choice here for customers. However, what is not clear is the efficiency with which the optimal route is chosen. In London, there is a rigorous requirement for a detailed knowledge of street routes and places of interest, known as the "knowledge", as a condition for the driver gaining a black cab licence. There is limited evidence as to whether this is superior in practice to satnav that takes account of traffic congestion in real time, as used by ride-hailing drivers. One small-scale trial in London found that black cabs took on average 88 per cent of the time of Uber but were around 35 per cent more expensive. This was attributed to a licensed taxi driver being able to use bus lanes (not available for others) and more complex routes via side streets, it being suggested that satnav favours simpler routes as easier to follow.[30]

One common attraction of ride-hailing is fares that are lower compared to conventional taxis. Operators of two-sided platforms typically prefer lower prices than the drivers who provide the service. The maximum revenue of a taxi service tends to arise at low fares, given the price elasticity of demand. Shared use of ride-hailing – for instance, using UberPOOL – offers lower fares and hence generates more revenue. However, two-sided platforms have to satisfy both providers and users. Lower fares increase demand, which will attract more providers onto the system, a benefit to users. But lower fares also mean less income to drivers.

Drivers' conditions

Ride-hailing has rapidly penetrated urban taxi markets partly on account of the quality of the service and partly because fares have significantly undercut licensed taxis, at least in the absence of surge pricing. One seeming contributory factor is that operators may subsidize fares as a means of rapidly building demand and attracting drivers, but clearly this cannot be a long-term expedient. Another possibility is that ride-hailing drivers receive less remuneration than licensed taxi drivers.

Constraints on the number of licensed taxis in a particular city can mean that fares, and hence drivers' earnings, are higher than in the absence of such constraints. In London, mastering the knowledge typically takes three to four years of part-time study and practice, which limits entry into this activity. In New York City, the number of licensed taxis is constrained by the requirement for each to have a medallion to operate, a system introduced in 1937 with the object of limiting supply. This limitation resulted in medallions reaching valuations as high as $1 million on account of the income that could be generated, although the introduction of competition from ride-hailing has resulted in a drastic reduction in their value.

Typically, New York taxi drivers pay a fixed fee to rent their cabs from medallion-holders for a 12-hour shift, retaining all their revenues. Work hours are flexible – they can quit early and often do – and income fluctuates because of the weather and day of week effects. Many drivers say they set a daily income target to cover rental fee, fuel and desired take home pay, and quit when they reach that target. Such drivers will drive longer hours on low-income days and quit early on high-income days. This behaviour is the opposite of income maximizing in the longer term, and explains why a taxi may be harder to find on a rainy day (Camerer *et al.* 1996).

It is likely that many ride-hailing drivers also set target daily incomes, but they can be incentivized by surge pricing, which generates higher income per trip, to put in more hours when demand is high. (Indeed, it has been argued that regular taxi drivers in New York City also respond to increased earning opportunities and that more experienced drivers are better at doing this [Farber 2015]). But the desire of the operators to grow market share means that fares must be kept competitive, which limits the earnings of drivers. Operators benefit from increasing customer numbers since their revenue derives from commission, which leads them to recruit more drivers, but this conflicts with their drivers' desire to maximize revenue earnt per hour.[31]

There has been controversy about the treatment of drivers by Uber in particular. A legal action in London involved the question of whether drivers were self-employed or were workers for the company. Uber argued that it was not a taxi company in that it owned no vehicles: rather it was a digital platform not subject to regulation as a taxi operator. This argument was the basis for a buccaneering approach to roll-out the service in many cities and countries, without seeking permission of the authorities, justified by the popularity of the service (for an account of Uber in London, see Dudley, Banister & Schwanen 2017).

The London Employment Tribunal ruled against Uber, finding that drivers were "workers" and so were entitled to holiday and sick pay and the national minimum wage.[32] Uber appealed against this ruling, initially unsuccessfully, but intends to go to the UK Supreme Court. The European Court of Justice has ruled that Uber must be considered a transport service, not merely an intermediation service, and so must comply with regulations applicable to taxis.[33]

In September 2017, Transport for London, which regulates taxis, refused to renew Uber's operator licence on a number of grounds, including inadequate reporting of criminal offences, deficiencies in securing drivers' medical certificates and criminal record checks, and use of software that limited regulators from gaining full access to the app for enforcement duties.[34] Uber appealed against this decision and, in the meantime, continued to operate in London with some 48,000 drivers while at the same time modifying its working practices and changing its senior management. A court hearing in June 2018 recognized these developments and granted Uber a probationary 15-month operating licence.[35]

It is very likely that Uber will retain the right to operate in London in the longer term, given its great popularity: an online petition against the proposed ban attracted over 850,000 signatures. The success of the ride-hailing model does not depend on the factors rightly regarded by TfL as deficiencies in Uber's conduct, which means they can be remedied without prejudicing the business.

The question of pay and conditions for Uber drivers is one element of a much wider issue, in that self-employment is general for all kinds of taxi drivers, who typically pay for their vehicle and its operating costs, and pay a commission or a fee to a call operator that arranges a trip in response to a phone or other enquiry. In all cases, remuneration must be sufficient to attract an adequate number of drivers to meet demand. However, because driving requires qualifications that a large proportion of the working population have gained, it cannot be expected that the rate of remuneration would be much different from that of unskilled workers generally.

A study of Uber drivers in the US estimated that earnings are roughly at the tenth percentile of all wage and salary workers' wages, meaning that Uber drivers earn less than is earnt by 90 per cent of workers. This study also found a clear duality in that most drivers do so for supplementary income on a very part-time basis and frequently for a limited time. However, there is a core group who are full time, year-round and provide a large share of the services to consumers.[36]

A study of Uber drivers in London found the vast majority to be male immigrants, about half experiencing an increase in income compared to previous employment. Median earnings were estimated at about £11 an hour while on the app, after vehicle operating costs and Uber's service fee, at the lower end of the London income distribution but above the UK minimum wage. These drivers report higher levels of life satisfaction than other workers, plausibly reflecting a preference for flexibility and autonomy, yet they also report higher anxiety levels (Berger *et al.* 2018).

The journalist James Bloodworth spent six months working in low-paid employment in Britain, including a stint as an Uber driver in London, which he found preferable to the other jobs he took on: in an Amazon warehouse, at a telephone call centre and as a care worker. He estimated his earnings from driving, after expenses but before tax, as £18,000 a year, which did not seem to him a great deal of money, especially not in London (Bloodworth 2018).

The plight of workers in the "gig economy" has attracted much attention recently. The term refers to a labour market characterized by the prevalence of short-term contracts or freelance work, often found via apps, as opposed to permanent jobs. Supporters see this as a desirable working environment that offers flexible working hours. Critics say it allows exploitation with little workplace protection. A recent study of the gig economy in Britain found that half the self-employed were in low pay, compared with 22 per cent of employees (Broughton & Richards 2016). Prompted by such concerns, the British government in 2016 commissioned a review from Matthew Taylor, a former head of the prime minister's policy unit.

The Taylor Review reported evidence that 1.3 million people work in the gig economy in the UK, which is 4 per cent of all employment. Some 60 per cent of gig economy workers are permanent employees elsewhere, suggesting gig economy activity is used to top-up income. The Review judged that platform-based working offers welcome opportunities for genuine two-way flexibility and can provide opportunities for those who may not be able to work in more conventional ways. The Review proposed to continue the status of "worker" – to provide basic protections to less formal employment relationships – but proposed renaming it "dependent contractor" and clarifying the definition so individuals are clear about their employment status. It proposed that those in the gig economy should be able to earn the national minimum wage, a legal requirement specified as pay per hour, which would therefore need to be adapted to work based on tasks or output, rather than hours.[37] In its response to the Taylor Review, the government said it would consult on how definitions of working time should apply to platform working.[38]

At present, ride-hailing drivers are free to make themselves available when they choose, which is influenced by the likelihood that there will be demand for their services. Were there to be guaranteed minimum hourly pay, there would be an incentive to be available when there is little demand. It may be that the companies would need to limit the flexibility of drivers, to ensure that they were only on the road when there is sufficient demand from users to justify guaranteed minimum earnings. New York City has introduced a minimum wage for all ride-hailing drivers, which is based on estimates of the time spent on trips, rather than time on the app when available but not earning income, although the arrangements have been contested by the smaller ride-hailing companies who claim they would be disadvantaged. [39]

Trade unions could have a role in influencing pay and conditions in taxi markets. The employment tribunal case brought against Uber, referred to previously, was backed by the Independent Workers' Union of Great Britain, a small trade union whose members are predominantly low-paid migrant workers in London. The revenues of businesses providing transport services are time-sensitive and so vulnerable to industrial action, the threat of which can induce managements to recognize and negotiate with unions. For instance, Ryanair, a budget airline that had long resisted union recognition, agreed in 2017 to recognize unions for pilots and cabin crews, following the threat of strike action and earlier dislocations due to pilot shortages. In Mumbai, India, competition between Uber and Ola, a local ride-hailing business, has driven down fares and thus drivers' earnings, which has led to a strike by drivers, organized by established unions.[40] A major British trade union has succeeded in negotiating minimum hourly and holiday pay for drivers working for a large delivery company.[41]

Another approach to improving the earnings is exemplified by the Mystro app, which allows ride-hailing drivers in the US to switch between Uber and Lyft, to evaluate trip requests and reject the least rewarding, and to track overall performance.

It would seem sensible for there to be a level playing field in respect of essential terms of employment for those offering taxi and other transport services, including compliance with minimum pay legislation. As well as national legislation, taxi regulation could play a part, as considered next.

Taxi regulation

Taxi services have long been regulated in developed economies. Digital platforms are now having a big impact and it is clear that the regulatory regimes need to be reconsidered. The UK Department for Transport recently commissioned a task group comprising interested parties to review current practice and regulation. The report of the Chairman reflected a wide range of opinions in the group, sometimes polar opposites, in particular on the question of whether vehicle numbers in a locality should be subject to regulation.[42] This report, which omitted any economic analysis, served to identify the agenda without pointing to clear conclusions about the nature of a modern regulatory regime for taxis.

Unregulated taxi services are characterized by plentiful supply since barriers to entry are low, uncertain service quality, low customer loyalty, high variable costs and no economies of scale. Three main problems result: the quality of the driver and vehicle cannot be determined in advance, which may deter potential users; low remuneration of drivers may incentivize illegitimate charging and neglect of vehicle maintenance; and limited supply of taxis in a particular location may allow exploitation of customers when demand exceeds supply (Harding, Kandlikar & Gulati 2016).

Historically, these problems led to regulation – for example, the set fares and "knowledge" requirement for drivers of London's tightly specified black cabs – which allowed profitable operation, acceptable remuneration and an assurance of quality to customers. The ride-hailing platforms overcome or mitigate the problems that led to regulation: surge pricing attracts more supply, but estimated fares are made clear in advance; and the quality rating of drivers ensure consistent standards of service. So what now is the role for taxi regulation?

There is little debate about the need for regulation to protect the safety of passengers. Drivers should be of good character and medically fit. Vehicles should be fit for purpose and insured. Fares should be transparent and based on a tariff reflecting distance and time. Beyond such uncontentious basics, there are a number of other issues for consideration.

It has been common to distinguish different classes of licensed taxi within a city, with privileges granted to a high-quality standard vehicle with visible branding, such as London's black cabs (which are not required to be coloured black in practice) or New York's yellow cabs, although most cities permit a range of makes of suitable vehicle to be used as taxis. A general privilege is the right to pick up passengers in the street, which was more valuable before the advent of ride-hailing via an app.

Traditional taxi licensing could also protect the incomes of drivers by limiting numbers of drivers or vehicles. However, with competition from very popular ride-hailing, protection of income and conditions generally by means of specific taxi regulation now seems difficult. Instead, a more likely approach would be new legislation governing terms for low-paid workers that are not employees.

A general style of regulation of public services has developed in recent years, in response to the shift of some of these into the private sector. Regulation to promote competition between providers is seen as the best way of ensuring good outcomes for consumers of energy, telecoms and financial services. But where such competition is not feasible, some form of price control is adopted to prevent consumers being exploited by a monopoly supplier, as, for instance, is employed for provision of the pipes and wires that run under our streets to supply gas, water and electricity.

In the transport sector in Britain, buses outside London have operated in competitive markets for the past 30 years and, on the railways, private sector companies bid for franchises to run services on specified routes and regions for defined periods of time. However, there has been much recent criticism about the effectiveness of competition, and counterarguments made for more integrated service provision, as I will discuss in Chapter 7.

The balance between competition and integration is relevant for taxi services. One question is whether a dominant provider tends naturally to arise in any particular city: if so, regulation would be needed to prevent exploitation of users. Evidence of the dynamics of ride-hailing markets is mixed. Uber retreated from very competitive markets in China and Southeast Asia, although it remains active in India where it competes with Ola, a local rival.[43] In New York City, Uber, although still dominant, has seen its market share decline in the face of competition from Lyft and others.[44] A smaller competitor in New York is Juno (now owned by Gett, yet another competitor), which aims to treat its drivers better by charging them lower commission.[45] In London, driver licences for private hire vehicles grew by 50 per cent from 2015 to 2017, reflecting the growth of demand for Uber services, while black cab driver licences decreased only slightly, by 3 per cent.[46]

The theory of network effects for two-sided platforms, discussed above, does not predict unambiguously whether a dominant provider would generally emerge, whether in individual cities or in whole countries. Taxi markets tend to be complex, with a variety of customary services as well as one or more ride-hailing services. Ride-hailing operators may not offer advance booking or accounts for businesses, nor do they take cash payments, all of which offer opportunities to traditional providers. There is competition for drivers who may be able and qualified to drive for more than one provider. There are few economies of scale as regards vehicle and driver costs. Competitive advantage depends in part on response time following a booking, which is subject to diminishing returns.

At present, it seems possible that taxi markets in big cities may remain competitive, in which case a main aim of regulation should be to enhance consumer choice. However, such choice should not be limited to taxis but should be of all forms of mobility. This means that taxi regulation must form part of the governance of urban mobility generally (these wider impacts are less important in areas of low population density).

The other possibility is that a dominant provider might emerge in a taxi market, as, for example, could happen in London if the time and effort needed to acquire the knowledge were not adequately rewarded by the higher fares earnt by black cab drivers. In such a case, fare regulation might be necessary to prevent users being exploited.

One general approach to countering the emergence of market dominance is to ensure that customer data is made available to new entrants. An example is Open Banking, an initiative of the UK Competition and Markets Authority aimed at helping smaller and newer banks grow by allowing customers to share their data securely with other banks, enabling them to manage their accounts with multiple providers through a single app, to take more control of their funds and to compare products.[47]

The possibility of market dominance is crucial for valuation of ride-hailing businesses ahead of an initial public offering of shares. Indeed, fares seem often to be subsidized to help achieve dominance. Prior to the share offering in May 2019, there were suggestions of a valuation of Uber of more than $100 billion, although in the event less than $70 billion was achieved. Yet the uncertainties around future revenues and profits are huge. As well as competition in the taxi market, there are the impacts of regulation, of autonomous vehicle technologies and of electric vehicle propulsion, as well as the prospects for expanding the platform to deliver other transport services.[48]

One argument sometimes made is that the number of ride-hailing taxis should be limited to reduce road traffic congestion. New York has capped the number of ride-hailing taxis for a year while it studies the industry.[49] However, as noted above, ride-hailing is most popular in evenings and at weekends, rather than at peak commuting times. Moreover, as discussed in Chapter 1, congestion tends to be self-regulating, so that growth of ride-hailing vehicles at peak times would be expected to be offset by a decline in other vehicles, most likely private cars. Indeed, the ready availability of ride-hailing may reduce the attractiveness of car ownership: a survey in 2016 found that 28 per cent of Londoners who used to own a car said that they no longer do so because they can use alternatives like Uber instead.[50]

Another argument sometimes made for regulating the number of ride-hailing taxis is to constrain the loss of passengers from public transport, which is the most efficient form of urban transport. However, there is scope for complementarity between taxis and public transport, particularly for the "first and last mile", from the bus stop or station to home. In London parts of the underground rail system were opened all night at weekends from 2016, following which Uber found a decline in late-night trips from stations in the centre of the city and a marked increase in pick-ups from newly functioning suburban stations. Uber also cites cases from the US of partnership with city authorities and transport operators – for example, in Florida, working with Pinellas Suncoast Transit Agency jointly to subsidize fares to and from bus stops – to increase the use of public transport.[51] A review of recent such developments in the US found some 27 other communities that had joined with ride-hailing and other transport network companies to supplement or substitute existing public transit services, with the aim of providing quality mobility in areas where transit options fall short (Schwieterman, Livingston & Van Der Slot 2018).

Conclusion

Digital platforms are making a substantial impact on travel behaviour by achieving a better match of demand with supply for journeys by a single mode of travel – whether taxi, rental bike or the various shared ownership and shared use services. Digital platforms can also make possible multimodal trips, the basis of Mobility-as-a-Service, for which complementarity between taxi and public transport services is an important aspect, and which offers the prospect of seamless travel without private car ownership.

One area where digital platforms are as yet having only limited impact in matching supply and demand is the use of private vehicles on the road network outside urban areas. I discussed in Chapter 4 how route guidance apps that take account of congestion can help optimize the efficiency of the network. And I suggested in Chapter 3 that the general introduction of electric vehicles would be likely to require some form of road-user charging, to generate income to replace the lost fuel duty. Digital platforms would be the basis for future road-user charging since these would recognize a vehicle's location and time on the road network, and would provide means for charging.

Digital platforms represent an important advance in transport provision in the twenty-first century. Their application could increase with the advent of autonomous vehicles, as I will discuss in the next chapter. How taxi and other platforms might best be regulated to meet public policy objectives is a topic for the final chapter.

However, it is important to bear in mind that although digital platforms can improve our connectivity and planning, they have limited impact on the average speed of travel, and so will not effect a substantial change in how and why we travel.

6

AUTONOMOUS VEHICLES

A potentially very important development in motorcar technology is the autonomous vehicle (AV). Many anticipate that the development of a successful driverless car might lead to numerous changes in the operation of road networks and in travel behaviour, mitigating the adverse consequences associated with conventional vehicles, in particular crash deaths and injuries, and delays due to road traffic congestion.

There are many books, articles and op-eds on the practicalities and prospects for AVs. In this chapter, I will outline the key features of the technologies involved and how the safety of AVs would need to be regulated (cf. Lipson & Kurman 2016; Herrmann, Brenner & Stadler 2018). I will then focus on their impact on road traffic congestion, the most difficult challenge for surface transport operations.

Two routes to the development of vehicle automation are being pursued: evolutionary and revolutionary. The *evolutionary* route is being followed by the main vehicle manufacturers. Many anticipate that this involves developing a number of operational modes to assist the driver (known as advanced driver assistance systems, ADAS), such as adaptive cruise control, lane change assistance and automatic parking. These are generally introduced for high-end models and gradually move down the product range to mass-market models, costs reducing as scale of production increases and so more drivers gain experience of these feature. As more such systems are integrated, the role of the driver is reduced, with full automation the possible ultimate development. Before that point, there remains a role for the driver in circumstances where the automation cannot cope with road and traffic conditions. The potential difficulty of handing over to a human driver is the motivation for the *revolutionary* approach in which there is no role at all for a human driver.

Vehicle automation is very much in the developmental phase at present. The long-term prospects are far from clear. In this respect it is different from the technologies discussed in the previous chapters whose market prospects and societal impacts are considerably more evident. So I will first discuss the underlying technologies, since their scope for development and integration will determine the practicalities of AVs.

Technology for AVs

Conceptually, vehicle automation involves replacing the human driver with a robot able to carry out all the necessary tasks, gathering all relevant information and exercising appropriate judgements. This robot is not a humanoid sitting in the driver's seat, but rather a computer that operates through actuators able to replicate a human driver's performance. While robots are increasingly deployed in the well-defined environments of manufacturing industry, the open road is a complex, fast-changing and dangerous place where quick decisions need to be made, and hence a severe technological challenge (cf. Lipson & Kurman 2016).

Sensors are needed for the robot driver to recognize fixed objects, signs, signals and other road users. Digital cameras replace human eyes and are supplemented by radar, which detects the presence of physical objects by the reflection of radio waves. Lidar, also called laser radar, uses the reflection of laser light to detect objects and, although expensive, is widely used in AV development. However, it is possible that improved computing power would allow adequate three-dimensional imaging with cameras, obviating the need for Lidar. Software is required to fuse all the images, using inexpensive hardware, with minimum power requirements but high computing power for very fast data processing.

GPS location and high-definition three-dimensional digital maps aid fixed-object recognition. The better the map the less effort required of the robot to recognize the world around it. However, the more detailed the digital map, the more often it needs to be updated, which is an argument for placing increasing reliance on sensors as their performance improves. In the meantime, the ability to store map data within the vehicle may be a constraint on where the AV is allowed to go.[1]

Unlike a factory robot, the robot driver cannot be pre-programmed to deal with all situations that might arise. Accordingly, the robot driver must learn on the job. This is now possible with the rapid development of artificial intelligence in the form of machine learning (also known as deep learning), whereby robots can be trained with vast amounts of data to recognize and classify objects and so to manage the range of driving situations. Fleets of autonomous vehicles can learn more quickly by collectively sharing knowledge.

An AV has to interact with other traffic and road users, with very varied behaviour, under a range of weather conditions, and has to be able to manage merging lanes and exiting at junctions, a formidable challenge for the technology.

To clarify the possibilities, we need to distinguish different levels of attainment. The most widely used categorization of vehicle automation is that of the Society of Automobile Engineers, which has six levels.[2] In brief:

- Level 0: no automated driving function;
- Level 1: the robot driver performs either forward or sideways movements – for example, either adaptive cruise control or parking assist – but the driver must continuously monitor and be able to take full control at any time;
- Level 2: the robot can control both forward and sideways movement, but the driver must monitor continuously and be prepared to take over if needed;
- Level 3: the robot can recognize its limits so that the driver does not need to monitor but must be ready to take over on request;
- Level 4: the robot can perform all functions in a defined environment;
- Level 5: the robot can perform all tasks on all roads and speeds such that no driver is needed.

Below Level 3, the driver must continuously monitor the road. At Levels 4 and 5 the vehicle occupants are free to carry out non-driving activities. At Level 3, the better the system works, the less often humans have to intervene. But the less often they intervene, the less skilled they are likely to be at performing that intervention and less ready to do so. The design challenge is to be able to alert drivers in time to take control, and to avoid too much trust being placed in partial automation. The key distinction between Levels 3 and 4 is what happens when something goes wrong such that the trip cannot be completed safely, so a safe stop is required. At Level 3, the human driver takes charge, while at Level 4 the robot acts.

So Level 3 is particularly problematic. The difficulty in managing this handover of control reliably and safely leads some to conclude that the driver should never be in charge. This is the revolutionary route, the true driverless car, pioneered by Google (now branded Waymo). This approach requires the vehicle to operate without human control, at Levels 4 or 5. There is much competition among the tech companies and vehicle manufacturers to deliver full autonomy. Companies naturally talk up the prospects for their technology, to prepare customers for the future market, to help recruit talented staff, to keep their shareholders happy and to attract new investors.

While Waymo earlier demonstrated a pod-like vehicle lacking a steering wheel and other controls, the company's recent trials have involved adapted mass-produced vehicles. This allows the options of autonomous driving or full driver control, avoiding the Level 3 problem. Such an arrangement may be well suited to ride-hailing in that the cost of the driver could be avoided under conditions that permitted the driverless mode, but would allow a driver to take charge, for instance in poor weather. This approach to autonomy would be attractive to businesses whose purpose is to sell journeys rather than vehicles. Applying its development of autonomous technology to cars built by others suggests that Waymo does not intend to be a vehicle manufacturer but rather a maker of robot drivers, following the model of Google's Android operating system available for use in smartphones made by others. However, there are other new entrants that plan to manufacture electric vehicles, for whom automation would be a necessary next step.

Although there is widespread optimism that success will be achieved, what is not yet clear is the ultimate outcome: whether and when full automation – the driverless mode – will be demonstrated and validated as sufficiently reliable for general use. Many informed observers think Level 5 autonomy may be quite some way off (Mervis 2017; Shladover 2018). Level 4 – driverless in forgiving environments – seems near. Waymo has been trialling ride-hailing AVs in an urban location in Arizona, where the weather is good and traffic relatively light. But, regardless of timing, before AVs could be generally deployed commercially, they would need to be demonstrated to be safe.

Safety of AVs

Safety is the biggest hurdle in the way of developing the AV. Safety standards for motor vehicles have evolved over decades and involve three elements: the safe operational function of the vehicles, including crash avoidance and crashworthiness; the design of the road infrastructure, particularly modern roads intended for motor traffic that are safer than historic routes built to accommodate horse-drawn vehicles; and the competence of the driver. Drivers have to pass a test to gain a driving licence; they then generally improve their performance with experience, at least until loss of function develops in later life, while poor performance – if detected, for instance, by speed cameras – may be penalized.

The traditional approach to improving road safety takes a backward look, analysing the factors contributing to a crash in order to suggest how it could have been prevented. An extensive body of knowledge has been accumulated for conventional vehicles, but is lacking as yet for AVs. A study by the International Transport Forum argued that it is not clear whether the rate of build-up of experience of AV crashes can keep pace with technological developments, especially as these will increasingly involve rapidly changing codes and algorithms. A forward-looking view is needed, to consider what crashes might occur and how they could be prevented.[3] One possible approach is to formalize the rules for safe driving, including specifying safe distances between vehicles and how to allow for limited visibility, and specifying what is considered a dangerous situation and the appropriate response to evade it.[4]

The main novelty of the AV is replacement of human drivers by robots. Studies indicate that 90 per cent or more of fatal crashes are due to driver error. In the US, 94 per cent of all crashes were attributed to the driver, mainly due to errors in recognition, including inattention, and in decisions such as driving too fast.[5] UK data shows that driver loss of control contributed to 35 per of fatal crashes; failure to look properly to 26 per cent; carelessness, recklessness or being in a hurry to 20 per cent; with all driver errors totalling 89 per cent.[6] So, in principle, removing the human driver has the potential to reduce fatalities. How much reduction could be achieved would depend on the performance of the replacement robots.

Humans and robots have different strengths and weaknesses. Robots are more consistent and precise in tasks requiring high vigilance, when humans might get tired or distracted. Humans are better at perception involving high variability or alternative interpretations, are more dextrous and adaptable, and able to make subtle distinctions where choices are complex. These differences present a challenge for developers who will need to achieve outcomes such that normal robot driving performance is very similar to that of a human driver in order to ensure public acceptability. For instance, human drivers might take advantage of an AV that proceeded particularly cautiously to meet safety requirements, which would make such AVs less attractive to users. Likewise, cyclists and pedestrians could also exploit a predictably super-cautious robot.

There are three broad scenarios for crashes involving AVs. First, where sensors do not correctly detect or identify something critical in the vehicle environment; sensors may be deficient in extreme weather conditions, in low illumination, where dirt, snow or ice may limit visibility, or where dense traffic limits line of sight. Second, where the robot driver encounters something unforeseen by its software or about which it has not learnt from previous experience; in this situation, the vehicle would need to default to the safest situation possible, which may be just stopping.

Third are scenarios involving faulty human–machine interactions in situations where there remains a role for the human driver. It may not be clear what role remains for the driver at Level 3 operation. Automation could encourage the driver to place too much trust in the robot, leading to lack of cognitive engagement, loss of situational awareness and so longer reaction times.

A crucial issue concerns the safety requirements of a robot driver. It seems certain that robot drivers would need to demonstrate safe performance superior to that of human drivers. This is partly because in general we are less willing to expose ourselves to risk of death or injury when others are in charge, as on the railway or in the air, compared with being in charge of our own road vehicle. Also relevant is the novelty of AV technology, for which we will be less accepting of risk than for familiar technologies. Were the conventional motorcar to be invented today, with its current safety performance involving over a million fatalities a year worldwide, it surely would not be publically acceptable.

How might we assess the safety performance of a robot driver? At the moment, there are many places where on-road testing of AVs is permitted, including a number of US states and the UK. AVs under test usually involve back-up drivers who take over when the vehicle reaches the limit of its capabilities. The frequency of disengagement from automated driving is one measure for assessing perform-ance. As AV performance improves, disengagements will decline and attention will focus increasingly on crashes in the absence of a back-up driver. Very large distances driven under representative conditions would be needed to demon-strate good safety outcomes with statistical significance, which may not be easy, given the low frequency of crashes. For example, there were 1,800 people killed in road traffic accidents in Britain in 2016, half of which were vehicle occupants; and there were 250 billion vehicle-miles of motor vehicle traffic, which means one fatality per 140 million miles. If AVs do better than human drivers, crashes involving fatalities would be exceedingly rare events. Yet the political response to a single fatal crash involving an AV led to the suspension of testing in Arizona in March 2018, following the death of a pedestrian by an Uber-owned AV.

On-road testing of AVs is intended to allow performance to be improved to the point where general deployment is accepted by the public as safe and desirable. Safety performance standards for AVs will be needed. Being the first to achieve the required performance for mass-market models could be a big advantage for a vehicle manufacturer. Conceivably the safety standard could be zero fatalities or serious injuries, given that this is the aim of Vision Zero, a multinational road traffic safety project, pioneered in Sweden and endorsed by a number of national and city governments (Christie 2018). The AV developers would contend that this aim is unrealistic and would press for a more permissive regime, arguing that the best is the enemy of the good and that the technology will improve as experience is gained. So the question is how much safety is enough, bearing in mind that the higher the standard, the longer it would take to achieve, deferring the safety benefits.

It is sometimes argued that AVs would have to avoid hitting pedestrians who intentionally stepped into their path, and that this could allow pranksters to block their motion. People do not intentionally step in front of cars with human drivers because of the risk of being killed or injured. We could reasonably expect robotic drivers to have faster reaction times than human drivers. Yet requiring an AV to avoid all intentional miscreants would probably confine their use to dedicated motor roads that exclude pedestrians and cyclists.

One way to ensure the safe performance of an AV might be to extend the existing system of type approval of vehicles to cover the robotic functions, essentially an engineering approach. An alternative would be to relate safe performance to that of a good experienced human driver: for instance, one who drives the annual average distance and has not made an insurance claim for ten years. We might then require each model of an AV to be, say, ten or 20 times safer than that, before general use would be permitted. It is also to be expected that AVs would generally observe legal speed limits, which would contribute to their safe operation, even though that might make the AV option less attractive than manual control for more aggressive drivers.

There is a need to allocate responsibilities in the event of an incident in which injury or damage occurred, and for insurance arrangements to take this into account, recognizing that improved safety performance would reduce the cost of insurance. The UK government has recently enacted legislation that will make insurers liable for damage when a vehicle is driving itself.[7] Satisfactory safety performance of AVs would require that the vehicle be maintained to a high standard, in particular the sensors that substitute for human vision; software would also need to be updated. Responsibility for ensuring maintenance would presumably fall to vehicle owners, whether corporate or individual.

A new issue that arises with AVs is the scope for opting between different outcomes of crashes involving fatalities. Human drivers have very limited opportunities to make choices about who lives and who dies in such circumstances. It is often supposed that robot drivers may have options, according to how their software is programmed: for instance, to choose between hitting pedestrians or sacrificing passengers to save pedestrians. Responses to a US survey indicated a general preference to minimize the total number of casualties, but also a preference when purchasing a vehicle to choose one that protects passengers (Bonnefon, Shariff & Rahwan 2016). However, an online survey of 2.3 million people from 130 countries found differences between countries in relative priorities, according to religious background, strength of government institutions and economic inequality (Awad *et al.* 2018). What is unclear is whether robots that have been trained to drive using machine learning would be capable of being programmed to exercise such choices. If so, it would be for the safety regulators to consider how to reconcile the conflicting wishes of citizens.

As well as safety, we must be concerned about cyber security: the potential to compromise a vehicle's safe performance by cyber attack. Remote door unlocking has been hacked and standard on-board diagnostic units have been exploited to extract information. The ever-increasing connectedness of vehicles, and of devices generally (the "internet of things"), offers opportunities for malevolent interventions, especially problematic when the "things" can travel at high speeds. This will be a particular difficulty for connected AVs, as discussed later. The question is whether the potential safety benefits of connectedness between vehicles – for example, to see beyond line of sight – outweigh the risks of cyber attack.

Safety and security converge when AV manufacturers intend to update vehicle software, in the way that computers and smartphones have software updates to remedy faults and improve performance. The safety of the update would need to be demonstrated to the safety authority, as would the invulnerability to unauthorized interventions.

The detail of measures to respond to the cyber security threat would not generally be made public by vehicle manufacturers. The British Department for Transport has set out high-level design principles.[8]

Since road vehicles travel across national boundaries, both safety and security regulation would need to operate at continental level. The United Nation's Global Forum for Road Traffic Safety has begun to consider the implications of AVs. The ultimate need for international agreement on safety standards is in marked contrast to the present situation in which AV developers are reluctant to divulge any of the vast amounts of data they are collecting in vehicle trials, impeding consideration of approaches to safety standards. Some progress is being made in setting voluntary industry-led engineering standards: for instance, to validate the safety of electrical and electronic hardware and software systems in the event of malfunction. However, compliance with such engineering standards, while necessary, would not be sufficient for public acceptability (Fraade-Blanar *et al.* 2018).

While safety criteria will be decided internationally, each country has its own laws governing road traffic offences and civil liabilities. The Law Commissions responsible for reviewing law in Britain are applying themselves to the comprehensive development of legislation required for AVs.[9]

Any noteworthy crash involving an AV made by one manufacturer is likely to discourage potential users of all such vehicles. There is therefore a good case for developers to address collectively the challenge of achieving public acceptability by sharing safety data and working with the safety authorities to agree standards that the public would accept.

AVs and traffic congestion

A key question is whether vehicle automation will contribute to or lessen road traffic congestion. To the extent that this or any other innovation may be expected to reduce congestion, it could be encouraged. However, regulation would need to be considered if congestion is likely to be worsened. And if the overall impact were judged to be neutral, then market penetration of AVs would be driven by user perceptions of benefits in relation to costs.[10]

The main focus of the remainder of this chapter therefore is the possibilities for policy responses to the introduction of AVs as these seem likely to affect road traffic congestion. Given that AVs are at a fairly early stage of development as a publicly acceptable mode of transport, what can be said has to be fairly tentative.

I explained in Chapter 1 how congestion arises in densely populated areas with high levels of car ownership. In this situation, road capacity is often insufficient to meet demand for all trips that might be made, particularly during the morning and evening commute. Some trips that might be made at a particular time are therefore not made – are suppressed or deterred – on account of anticipated delays. Those so deterred may change the time of travel, the destination (where options exist, as for shopping), the mode of travel, or may decide not to travel at all.

Congestion is therefore substantially self-regulating. As traffic grows, delays increase and some potential road users make other choices. For the same reason, congestion is difficult to mitigate. Measures that aim to get people out of their cars initially reduce traffic, but the resulting reduction in delays attracts onto the road other drivers who had previously been deterred by the prospect of delays. Similarly, increasing road capacity initially reduces congestion, but this makes road travel more attractive to those whose trips were previously suppressed, hence the maxim that you cannot build your way out of congestion, which is known from experience to be generally true.

Levels of traffic congestion vary from place to place, from city to city, depending on population density, road capacity, choice of alternative modes of travel and traffic management technologies in use. We therefore need to consider how AVs might affect road use and travel demand, to assess the impact on congestion.

When considering the impact of AVs on congestion, the key question is whether there is a driver in charge of the vehicle. If there is, little is changed. As discussed above, there are essentially two levels beyond driver assistance: Level 4, where in defined circumstances the driver can disengage; and Level 5, where no driver is needed.

The current focus is on AVs that are essentially self-contained, although they generally communicate with the surrounding infrastructure for navigation purposes – using GPS for location, communicating location and speed to providers of digital navigation and receiving route guidance. A further development involves AVs that are also connected vehicles: vehicles that communicate among themselves (V2V) to improve safety, smooth traffic flow and increase road capacity by reducing headways between vehicles, as discussed later.

The nature of the infrastructure is relevant for the performance of AVs. Segregated roads (freeways, motorways) are favourable for assistance systems that allow the driver to relax or to carry out other tasks. Lanes dedicated to AVs may be helpful, analogous to high occupancy vehicle lanes, common in the US. Separate lanes for AV cars and trucks may be necessary for reasons of safety and efficiency, which would limit these to wider highways. Vehicle entrance and exit from such highways would need to be managed safely.

Another type of favourable context for AVs would be low-speed operation where access by general traffic is controlled, such as campuses, resorts, business parks, airports and other kinds of terminal. An example is the French-designed NAVYA low-speed autonomous shuttle able to accommodate up to 15 passengers at a maximum operating speed of 25 km/hour, in operation on defined routes in a number of locations around the world.

Generally, it seems likely that the scope for dedicated road space for AVs would be limited, particularly at the earlier stages of deployment. Accordingly, most AV use would be on roads with mixed traffic: conventional, partially assisted and fully automated vehicles on main highways, plus bicycles and pedestrians on urban streets and local roads. It may be demanding to demonstrate sufficiently safe AV operation in such environments, particularly in historic towns and cities with narrow residential streets that have parked cars on both sides and too little space for vehicles to pass without negotiation. More recent urban settings with gridiron or similar road networks, and with light traffic, would offer better opportunities for general use of AVs. Good weather to aid visibility is also helpful.

How AVs are used would be affected by ownership, whether individual or shared. The evolutionary route pursued by the main vehicle manufacturers would fit the traditional model of individual car ownership. Indeed, for manufacturers of brands whose attractions are based on superior driving performance, the possibility of full autonomy would send a mixed message. Tesla, a new entrant to mass-market vehicle manufacture, offers an electric car with an option for overnight home charging from solar-powered electricity generated during the day and stored in domestic batteries, consistent with personal ownership incentivized by near-zero running costs.

The revolutionary route to full automation offers the possibility of car-based door-to-door travel without individual ownership, in that empty vehicles could be summoned when needed and left when no longer required. Essentially this would be a taxi with a robot driver: a "robotic taxi". Conventional taxis are useful and would be more used if robots replaced human drivers at lower cost.

On the one hand, shared ownership spreads the capital cost of the vehicle over much higher annual distance travelled, contributing to cost reduction compared with personal ownership, given that most cars are parked for some 95 per cent of the day. On the other hand, intensively used vehicles would be expected to have a shorter life, all else equal. Possibly more important would be cost reduction from electric propulsion of AVs as battery costs decline, and because the simpler technology, operating at lower temperatures than internal combustion engines, is expected to extend vehicle life, increase reliability and lessen maintenance expenditure.

Altogether, the cost reduction obtainable with shared used electric AVs seems likely to make them economically attractive. However, vehicle sharing depends on the supply being able to meet demand, particularly at times of peak demand. Thus car club vehicles, which are shared by members, are not generally used for commuting, for which supply would be limiting.

Shared use AVs are often proposed as a solution to the "last mile" problem: travelling between home and the suburban railway station or other transport hub. However, if there were sufficient AVs to replace all the commuters' cars in the station car park, these would be likely to be under-utilized at other times, detracting from economic viability.

So the attraction of shared use AVs may be limited, such that both personal and shared vehicles may be widely used, in proportions that would depend on factors such as availability of home parking and electric charging, and of alternative modes for urban travel under congested conditions. Personal ownership may be attractive, despite the cost, for the convenience of having the vehicle when we want it. Shared use launderettes declined in popularity as home washing machines became more affordable and reliable.

In the light of the above consideration of the performance of AVs, both individually owned or shared, I now consider how AVs might affect the level of traffic and congestion. An AV takes the same amount of road space as a conventional vehicle of similar capacity. It is possible that AVs could operate at reduced headways (the space between vehicles), as well as on narrower lanes, and they might be more efficiently managed at junctions, all of which could increase effective road capacity. A constraint would be how comfortable occupants would be with short headways. The implications of varying levels of AV deployment and styles of behaviour have been explored in traffic simulation modelling. A recent review concluded that most such studies show little impact on traffic flow and capacity until relatively high penetrations of vehicles with high levels of automation (which would not be the case at best for many years); moreover, it is to be expected that demand for travel would rise as capacity increases, analogous to induced demand associated with new transport infrastructure.[11]

Individually owned AVs operating in mixed traffic are therefore likely to be operationally neutral as regards traffic congestion, certainly until they account for a high proportion of traffic. However, there could be wider impacts of driverless vehicles on demand for travel. Individually owned AVs could extend car use to those who are not able or qualified to drive, including children, older people and those with disabilities. This could increase the demand for car use, for which one upper-bound estimate is 14 per cent more vehicle-miles travelled, potentially worsening congestion (Harper *et al.* 2016).

Individually owned AVs would offer new options to households, such as taking one member to work in the morning, returning unoccupied for use by others during the day, then travelling back to the workplace for the return commute trip. This might obviate the need for a second car for household use, but would double the distance travelled for work journeys, half of which would be running empty. Analysis based on data from the US National Household Travel Survey suggests that average household ownership could be reduced from 2.1 to as few as 1.2 vehicles per household.[12]

Use of driverless vehicles would allow occupants to engage in other activities, including working online. The ability to work online is likely to have contributed to growth of rail passenger numbers, which have doubled in the UK over the past 20 years. The ability to carry out activities other than driving while in a car could lessen the time constraint on personal travel, the average of an hour a day that I reported in Chapter 2. This could result in increased distance travelled and suburban sprawl, which, however, would add to traffic congestion, thus slowing speeds and negating the benefit from more time on the move. Nevertheless, individually owned AVs could be particularly attractive to drivers who are already committed to long daily commutes through choice of residential and work locations.

Individually owned AVs would be expected in these ways to add significantly to overall distance travelled by car and hence to increased traffic levels. In contrast, AVs operating as robotic taxis would not be expected to have such an impact, given that conventional taxis travel without passengers between paid trips.

I discussed in the previous chapter how shared use of cars and taxis by unrelated people – ride sharing – has been made generally feasible by smartphone apps, incentivized by lower cost for individuals. Shared vehicle use at present involves cars with drivers. If and when AVs are permitted for general use and drivers are not needed, costs could be further reduced, which should increase demand for sharing. This would increase vehicle occupancy, which might be expected to reduce the number of cars needed to meet the travel needs of a given population and hence would reduce traffic congestion. However, I have explained that reduced congestion would tend to attract onto the road network trips previously deterred by anticipated delays. Moreover, the lower travel costs associated with shared use would be expected to attract passengers from public transport, increasing demand for car and taxi use. So the net effect of shared use AVs on congestion may not be substantial, given the self-regulating nature of road traffic congestion.

As well as affecting moving traffic directly, AVs may have an indirect impact through lessening the need for parking space. Individually owned driverless vehicles could return home after the morning commute, as noted above, so not needing parking space at or near the workplace. A similar effect on parking space would occur if robotic taxis were to replace personally owned vehicles.

Reduction in parking adjacent to the workplace would permit development opportunities for land no longer required. These could be substantial in cities where a considerable part of the central business district is dedicated to parking. For instance in Seattle, Washington, there is a total of five parking places per household overall, and utilization of public parking has been declining, with average daily occupancy in the central business district now 64 per cent.[13] The reduced need for parking would reduce the contribution to congestion of vehicles in search of vacant parking spaces.

More generally, robotic taxis that are used for a substantial part of the day would need much less parking space than individually owned vehicles, and such capacity as is needed could be on low-value off-street sites, thus freeing up kerbside space. Such off-street parking would be suited for recharging electric robotic taxis. Reduction in the high demand for kerbside parking space in city centres would be helpful in lessening congestion arising from double parking by goods vehicles unloading and by taxis picking up and setting down. Reduced parking in narrow inner-city residential streets could help AVs to pass through.

For conventional vehicles, parking involves finding a suitable space for a stationary vehicle. However, individually owned AVs might be programmed to cruise round the block while the owner was doing business. This would contribute to congestion, and might therefore need to be regulated in city centres and other areas prone to congestion.

Let me now summarize the likely impacts of AVs on congestion. Vehicles that are highly but not fully automated would probably not behave significantly differently from normal vehicles. For fully automated vehicles, these factors would tend to increase congestion:

- individually owned AVs travelling unoccupied on return trips or while "parked" on the move;
- increased demand for car use from those unable to drive;
- increased demand arising from the relaxation of the time constraint on daily travel, if work could be carried out on the move;
- increased demand for lower-cost robotic taxis by former users of public transport.

Factors that might mitigate congestion:

- possible scope for reduced headway and lane widths on dedicated highways;
- reduction in city kerbside parking;
- shared use of robotic taxis and less individual car ownership.

All these factors would play out in the context of congestion that is self-regulating on account of the time constraints to which road users are subject. So the net impact is an open question, but may not be substantial either way.

To reduce urban traffic congestion substantially, it would be necessary to limit car ownership to within the capacity of the road network. The availability of driverless taxis may encourage city dwellers to give up personal car ownership, and indeed may change how we think about personal car ownership and use.

A number of simulation studies have been carried out to explore the scope for reducing urban traffic through sharing of vehicles. For example, the International Transport Forum modelled the impact of replacing all car and bus trips in the city of Lisbon with fleets of shared vehicles, both shared taxis and on-demand minibuses, plus existing rail and subway services. It was concluded that the travel needs of the population could be met without use of private cars in the urban core area and hence without congestion.[14]

Such modelling studies suggest that high levels of shared use vehicles could result in a substantial reduction in congestion, thus improving speed and reliability of road travel. The challenge is to reduce car ownership in societies where this is already high. In successful cities with growing populations, car use as a share of all trips tends to decline, since limited road capacity prevents any increase in car traffic. For instance, 50 per cent of all journeys in London in 1990 were by car, which has reduced as the population has grown, currently to 36 per cent as reported in Chapter 2. In London's central congestion charging zone the composition of four-wheeled (or more) traffic is: private cars 22 per cent, taxis and private hire 39 per cent, goods vehicles 31 per cent and buses and coaches 7 per cent. This indicates a significant scope for reducing traffic if private cars could be discouraged.[15] The ambitious aim of the Mayor of London is to reduce the share of trips by car, taxi and private hire to 20 per cent by 2041. So it may not be impossible to reduce urban individual car use to the point where alternatives, including shared AVs, offer effective Mobility-as-a-Service under reduced congestion.

Connected vehicles

Adaptive cruise control, available in some production vehicles, adjusts the gap to the vehicle in front using sensor data to vary speed. Connected (or cooperative) adaptive cruise control (CACC), an emerging technology, takes data from vehicles further ahead using vehicle-to-vehicle communication, which allows shorter headways and attenuates traffic disturbance to achieve smoother flow. The shorter the headway, the less scope for driver control. In the limit, CACC allows platooning of vehicles on inter-urban roads: "road trains" involving vehicles in close proximity with a lead driver in control. The benefits of platooning include better fuel economy and decreased emissions resulting from lower aerodynamic drag, improved traffic flow and capacity, and lower labour costs.

A number of truck manufacturers have initiated trials and more are planned. The 2016 European Truck Platooning Challenge involved six manufacturers sending platoons from starting points in five different countries to end at Rotterdam, gaining valuable practical experience.[16]

Unlike truck drivers, the generality of drivers of AVs would be able to choose the gap to the vehicle in front. To increase road capacity by reducing headway there would need to be some incentive for individuals to drive in such a fashion. This might be a road-user charging regime that charged on the basis of the length of carriageway effectively occupied. Another kind of incentive to reduce headway would be dedicated lanes that are less congested and faster flowing than other lanes, analogous to high occupancy vehicle lanes on US highways. Acceptable incentives would be needed if manufacturers were to go beyond equipping vehicles with the existing adaptive cruise control. Manufacturers are likely to be held to be responsible for the safe functioning of AVs. Adding V2V or vehicle-to-infrastructure connectivity to reduce headway would exacerbate this responsibility by introducing functionality that depends on that of other manufacturers and suppliers, and that increases the risk of security breaches.

More generally, connected vehicles operating at short headways would require reconsideration of the safety regime, which at present is concerned with the crash-worthiness of individual vehicles. A system of connected vehicles would require consideration of fault modes at system level: for instance, the consequences of faults in individual vehicles in a platoon and of faults in connectivity. Such faults might arise from hostile interventions, pointing up the need for cyber security. It would not be surprising if there were trade-offs between headway and safety that limited possible increases in effective road capacity.

Much of the past impetus for the development of connected vehicles came from research funding provided by the US Department of Transportation. The main motive was to improve safety through vehicles exchanging data about speed and location, and vehicles acquiring data from roadside infrastructure about road conditions (Shladover 2018). There are two competing telecoms technologies under consideration: short-range Wi-Fi for V2V being developed by the car manufacturers for platooning; and a system based on the next generation 5G mobile phone technology, to be installed in both vehicles and infrastructure, and able to signal at longer range.[17]

However, the current industry-wide technological thrust is directed towards vehicle autonomy, not connectedness. The logic is that the general application of V2V connectivity would need to follow on from the successful adoption of vehicle autonomy because the benefits of such connectivity largely depend on response times of connected vehicles that are faster than achievable by human drivers. There will then be a question of whether access to certain classes of roads should be limited to vehicles equipped with V2V technology. However, the efficiency gains from such dedicated infrastructure use would depend on widespread adoption of V2V communications, for which, as noted, there may be a lack of incentive for vehicle manufacturers to develop (see Lipson & Kurman 2016: 128–31).

Implications for policy

Politicians are generally enthusiastic about autonomous vehicles. Governments in many developed economies are already playing an active role in supporting the technological development of AVs, based on expectations of a range of potential societal benefits that are yet to be proven or demanded by the market.

For example, the British government has stated its aim of ensuring that the UK is at the forefront of the testing and development of the technologies that will ultimately realize the goal of driverless vehicles. The government has established a Centre for Connected and Autonomous Vehicles to support research, development, demonstration and deployment; is funding driverless car projects in four cities; has published codes of practice for on-road testing and for cyber security; and has enacted legislation to clarify the liability of insurers when a crash involves an AV.[18] This government support for AVs seems mainly motivated by considerations of industrial strategy since the transport benefits remain uncertain, given the lack of evidence beyond that from as yet quite limited pilot testing and simulation studies, discussed above.

Autonomous vehicles are one of four "grand challenges" specified in the UK government's 2017 industrial strategy (the others being artificial intelligence, clean growth and the ageing population): "The government wants to see fully self-driving cars, without a human operator, on UK roads by 2021."[19] However, the funding to support this ambitious policy intervention is arguably too little and comes too late, given the scale of worldwide effort to develop and deploy AV technology. Moreover, although Britain is the location of major motor vehicle manufacturing plants, none are British owned. Generally, research and development is carried out in the countries where company headquarters are located. In Britain, the nearest there is to an endogenous manufacturer is Jaguar Land Rover (JLR), which is a subsidiary of Tata Motors, the Indian automotive company. JLR is developing AVs but has also agreed to supply up to 20,000 of its I-PACE, an electric premium car, to Waymo for its driverless fleet, as part of a long-term partnership.[20] Given that Waymo has probably the most advanced AV technology, this suggests that JLR does not plan to rely on UK-developed technology.

A good example of a timely and far-sighted governmental-led industrial strategy followed from a mandate from the US Congress in 2001 to require that one third of vehicles used in military war zones should be fully autonomous.

The Defense Advance Projects Research Agency (DARPA) sponsored a series of road races with cash prizes where researchers could contest their efforts at building autonomous vehicles. By the end of the third race in 2007, six of the 11 competing vehicles finished the 60-mile course, demonstrating that AVs could become a viable technology (Lipson & Kurman 2016).

The potential contribution of AVs to transport policy needs to be considered as one of four new technologies that will be important in meeting future demand for travel, which are the subject of Part II of this book, those considered previously being electric propulsion, digital navigation and digital platforms. In this context, the key development for AVs is full autonomy – driverless vehicles able to operate in general traffic, whether on a substantial defined road network or on all roads. Developments short of this seem likely to have little impact. Driver assistance does not change the basic behaviour of the vehicles; and autonomy in limited circumstances, such as in low-speed environments, would not have general impact. Given the maturity and scale of existing road networks in developed economies, there would seem to be limited benefit in considering changes to the design of any new road infrastructure to accommodate AVs.

While the timing of driverless vehicles operating in general traffic is unclear, it is nevertheless possible to anticipate the implications of such deployment for the transport system and for transport policy. I summarize the main considerations.

In some situations, driverless vehicles do not change basic features of the transport system:

- driverless shared ownership cars are essentially taxis with robot drivers, not fundamentally different from taxis with drivers. Costs could be lower through not having a paid driver, making such services more attractive, thus increasing demand;
- autonomous on-demand minibuses could fill the present gap between high-capacity, low-cost bus and rail services and low-capacity, high-cost taxis. The main impact of autonomy is cost reduction, permitting a wider range of publicly available services, in areas of both high and low residential densities;
- driverless vans and trucks in general traffic would not be fundamentally different from their conventional counterparts. Their practicality depends on being able to arrange for offloading at customers' premises.

While driverless vehicles for these purposes would not result in novel behaviours, the volume of traffic may tend to increase in already congested locations, requiring additional urban road management measures.

In contrast, individually owned driverless cars are different from conventional vehicles in that they could travel without occupants, for instance returning empty to base after dropping the user at their destination, or "parking on the move" when no stationary parking is available. Such unoccupied vehicles would add to traffic congestion and their presence might need to be regulated in areas and at times when congestion was a problem. Cities will need to manage the urban deployment of AVs using powers to regulate taxis, support public transport, manage traffic and charge for road use.

Employment impact of AVs

A general concern about the impact of automation and artificial intelligence is the impact on employment. Technological development generates innovations that offer better experiences or lower costs, and the structure of the economy changes as people take advantage of the new offerings. Employment responds to changes in technology and consumer demand. For example, mechanization resulted in a long-run decline in the UK agricultural workforce, from 1.7 million in 1851 to fewer than 200,000 currently.[21] In the short run there may be dislocations requiring response from governments. But much depends on the pace of change, which can be quite rapid, as with word processing that displaced traditional typists and secretaries, and which arguably led to improved quality of work for those previously so employed.

A study by the intergovernmental Organisation for Economic Co-operation and Development (OECD) concluded that nearly half of all jobs in the developed economies are either highly automatable or could face substantial change in how they are carried out. Automation mostly affects manufacturing and agriculture, but some service sector jobs are highly automatable. For the land transport sector, it was judged that the mean probability of automation is 54 per cent (Nedelkoska & Quintini 2018). A study of the long-distance road freight sector by the International Transport Forum suggested that rapid automation could reduce demand for drivers by 50–70 per cent by 2030.[22]

However, much hangs on precisely what may be technically feasible: for instance, whether driverless delivery trucks would be able to unload in the absence of a human and whether driverless taxis could navigate narrow urban streets. Uber sees driverless trucks mitigating the impact of an ageing US workforce, with local delivery drivers, able to navigate tight and crowded city streets, complementing long-haul driverless trucks.[23] The latter are analogous to rail freight.

The impact on employment depends also on the rate of introduction of new technology. In the transport sector this has been quite measured, reflecting both the scale of past investment in infrastructure and the cost of new build. I described in Chapter 2 the coming of the railway in the early nineteenth century. The historian Ulrich Raulff, in his magisterial book *Farewell to the Horse*, depicted the subsequent full century over which the horse as a mode of transport was gradually phased out, and with it the employment of those who tended the horses and built the horse-drawn vehicles (Raulff 2017). The phasing out of the human driver may well be less leisurely, but is unlikely to be as rapid as the demise of the shorthand typist.

Conclusion

It seems likely that the main impact of AVs on the transport system will only be seen when driverless vehicles have developed to the point that general deployment occurs on roads that accommodate mixed traffic, the timing of which is unclear. There is much optimism on the part of protagonists of the technology, both inventors and investors. Those not so involved may be sceptical. Christian Wolmar, a seasoned British commentator on transport matters, has authored a book entitled *Driverless Cars: On a Road to Nowhere*, in which he vents considerable doubt about the hype surrounding AVs (Wolmar 2018). I myself am cautious about pronouncing on the likely outcome of current developments, given the huge uncertainties about both technological feasibility and public acceptability. But if AVs come to be deployed at scale, then we can take an initial view of the probable main consequences.

Prior to full autonomy, driver assistance features will be increasingly offered by traditional vehicle manufacturers to meet the preferences of users, subject to demonstration of safe performance, but without much impact on traffic levels. Driverless shared ownership vehicles would both reduce the cost of taxis and stimulate demand, and a wider range of public transport vehicles would be economic. Driverless individually owned vehicles could add to traffic when unoccupied and their use in congested urban areas may need to be regulated.

Autonomous alternatives to the private car could reduce the cost of travel. As these alternatives develop, car ownership in urban areas may decline to the point at which congestion ceases to be the main problem for surface transport. This prospect should encourage city authorities to begin plans for a driverless future, or at least not unreasonably hinder the introduction of AVs.

Successful deployment of AVs would, I anticipate, be likely to occur first in low-speed ring-fenced environments and in urban locations where the street pattern is simple, parked cars are few, the traffic is light and the weather generally good. Subsequently, I would expect to see AVs on dedicated motor roads from which cyclists and pedestrians are excluded. Historic cities, often with heavily used and complicated streets of variable width, would be the most challenging environment. Yet such densely populated, congested locations are where there is greatest need for innovative approaches to improve the efficiency of the transport system. It is noteworthy that Ford is trialling AVs in downtown Miami, which suggests considerable optimism by that manufacturer.[24]

At present, it does not seem likely that deployment of AVs on the road network would have much, if any, impact on the speed of travel. Accordingly, there would not be much impact on how and where we live.

TRAINS, PLANES, BUSES AND ROADS

The historic high cost of personal vehicles led to the growth of demand for new shared modes of travel at much lower cost, in the form of mass-market public transport: trains in the nineteenth century, buses in the first half and air travel in the second half of the twentieth century. The heyday of public transport was reached in the middle of the last century. Subsequently, there was a very substantial shift to personal means of transport as the auto makers drove down costs through efficient assembly line technology, to the point where the car is now the main mode of travel in developed economies.

Yet public transport is far from being down and out. These traditional shared modes of travel are far more efficient at moving people in their use of road and rail infrastructure. The capacity of the road network constrains car use. Rail in all its forms has undergone a major revival in Britain and elsewhere, largely because it offers fast and reliable journeys compared with cars and buses on congested roads. In contrast, the situation of buses is far more variable and depends on local circumstances. Long-term decline in passenger numbers is common. Yet in some cities passenger numbers are growing, aided by policies that prioritize buses over cars.

The main question to be considered here is the likely impact on public transport modes of the new digital technologies that I discussed in the previous chapters. I will also review technological possibilities for extending the realm of public transport, above and below congested surface networks.

Digital railway

Digital technologies are having a profound effect on the railways, both in how we interact as consumers and the way in which trains are operated and managed. The convenience of making arrangements through well-designed websites has contributed to the growth of longer-distance rail travel, eliminating the need for intermediation by travel agents. The ability to flex fares and offer choices to passengers helps contain costs by matching demand with supply to gain revenue from seats that might otherwise remain empty, although often prompting criticism of an over-complex fare structure. Digital technologies also make possible cashless ticketing for urban public transport, initially via a card for that specific purpose (for instance, London's Oyster card system) and subsequently via standard contactless bank or credit cards (Verma 2014).

Autonomous vehicles are not new to the railway. The metro in Lille, France, which opened in 1983, pioneered driverless trains. A similar technology is used to operate London's Docklands Light Railway, a purpose-built low-speed route opened in 1987, on which there have been no incidents involving injury to passengers. There are now many such systems around the world in which the driver is either absent or present only in a back-up role.

On established railways, partial automation can achieve more precise control and closer running of trains, increasing the capacity of existing tracks to meet growing demand for rail travel. We are moving away from the historic track-based signalling employing visible signals to train-based systems that receive instructions transmitted by the signalling control system. This enables trains to run more consistently and closer together while maintaining safety.

A good example is the renewal of signalling and rolling stock on London Underground's deep Tube lines, which has allowed up to 36 trains an hour to operate at as little as 100-second intervals, increasing capacity of the existing tunnels by some 30 per cent.[1] Investment is underway in the sub-surface lines where an average capacity increase of 33 per cent is expected, three-quarters of which will be from new signalling that allows trains to run both faster and closer together, plus a quarter from new rolling stock.[2]

The "digital railway" concept is being implemented on Britain's national rail system to increase capacity within the space taken by existing track and tunnels. Unlike the road system, which is open to all who are qualified to drive, the railway is a closed system, with trained drivers subject to oversight by the system operator. This means, on the one hand, that the potential for reducing headways (the gap between trains) and increasing capacity on the railways is greater than on the roads, with their mixed traffic and largely non-professional drivers. On the other hand, the basic technology of steel wheel on steel rail, with limited grip compared with rubber on tarmac, requires greater separation of vehicles for safe stopping in emergency. The building blocks of the digital railway concept include: the European Train Control System, which allows trains to run closer together while maintaining safe braking distances; support for drivers, either through advice or automatic train operation, to improve performance and safety; and traffic management to optimize flow across the network and aid recovery from dislocations.[3] Because trains cross national borders, a Europe-wide approach is appropriate.

There is political enthusiasm in Britain for the digital railway as a means of improving productivity and holding down costs (despite some expert scepticism).[4] Many commuter routes operate with only a driver, while others have a guard on board as well. The trade unions tend to resist innovations that are intended to reduce costs by cutting on-board staff requirements, arguing that passenger safety would be prejudiced, although the safety regulator accepts that driver-only operation is permissible.[5] Efforts by the train operating companies to move to driver-only operation have led to strikes that have hit rail users hard, prompting parliamentary criticism of government ineptitude.[6]

Nevertheless, digital rail technologies could hold some of the answers to the problems arising from the growth of demand for rail travel, by making more efficient use of existing rail routes. Rail passenger numbers in Britain have more than doubled in the past 20 years. Significant growth in rail-km travelled has also occurred in other European countries, including France, Germany, Spain, Sweden and Switzerland, while substantial growth has taken place in China and India.[7]

This doubling of demand for rail travel in Britain had not been anticipated. It followed a long period of decline in rail use, reflecting strong growth in car ownership, lower road fuel and operating costs, and a substantial programme of road construction. The reversal of trend is attributed to a number of distinct developments: congestion on the roads; saturation of growth of car ownership; a shift in the wider economy from manufacturing to business services (the "knowledge economy") that tend to be located in city centres served by rail; digital connectivity that allows productive work by rail passengers; less interest by young people in the car, leading to more rail travel; as well as improvements made by the rail industry such as new rolling stock and online reservations.[8] It is noteworthy that 30 per cent of those who work in finance and insurance commute by rail, but only 2 per cent of those in manufacturing, hence employment growth in London's service sector has contributed to the increase in both commuting and business travel by rail.[9]

This growth of demand is the consequence of a substantial increase in the proportion of the population making rail trips, with little change in the number of trips per rail user.[10] A further factor contributing to the new growth of rail travel may have been a change of ownership of the railway industry, discussed below.

Growth in rail passenger numbers in Britain has plateaued since 2015–16.[11] It is not yet clear whether this is the initial signal of a break in the growth trend, or just a pause. It is possible that behavioural and technological changes, such as increased home working, are eroding peak demand. One suggestive indication is a modest downward trend over the past five years in passenger journeys using season tickets, offsetting continued growth in other kinds of journey.[12] It is possible that further capacity increases to reduce commuter crowding may attract people back to the railway for journeys to work.

Ownership: the public–private debate

The railways in Britain were initially developed by private companies in the nineteenth century, but went into decline in the twentieth century, as I described in Chapter 2. The railways were taken into public ownership in 1948. There was a substantial reduction in routes in the 1960s, mainly those in rural areas that were little used. The railways were privatized in 1997, half a century after being taken into public ownership, with the track in the single ownership of a company known as Railtrack, and private companies bidding to operate trains for particular routes and regions (although the track infrastructure was taken back into public ownership in 2002, following one of the worst crashes in Britain in which 31 people were killed). This change of ownership, with some degree of competition between train operators, contributed to expanding supply to match the growth of demand. The general approach of opening the railway to competition has been endorsed by the European Union as a means to create an integrated European railway system and a more customer-responsive industry.[13]

There has been substantial and continuing investment by the private sector rail operators in new rolling stock, and by the public sector Network Rail (Railtrack's successor) in track, signal and station improvements. Major investments in new lines are contentious on account of cost and environmental concerns, particularly High Speed 2 (HS2), currently under construction, linking London to the cities of the Midlands and the North, the high cost in part the consequence of the amount of tunnelling needed to reduce environmental impact. Another high-cost tunnelling project is Crossrail under central London, expected to open in 2020, albeit after some delay and cost-overrun against an optimistic budget. This new route will run up to 24 trains an hour at peak times, made possible by digital signalling and train control. A number of other substantial new rail investments are under consideration, including improved routes across the North of England, linking Liverpool to Hull via Manchester and Leeds; and reopening disused links between Oxford and Cambridge via Milton Keynes, with the aim of making land accessible for housing to assist growth of technology businesses in these attractive cities.

Despite investment in new and upgraded routes, there have been quite a number of problems with Britain's railways in recent years, caused in part by the growth of demand for rail travel. This has resulted in crowding and the need for some passengers to stand at peak times, especially on commuter routes. It has proved difficult to modify timetables to accommodate more trains on existing tracks. The investment to upgrade track requires temporary line and station closures, which, however necessary, disrupt journeys. There have been cost and time over-runs on investment projects due to inadequate planning. And there have been quite serious industrial disputes arising from proposals by management to reduce staffing levels. An attempt to bring into operation substantial infrastructure and rolling stock investments in a north–south route through central London, while at the same time dealing with a long-running industrial dispute, resulted in a major disruption of services when the new timetable was introduced in May 2018. A subsequent inquiry by the rail regulator found that there were systematic weaknesses in the planning and delivery of such major network changes.[14]

The system for allocating franchises to the private sector rail operators has been problematic. Competitive bidding requires prospective operators to commit to make payments to the government in return for award of the franchise (or, in the case of loss-making routes, to receive subsidies). To make a winning bid, an optimistic view of future passenger numbers is likely, which if not borne out leads to unsustainable finances for the operator.[15] This has resulted in franchises being abandoned before the end of the contact. The East Coast Mainline franchise was abandoned on three occasions by three private sector operators on account of financial losses. The government was then required to make alternative arrangements, effectively to renationalize. Such experience has deterred potential operators from bidding for new franchises, lessening the benefits of competition. A further problem has been the late delivery of improvements to the infrastructure operated by Network Rail, which has had an adverse impact on the performance of the train operating companies, with promised enhancements to services being delayed and disrupted, leading to passenger disappointment and discontent.

The Department for Transport is responsible for operating the bidding system for rail franchises. This has not been without problems. In 2012 the award of a key franchise had to be cancelled after discovery of significant flaws in the bidding process. More generally, the Department has had to take a remarkably detailed interest in the availability of new rolling stock in order to specify the improvements to be achieved through issuing new franchises.[16] The ability of the Department to manage the franchising process is in question. The House of Commons Public Accounts Committee concluded that the Department's management of two of its most important franchises "has been completely inadequate and could be indicative of wider weaknesses in contract management capability".[17]

All this has led to continuing political debate about the structure and ownership of the rail industry, with opinion polls suggesting substantial public support for taking the operating companies back into public ownership, the longstanding position of the Labour Party. It is clear that the theoretical benefits of competition, as seen by the European Union, may be difficult to deliver in practice, in part on account of the dependence of train operations on the state of the track and signalling infrastructure. The position is different from that of air travel, where good airport infrastructure and air traffic management is certainly required, but nothing analogous to the demands of steel wheel on steel rail and maintaining train separation throughout the journey. The arguments seem finely balanced as between a competitive railway and an integrated system. However, any change in ownership or structure would not resolve two fundamental issues – the scale of subsidy and workforce productivity.

Railway operating costs

Passenger railways are rarely able to cover all their costs while being competitive with road transport. Generally, receipts from fares and freight at best match the operating costs, with the budget for new investment to meet the growth of demand having to be funded by governments. Thus the British government is providing Network Rail with £35 billion over a five-year period to overhaul and renew track, structures and systems, plus £450 million to fund deployment of digital technology.[18]

There is a question of the balance between the contribution of fares from those who use the railway and taxpayers at large, most of whom make little use of rail – only 10 per cent of the average distance travelled per person in Britain is by rail. The railways in Britain currently spend about £20 billion a year to operate the system, funded mainly by £11 billion from passenger fares and a net contribution of about £4 billion from the government. It has been the policy of successive governments in recent years to reduce the contribution of the taxpayer by increasing rail fares faster than both the rate of inflation as measured by the Consumer Price Index and wage growth. In fact, over the five years to 2017–18, net government funding decreased only modestly, by 10 per cent.[19]

Fare increases are naturally unpopular with rail users, particularly those who commit to long, relatively costly commutes to gain access to homes they can afford in agreeable environments. Fare increases have varied according to ticket type and location: for instance, the real increases (after allowing for Retail Price Index inflation) in fares for all tickets since 1995 have been 12–14 per cent for London and the Southeast and for other regional railways, but 36 per cent for long-distance journeys.[20]

Fare increases are likely a factor contributing to the disaffection with the private rail operators, although in reality it is the consequence of government policy that is concerned with equity as between rail users and taxpayers generally; and between rail users who live mainly in prosperous London and the Southeast of England and the populations of cities and regions beyond the Southeast who complain that they are not getting a fair share of national funding of transport investment. Certainly, the disparity in public expenditure by region on the UK railways in 2016/17 appears substantial: £773 per capita in London compared with other regions receiving £70–175. However, such comparisons at a single point in time can be misleading, given the long life of assets and the cyclic nature of their replacement.[21]

One answer to the problem of rail fare increases would be to improve productivity, getting more outputs from the same inputs. A 2011 study of the costs of the railway in Britain estimated staff costs at some 35 per cent of the total and suggested that a reduction in cost per passenger-km of 30 per cent should be achievable through realizing best practice across the whole range of functions.[22] However, it seems that little progress has been made so far. One approach is to increase the productivity of infrastructure by means of digital technologies. Where headways can be reduced, and more trains run, both capacity and employment are increased. However, automation would reduce the labour requirement, which tends to be resisted by the trade unions representing a well-organised workforce. A key challenge for the management of a successful rail operator, whether in the private or public sector, is to take advantage of new technologies to increase labour productivity, thereby constraining increases in costs and fares. This would make rail a more attractive mode of travel and thereby increase passenger numbers and revenues from ticket sales: a virtuous circle.

High-speed trains

Digital rail technologies permit infrastructure capacity to be used more effectively. Another important technological development has been to increase the speed of rail travel. High-speed rail was pioneered in Japan in the 1960s and subsequently pursued in France and other European countries. China has invested in a substantial network, operating two-thirds of the world's high-speed tracks. High-speed rail employs specialized rolling stock and dedicated tracks, operating generally at speeds in excess of 250 km/hour (155 miles/hour). It offers an attractive alternative to air travel for city centre to city centre travel over moderate distances. The feasibility of such new routes depends on geography, governance and financing. In the US these factors have inhibited investment, such that air travel remains unchallenged.

There are other rail-like technological developments that may offer even higher speeds for surface travel, potentially replacing air travel over longer distances.

Magnetic levitation (Maglev) dispenses with wheels. The vehicle is raised above a track by magnetic repulsion, thus avoiding frictional resistance between mechanical components. Magnetic means are also used to propel the vehicle, permitting speeds of 500 km/hour. Although in development for half a century, with a number of low-speed versions demonstrated, commercial deployment at high speed has been limited so far to Shanghai. Here a Maglev train operates at a top speed of 430 km/hour to link the airport to a terminal on the eastern edge of the city in seven minutes, in competition with the conventional metro that takes passengers from the airport to destinations throughout the city at lower cost. In Japan a long-distance Maglev route is under construction, from Tokyo to Osaka, 80 per cent of which will be in tunnels.[23] Yet the prospects for the general adoption of Maglev technology do not seem promising given high costs and inflexibility, unlike high-speed rail where the trains are able to travel on conventional rail routes for parts of journeys.

Another high-speed surface transport concept that has attracted much interest is the Hyperloop, designed to convey capsules carrying passengers in tubes from which air is evacuated to reduce frictional resistance, so permitting sub-sonic speeds of around 600 mph. The concept was first proposed by Elon Musk as a means for connecting cities several hundred miles apart where passenger numbers are high.[24] The tubes would be largely located above ground, along existing inter-urban roads, likely more feasible in the US than in Britain. The very limited US passenger rail system provides an incentive to develop a new fast form of land transport, rather than improve and extend an existing rail network, as in Europe. The single-point origin-to-destination of Hyperloop is a limitation, particularly if these are outside city centres, the time for travel to final destinations negating some of the benefits of sub-sonic speed.[25]

All faster rail technologies are powered by electricity, as is much of the standard-speed rail network. In principle, all rail could be electrified, although there may be practical or economic reasons why this is not done. In such cases, decarbonization may he achieved using batteries or hydrogen fuel cells, as discussed for road vehicles in Chapter 3.

Urban rail

Because rail is a closed system with vehicle movement constrained by design, congestion is avoidable in well-managed operations, so passengers benefit from speed and reliability, compared with travel on traffic-congested roads. Overcrowding can be a problem at peak times, the remedies being longer trains and platforms, and improved signalling that allows more trains to be operated with shorter distances between them.

New technologies offering high speeds are not relevant for short distances within cities. The challenge is one of space, not speed. Old rail routes can be successfully modernized, a good example being London's Overground, an inner orbital service created by linking an assortment of under- or disused routes; renewing the track, signalling and station infrastructure; and introducing new trains with frequency of least four an hour, so that travellers need not check the timetable: they simply "turn up and go". Since opening in 2008, passenger-km have increased three-fold, well in excess of expectations, reflecting both extensions to the network and the popularity of the new service in enlarging the choices of homes accessible from where people work.[26] One result has been a significant increase in house prices in previously relatively low-cost areas (for London), now better connected by the Overground to where people work.[27]

Vehicles running on rail on city streets, variously known as trams, streetcars, or trolleys, were the earliest form of urban public transport, initially drawn by horses, taking advantage of the low rolling resistance of steel wheels on steel rails. Electric trams were first introduced in the 1880s and have remained an important mode of public transport in many European cities, although elsewhere, including Britain, they were generally scrapped to create more space for cars and for buses, which were seen as a more flexible form of public transport. With hindsight, we can see that the abandonment of urban trams was a mistake, the result of a failure to anticipate the magnitude of traffic congestion, from which trams are largely exempt.

It can be difficult to introduce wholly new rail routes into established cities, given the existing built environment that is generally valued by citizens. Light rail (trams, streetcars) is more feasible than conventional heavy rail. France has implemented tram schemes successfully in a number of medium-sized cities, finding that the improvement in public transport permits more pedestrian space to be created, which has had a revitalizing effect. I was much impressed by the modern tram system on a visit to Bordeaux, where three lines, totalling 66 km with over 100 vehicles, have made possible a reduction in car use in the city centre, enhancing the seventeenth-century architectural and urban heritage, as well as improving the connection between peripheral neighbourhoods and the core (Boquet 2017).

There is much interest in implementing such schemes elsewhere, to promote sustainable urban development (Ferbrache & Knowles 2016). The surface light rail technologies seem well established, with little innovation in prospect that would have much impact on cost or performance.

Elevation above the surface is a way of inserting rail into cities that was widely used in the past, leaving a legacy of railway arches for low-cost business premises. The Vancouver Skytrain is a recent example of a substantially elevated metro system with automated trains. The alternative to visually intrusive elevation is to head in the opposite direction: underground. Putting trains in tunnels is a well-established technology for urban public transport. Road traffic congestion is a problem limited to two dimensions, so taking advantage of the unoccupied third is attractive.

Tunnelling involves the large-scale shifting of earth and pouring of concrete, and is costly, like much civil engineering. Nevertheless, the economics can be justified for large, densely populated, growing cities. In London, Crossrail, renamed on inauguration the "Elizabeth Line", is a 73-mile-long east–west route tunnelled under central London, adding 10 per cent to the rail network serving the centre of the city. The tunnels are wide-bore to accommodate standard rolling stock, 6.2m internal diameter, compared with 3.8m for an existing Tube, a cross-section area 2.7 times greater and hence that much more material to remove for a tunnel of given length.

More underground rail routes would be built if the cost of tunnelling could be cut. Elon Musk, the innovator responsible for the Tesla electric car, has established the aptly named "The Boring Company". Its aim is to increase the speed of tunnelling and reduce costs by a factor of ten, thereby making underground travel by a variety of vehicles feasible (including bringing the Hyperloop into city centres). The main means are to reduce tunnel diameter and increase tunnelling speed (and so reduce labour costs) through increased power and automation. The small-diameter tunnel is designed for autonomous "electric skates", carrying either eight to 16 passengers or a single car.[28]

The Boring Company has been selected, subject to contract, to build a high-speed link between Chicago's O'Hare airport and the city centre.[29] It is reported that the proposed cost is less than $1 billion for an 18-mile tunnel, which compares with costs in excess of $600 million *per mile* for recent US subway tunnels, suggesting substantial appraisal optimism.[30]

There is a trade-off between the cost of a tunnel and its capacity for moving people. It is not obvious that Musk's concept of narrow-gauge tunnels (4m diameter) would be more cost-effective than the large-bore Crossrail model. Indeed, the larger Crossrail tunnel was selected in preference to a smaller Tube-type tunnel to provide the desired capacity. Irrespective of diameter, there would be benefit from technological innovations that reduce tunnelling costs, the scope for which is far from clear at present. The prospects for mitigating the impact of urban road traffic congestion may depend as much on improved tunnel boring technology as on digital innovations.

Up in the air

The advances in surface transport discussed above and in previous chapters contrast with limited innovation in conventional civil aviation, where aircraft have not changed fundamentally since the commercially successful Boeing 707 was introduced in the late 1950s. Long-haul travel times have been somewhat reduced as range has been extended through use of lightweight materials and improved engine efficiency, thus reducing refuelling stops. The supersonic Concorde was environmentally problematic and commercially unsustainable, although efforts continue to develop a marketable aircraft.[31] Achieving economies of scale through increasing aircraft size has reached its limit with the decision of Airbus to end production of the superjumbo A380, capable of seating up to 850 economy-class passengers. Innovation in the civil aviation sector is now focused on operational aspects, where budget airlines have entered long-haul markets, using modern fuel-efficient narrow-bodied aircraft.

The prospects for any major development in conventional aircraft technology seem limited, although there is a need for improvements in fuel efficiency to meet climate change targets. The international aviation industry has adopted the unambitious goal of carbon neutral growth from 2020 through purchasing emissions reduction credits from other sectors, as well as through the use of sustainable aviation biofuels.[32] Liquid biofuels, derived from crops grown for the purpose or from biomass waste, have long been seen as a potential replacement for oil-based fuels for transport. The recent commitment to electric propulsion has lessened the need for biofuels for road transport, but they remain an important means for aviation to reduce net carbon emissions.

The future contribution of the aviation sector to climate change mitigation will depend not only on technology, but also on future demand growth, which may turn out to be less than generally supposed. There are signs of maturity in certain market segments. For instance, while passenger numbers travelling by air between the UK and the US grew rapidly in the last century, there was a break in trend around the turn of the century, when growth ceased, as shown in Figure 7.1. Between the UK and Japan, passenger numbers grew prior to peaking in the late 1990s, after which they fell substantially, mainly the consequence of a fall in Japanese tourists visiting Britain; a similar peak and fall were experienced in travel between the US and Japan, as shown in Figure 7.2. These market segments are not typical; most show continuing growth in passenger numbers. But the UK–US, UK–Japan and US–Japan segments are long-established routes between developed economies, and cessation of growth suggests that we are seeing the emergence of the phenomenon of market maturity in air travel. Market maturity is a general phenomenon of all markets in goods and services; innovative offerings stimulate new demand, but over time growth slows and ceases as demand becomes saturated (Graham & Metz 2019). I discussed the evidence for saturation of daily travel demand in Chapter 2.

While market maturity in long-distance air travel may be emerging, the reverse is the case in the use of the air space above cities. There is currently

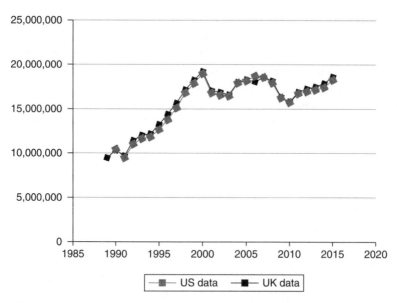

Figure 7.1 Air passengers travelling between UK and US (annual numbers)
Source: Airline data provided to UK and US authorities; Graham and Metz (2019).

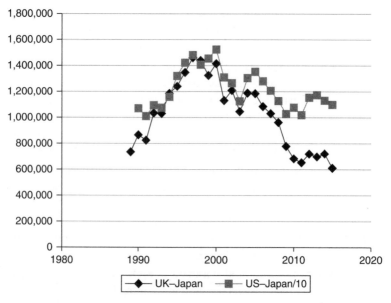

Figure 7.2 Air passengers travelling between UK and Japan, and between US and Japan
Source: Airline data provided to UK and US authorities; Graham and Metz (2019).

much interest in innovative technologies to take advantage of the third dimension upward. Traditional helicopters, powered by internal combustion engines, are noisy, fuel-intensive and costly to operate. Their use in cities has generally been limited. Exceptionally, São Paulo, the largest city in Brazil, has long had a helicopter service with a dedicated urban air traffic control system for a fleet of 500 helicopters. Use of this mode by the wealthy is prompted by severe traffic congestion, inadequate public transport, anxieties about street violence, and the status implied by helicopter travel. Protesting middle-class residents in neighbourhoods with helipads experience the noise. Helicopter accidents often involve celebrities, which gain them media coverage (Cwerner 2006).

The development of batteries for electric road vehicles has opened possibilities for short-distance electric-propulsion air travel. Already in wide use are pilotless drones that use multiple rotors: for instance, for remote monitoring and for delivery of urgent medical supplies.[33] Drones are being trialled for: parcel deliveries away from built-up areas – for example, in rural China where 100 villages are supplied by remotely piloted drones; orders being placed by smartphone; and distribution to individual households by the village "drone postman".[34] Amazon has well-publicized plans for drone delivery in the US, although Federal Aviation Administration rules are restrictive, requiring, for instance, a drone to be kept within sight of the controller.[35]

To increase distance travelled, the vertical take-off/landing rotor technology can be supplemented with fixed wings, which provide lift more efficiently than rotors in forward motion and permit higher speeds. Multiple rotors (typically six or more), driven by electric motors, are a safeguard against engine failure. These rotors are of smaller diameter than the single helicopter rotor and rotate more slowly, generating substantially less noise. Moreover, electric motors are far quieter than internal combustion or turbine engines.[36]

The possibilities for opening up urban airspace for personal travel and goods delivery very much depend on the development of battery technology: increasing energy density, reducing weight and cost. A number of prototype vertical take-off aircraft are under development.[37] Uber is ambitious to operate a ride-sharing air taxi service, to be known as UberAIR, and has issued a set of requirements for aircraft performance, with the aim of demonstrating acceptable functioning for revenue-producing operations from 2023.[38]

More generally, there are around 100 electric aviation projects announced, most from new entrants, including ideas for regional aircraft using hybrid technology to increase range, as for electric vehicles. The weight of the battery is the main constraint, in contrast to kerosene, which is 60 times more energy dense, the weight of the fuel reducing as it is used. Another limiting factor may be the time to recharge batteries while the aircraft is on the ground.[39] A further issue is the acceptability of the noise from large numbers of such aircraft.

If general use of such devices proves feasible, some form of urban air traffic control would need to be developed, to ensure that operations were safe and environmentally acceptable. This would need to apply to both passenger-carrying aircraft and unmanned drones in the same airspace. Given that battery capacity would be a constraint, direct point-to-point travel would need to be accommodated, complicating the management of airborne traffic. It is likely that advances in vehicle autonomy would be applicable to air travel, removing the need for trained pilots and allowing tight traffic control.

What is far from evident is the economics of urban air passenger travel: will it be a high-priced premium service or for the mass market? If costs were to reduce as scale of operations rose, safety and environmental considerations could limit availability, such that the service would nevertheless be priced at a premium. At this stage, the outcome is unclear, but it seems possible that in five to ten years some cities will have an urban air taxi service arranged through a smartphone app. This may seem slow progress in relation to expectations raised by half a century of science fiction movies, their skies filled with craft darting to and fro. For the present at least, we are confined to the surface by the weight of electric batteries, although we may live in hope of higher things.

One other approach to utilizing the space above cities is to employ cable cars, familiar from ski resorts, as adopted by a number of South American cities. In Medellin, Columbia, cable cars allow access to bus routes from informal settlements located on steep hillsides with poor road connections, which has doubled access to employment opportunities (Bocarejo *et al.* 2014). At present, the case is unproven for cable cars in developed cities with road networks suited for buses. There may be opportunities to link areas of cities severed by rail, road and rivers at relatively low capital cost. A cross-river cable car that opened in London in 2012 offers tourists a great view but is regrettably little used by residents.

Buses

Trains and planes have always provided shared travel, and shared taxis accessed via apps offer further possibilities for urban travel. However, buses are still a mainstay of public transport. In Britain, for instance, although half the population never or rarely use local buses, a quarter makes bus journeys more than once a week.[40] In some developed economies, bus (mass transit) use tends to decline as car ownership becomes more affordable. In the US, although ridership has been growing, the rate of increase has been less than population growth (Polzin & Sperling 2018). In contrast, bus use has been increasing in a number of European cities – Hamburg, Munich, Vienna, Berlin, Zurich – facilitated by the integration of public transport services over a large metropolitan area (Buehler, Pucher & Dummler 2018).

In Britain, bus travel outside London declined by 20 per cent in the period 2002–17.[41] In London, bus travel grew by some 80 per cent from 1996 to 2011, but has since fallen back.[42] There are a number of factors that have contributed to decline: growth of competition from increasing car ownership outside London, and from rail use, particularly within London; the scale of public subsidy, which makes fares more affordable but which has been generally decreasing; and road traffic congestion, which makes buses slower and less reliable. Congestion and subsidy are related in that slower speeds lead to higher costs (more vehicles needed to maintain service frequency) and fewer passengers, requiring more subsidy for a given level of service, which if not forthcoming leads to a spiral of decline (Begg 2016).

Efficient operational arrangements can help counter the trend away from bus use: for instance, London's integrated public transport system with a common payment system and real-time information about bus arrivals on apps and at bus stops. A study in Seattle found that real-time bus information reduced perceived waiting time, since those reliant on traditional arrival information overestimated waiting time by about 30 per cent (Watkins *et al.* 2011).

Low-floor buses that facilitate wheelchair use also speed entry of all, allowing faster journeys, as does cashless ticketing. Giving buses priority at traffic signals helps. However, bus service speed and reliability are adversely affected by road traffic congestion, which can worsen as happened in London with the opening of "cycle superhighways", a flagship programme of the previous mayor, Boris Johnson, to boost cycling.

The best means of attracting people onto buses is to increase speed and reliability by separating them from the congestion caused by general traffic. Bus Rapid Transit (BRT) employs buses on segregated routes with priority at intersections – for instance, in central lanes of wide boulevards – as pioneered in a number of Latin American cities beginning in the 1970s. At their best, such systems can perform comparably to light rail, but at lower cost (Ingvardson & Nielsen 2017). In Britain, the Cambridge Guided Busway, at 16 miles the longest in the world, takes advantage of disused rail routes north and south of the city. When it opened in 2011 there was an immediate doubling of passenger numbers in the corridor served (Brett & Menzies 2014). However, as with other historic cities, the part of the route through the centre of Cambridge is on conventional roads, which are too narrow to permit segregation.

Measures short of complete separation, such as priority bus lanes on main roads, are, of course, helpful, if less effective than BRT. This requires supportive policy by local government and has been a factor contributing to growth of bus travel in a number of British towns, contrary to the national trend, including

Brighton and Reading.[43] However, there is competition for segregated road space between bus lanes, cycle lanes and pedestrian space, which limits the scope for giving more priority to buses (Leeder 2017).

Buses are an efficient means of moving people in urban areas when demand is sufficient to ensure good occupancy levels and frequent services. There are opportunities to improve services through investment in digital technologies and in infrastructure. Suitable organization and governance are also important. There is, however, some tension between the advantages of integrated public transport provision over large metropolitan areas and a competitive market that allows new entrants and encourages innovative offerings (a similar situation to the railways, discussed earlier).

Road investment

The trains, planes and buses discussed in this chapter need infrastructure on which to operate. In some cases, private sector operators of infrastructure make investment decisions based on assessment of the commercial prospects, such as at privately owned airports. Public sector investment in road and rail infrastructure is subject to its own rules, aimed at ensuring that value for money is obtained when using funds ultimately provided by taxpayers. Such investment decisions are evidently important for the development of the transport system, but in practice are quite problematic, as I will explain.

Making the case for investment in the railway is more straightforward than it is for roads. We have data from ticket sales on the origins, destinations and timing of trips, so can infer the kinds of journey: commuting, business or leisure. The ability to control timetable and fares helps in projecting future travel demand and revenues. Of course, there are many uncertainties, some of which are not within the influence of the rail industry, particularly the future state of the economy. And control of the cost of new infrastructure has been challenging, but is capable of improvement. In relation to the new technologies discussed in previous chapters, the rail industry already recognizes the benefits of digital technologies to increase the capacity of existing track infrastructure, and of digital platforms for ticket sales and journey guidance. The railway can be carbon free through track electrification, or, where that may not be economic, by means of battery power or hydrogen (although long-distance freight in the US and elsewhere remains problematic). And driverless trains are already with us and may be expected to become more common.

Making the case for road investment is less straightforward, particularly in a developed economy with a mature road network. While we have extensive data on traffic flows, there is little on origins, destinations and purposes of journeys.

Because the road network is open to all qualified users, demand can exceed supply, resulting in traffic congestion. Congestion on Britain's strategic road network, comprising the main inter-urban routes, is found very largely in or near centres of population, not surprisingly. Remote from areas of high population density, the traffic mostly flows freely for most of the time (holiday destinations in the summer are an exception).[44] The weekday traffic pattern on roads prone to congestion displays morning and late afternoon peaks corresponding to commuter traffic, with typically 40 per cent of the morning peak being commuting.[45] While the stated aim of adding capacity to such congested strategic routes is to alleviate congestion and improve connectivity between cities to boost economic growth, in practice the outcome is more car commuting. The extra capacity initially reduces delays, allowing longer commutes and more people commuting by car, which adds to traffic and negates the expected congestion relief and better inter-city connectivity. Another consequence may be housing development on land made more accessible to employment in the city centre.

The failure to distinguish between commuter and long-distance traffic is a serious shortcoming of decision-making for investment in the road network. This is a consequence of the standard approach to the economic appraisal of transport investments.

In Chapter 2 I discussed the seeming inconsistency between the unchanging hour a day of average travel time and the assumption of orthodox transport economists that the benefits of investment that allows faster travel can best be estimated by multiplying the time saved per person by the number of people benefiting, and then converting the total time saved to a money value by multiplying by an estimate of the value of time (in £ or $ per hour). Time savings from typical road improvements, evaluated five years after opening, are quite small, generally three minutes or less at peak hours.[46] So the estimation of benefit involves multiplying small time savings per person by a large number of persons, despite such time savings being in practice an immaterial benefit to road users.

The economists justify their approach by arguing that the immediate impact of an improvement must be a reduction in journey time, which can be estimated from models; and while that time saving is likely to be converted into other forms of benefit – for instance, higher property prices and rents for locations made more accessible – this conversion process does not alter the total value of economic benefit. They also argue that to include uplift in land and property values would be to double count benefits included in the travel time savings estimation.

There are a number of difficulties with the orthodox approach. The time savings are based on the output of transport models that compare outcomes for the "do something case" (making the investment) with the "do minimum case" (not making the investment). The supposed time saved travelling that allows more productive work or valued leisure is not observed in reality. Evaluation of the outcome of completed road investments is limited to traffic volumes, vehicle speeds and journey time reliability, aspects that can be measured from the roadside. The actual impact on the behaviour of road users is not determined.[47]

I characterize the orthodox approach as "theory based", being based on the output of transport models for which simplifying assumptions are made, most commonly that land use remains unchanged. What is needed is an "evidence-based" approach that takes account of observable changes, including changes in land use and value. An evidence-based approach avoids double counting benefits because people can only do one thing at a time. If they take advantage of faster travel to reach most distant destinations, they cannot also be saving travel time, and vice-versa. Time savings should be counted when they can be observed, which generally would be in the short run. But to justify investment in long-lived infrastructure, it is the long-run benefits that we must estimate, much of which would be seen as changes in land and property values.

There is growing interest in Britain in how investment in infrastructure can benefit the economy, including how transport investment can make land accessible for new housing and can contribute to transforming the prospects of lagging cities and regions. The shortcomings of conventional transport investment appraisal in relation to these aspects are recognized by the government, which may be the first step to a better approach.[48]

There is also increasing interest in how to capture some of the uplifts in land and property values resulting from transport investment that increases access, as a means to help fund the investment. The argument is that land and property owners make windfall gains, which it would be reasonable for them to share with the infrastructure provider, for mutual benefit. Land value capture has long been employed in Hong Kong as a means to fund urban rail construction: the government gives the rail operator, in which it has a major shareholding, exclusive rights to develop property in defined catchment areas along a new route, the proceeds of development being used to fund the rail investment. Other Asian cities are following this approach. In Britain, existing mechanisms extract only a small fraction of land value gains from transport investment, and accordingly proposals have been made for how more could be achieved, particularly in London where the boost to land values would generally be greatest.[49] The focus of orthodox transport economists on time savings as the main benefit of investment has hitherto diverted attention from the potential to capture part of the uplift in land value.

These shortcomings in the investment appraisal methodology have distorted transport investment decisions in Britain. There has been too little investment in urban rail because the benefits arising from changed land use and property development have not been recognized. Moreover, much investment in inter-urban road schemes is justified as contributing to economic growth although improving connectivity and reducing congestion. Yet the amount of new traffic induced by the additional capacity is underestimated in the methodology based on time savings, and in practice congestion relief is generally quite short term. New road capacity tends quickly to fill with traffic, much of it car commuting, a consequence of the fact that people take the benefit of faster travel to reach more distant destinations and so to gain more opportunities and choices.

A further shortcoming of orthodox transport investment appraisal is that it disregards or underestimates the benefits of improved journey time reliability, where low-cost digital technologies are more effective than high-cost civil engineering. The highway engineers responsible for road networks have always seen investment in additional capacity as the "solution" to the ubiquitous problem of road traffic congestion. In cities, this approach has had its day, and the current approach is to push back the car, especially for commuting, to foster more vibrant city centres. However, beyond cities, adding road capacity still predominates.

The highway engineers in charge of the inter-urban road network understandably focus on travel between cities and turn a blind eye to the role of these major roads in local travel, where commuters may use quite short sections for short journeys. Local authorities responsible for local roads often grumble about the difficulty of coordinating operations and investment plans with the strategic road network, yet road users experience a single network that should be managed effectively for all.

The highway engineers have been slow to recognize the potential for digital technologies to optimize the operation of the network and mitigate the impact of congestion on road users by predicting journey times in advance of travelling. They display little recognition of the importance of decarbonizing the road network. And they have taken advantage of the orthodox approach to investment appraisal that sweeps under the carpet the impact of induced commuter traffic on efforts to alleviate congestion and improve connectivity between cities. As a result, much ineffectual expenditure is incurred attempting to build our way out of congestion, which we know from experience we cannot do.

To better plan long-term investment in infrastructure, the British government has established an independent National Infrastructure Commission. This has a remit to set out every five years an assessment of long-term infrastructure needs, with recommendations to the government. The first assessment, published in 2018, included the important recommendation that cities should be provided with long-term funding to implement integrated strategies for transport, employment and housing, recognizing that new housing requires new transport infrastructure to connect homes to jobs.[50] (Such an integrated approach already exists in London.) Joint planning of investment in housing and transport would require a new approach to transport investment appraisal. It no longer makes sense to consider transport improvements in isolation from their wider impact on employment and regeneration, and on their scope for making neighbourhoods accessible for homes within reach of employment.

The National Infrastructure Commission has also carried out a study on the government's wish to maximize the potential of the Cambridge–Milton Keynes–Oxford corridor as a knowledge-intensive economic cluster by improving the rail and road infrastructure that connects these cities. Shortage of housing is the main risk to economic growth. While rail provides commuter routes to city centres, more road capacity is seen as allowing travel to the fringes of cities where there are expanding employment sites and science parks.[51] However, while the Commission emphasized the need for a long-term vision for development of the corridor, it sidestepped the question of where to locate additional housing, whether near to railway stations or remote from them such that car commuting would be required.

Although it is a generally established practice for governments to have a department or ministry dedicated to transport, this tends to lead to investment decisions that focus on the supposed benefits to users of the transport system. The impacts on the wider economy and on people's quality of life receive insufficient attention. The focus on estimating the value of notional time savings distorts decisions. While it suits the civil engineers in the business of building new road capacity, what is needed is recognition of all the real impacts, including those beyond the traditional policy responsibility of a transport ministry.

Conclusion

Shared travel of the traditional kind – buses, trains and planes – is an efficient means of moving people when space is limiting, as in urban centres and on busy inter-urban routes. While there is much interest in shared taxis, as a more efficient means of moving people than individually occupied or owned cars, it is hard to see this making much impact on demand for conventional public transport modes.

Given that road traffic congestion is a problem in two dimensions, there are attractions in developing options for mobility in the third. Making better use of existing underground rail routes through digital signalling is cost-effective. New tunnels can be justified in economically dynamic cities, and would be more attractive if tunnelling costs could be reduced, which is conceivable. Use of urban airspace for passenger travel may also be feasible if battery technology improves sufficiently.

There is scope for improving bus services through digital technologies for information and payment, but the main constraint is the difficulty of creating segregated routes in limited urban spaces. City authorities can take a leading role in improving public transport by investing in new technology and infrastructure.

The case for public investment in new transport infrastructure needs to look beyond the traditional benefits as supposedly seen by travellers, to take account of impact on employment, housing and land use. Capturing a share of uplift in land values would permit more investment in urban transport infrastructure.

The railways have recognized the potential of digital technologies to improve performance. The public highway authorities are lagging in comparison, remaining committed to costly civil engineering technologies.

There are opportunities for employing new technologies to travel faster: for instance, underground urban rail, high-speed inter-urban rail and urban electric air travel, as well as more adventurous ideas such as the Hyperloop. However, all these seem costly where technically feasible, and so deployment is likely to be largely limited to high-density locations and routes, or to niche markets where premium fares could be charged. The impact on the average speed of travel across the population seems likely to be small, and hence not transformative.

8

TWENTY-FIRST-CENTURY TRAVEL

The benefits of greater access offered by the invention of the railway in the nineteenth century were very substantial, which justified the huge investment in rail networks. Subsequently, the advantages of door-to-door travel made possible by the motorcar vindicated the vast investment in vehicles, roads and fuel supply in the twentieth century. The bicycle in its heyday also had a major impact on access to employment and leisure opportunities, in the decades between becoming generally affordable and the beginning of the era of motorized mass mobility. All these innovations were transformational in that they allowed us to travel faster and so farther, to gain access to new destinations, opportunities and choices.

Electronic innovations have also been responsible for transformational changes in access to people and services: the telegraph, telephone, radio and television. Digital technologies are changing behaviour globally through access to the internet via ubiquitous smartphones, which allow us to shop online and to communicate to friends and foes through social media.

Now we have innovative transport technologies making an impact on how we travel – electric and autonomous vehicles, digital navigation and platforms. The question is whether a step change in access is likely to arise from any of these transport technologies. In previous chapters I have argued that this appears unlikely because they do not offer any general increase in the speed of travel, unlike the trains and cars that came earlier.

There are, however, some new transport technologies that allow faster travel, as I discussed in Chapter 7: high-speed rail, magnetic levitation, the Hyperloop and electric-powered urban aviation. But none of these seem likely to be economically viable beyond limited markets at best, and not on a mass-market scale that would increase the average speed of travel significantly. The one that could conceivably be transformative is electric urban air travel, given the volume of airspace available above cities, but the requirements for battery technology and safety would be very demanding and achievement is far from certain.

Beyond economic considerations, an important constraint on new transport technologies achieving transformational change is the long-lived nature of the man-made built environment, together with our attachment to historic buildings and places and to the countryside. Transport systems are also long lived, as well as being "path dependent", in that once we commit to a technology it is hard to switch to what might have been a better approach. Proposals for wholly new road and rail infrastructure commonly generate strong local opposition, in contrast to digital technologies that do not obtrude. Only those with the opportunity to build a new city from scratch with unlimited funds could indulge in blue sky thinking about the best transport system that might be managed with innovative technologies.

The development of digital technologies generally tends to be fast and is often disruptive to existing businesses. Yet their applications to transport are constrained by historic investments that cannot be written off. The digital hare must travel at the speed of the civil and mechanical engineering tortoise. What can be achieved through the application of digital technologies is more efficient, seamless travel along optimal routes; better matching supply to our demand; and reducing the cost, both by extending the scope for sharing with others travelling in the same direction and reducing labour requirements. These are useful and desirable improvements to the quality of the journey, if not transformative of our lifestyle.

The impact of the new transport technologies has to be assessed in the context of our existing patterns of travel behaviour. In the nineteenth and twentieth centuries we harnessed the energy of fossil fuels to travel faster and farther. As we moved into the twenty-first century there were significant changes in our collective travel behaviour, seen as breaks in long-run trends, as we ran out of ways of travelling faster. Car ownership ceased to increase. Travel on uncongested roads at higher speeds is limited by concerns about safety. Traffic congestion increasingly limits the speed of road travel.

At the same time, there have been demographic developments: population growth, particularly in cities, and the ageing of the population. Urbanization at higher population density adds to congestion, but at the same time increases the accessibility of services and makes public transport, walking and cycling more feasible, of which young adults in particular take advantage.

We are in transition between an era characterized by growth of travel, based on established technologies, and a new era in which innovative technologies will make their impact on how and where we travel. We need to ask about their likely influence on our travel behaviour, and then consider how these changes can be managed to achieve better outcomes for users of the transport system and for society as a whole.

Travel behaviour

An important characteristic of travel behaviour is that personal daily travel has stabilized in recent years, after nearly two centuries of growth. Each person in Britain travels on average about 6,500 miles a year for all purposes (other than international air travel), spread over about 1,000 journeys, and taking on average an hour a day. This pattern has persisted for the past 20 years. There is no certainty about the future, but it would be sensible to plan on the basis of continued stability as a central forecasting scenario, with variant cases to reflect other possible outcomes.

The hour or so a day of average travel time is found generally for settled human populations. It is a striking finding whose significance is insufficiently appreciated, in part because of the assumption by transport economists that the main benefit of investment that permits faster travel is the saving of travel time. In fact, the availability of time, within the 24 hours of the day, limits the amount of travel we can undertake. I regard the continuing stability of travel time, averaged across the population, as the least uncertain of all future aspects of travel behaviour.

Given unchanging average travel time, it follows that the average distance travelled cannot be expected to increase unless we are able to move at higher speeds. But the new transport technologies do not offer this prospect. Accordingly, we have entered an era of relative stability as regards personal travel.

Given stable travel per person, total travel demand, and the pattern of that demand in the future, will reflect demographic changes: population growth, where the additional inhabitants are located and population ageing. Most importantly, on the one hand, where new homes are built on greenfield sites, the occupants would make good use of cars and additional road capacity may need to be provided. On the other hand, housing more people within existing urban areas at higher population densities would require investment in public transport since there is little scope for additional car use in most larger towns and cities at times of peak demand.

The inability of cities to add road capacity without damaging the urban fabric has led to the phenomenon of what I have termed "peak car in the big city", seen where cities have historic centres that are popular with residents and visitors. Such successful cities attract people to work, study and live, but car use is constrained by road capacity. So, as the population grows, people make more use of public transport, walking and cycling, and the share of journeys by car declines. During the twentieth century, increasing prosperity was associated with increasing car ownership and use. However, in the twenty-first century increasing prosperity is associated with *decreasing* car use in successful cities.

Beyond the cities, the car will remain popular where there is space to drive and park, but car use per person in developed economies is unlikely to increase.

The growth and subsequent decline of car use in growing cities is mediated by road traffic congestion. Congestion arises in places where population density and car ownership are both high. Potentially more trips could be made by car than the road network can accommodate. Given the constraint on the availability of time for travel, people are deterred from car use by the prospect of delays due to congestion. Accordingly, they make other choices – of mode, time or destination of travel – where there are such choices, or not to travel at all. This means that congestion is substantially self-regulating since if traffic increases, delays worsen and more trips that might previously have been made are not undertaken. Gridlock is rare in well-managed cities where there are alternatives to the car available. For the same reason, mitigating congestion proves difficult. Adding road capacity initially reduces delays but this induces more traffic – trips previously deterred – consistent with the experience that we cannot build our way out of congestion. Encouraging drivers to switch to walking, cycling or public transport has little impact on congestion since previously deterred drivers take advantage of the road space freed up by those who switch. Congestion charging – charging for road use under congested conditions – would be a solution if charges could be set high enough to deter sufficient potential vehicle users, as happens in Singapore. However, the charges in London are insufficient for this purpose, with substantially higher charges likely to prompt public and political resistance. High-income cities seem to be the most difficult places to achieve effective congestion charging.

Road traffic congestion is the most intractable problem of the transport sector and the one that has the biggest impact on our daily travel. It will tend to worsen since the global population is urbanizing, with economic, cultural and social activity increasingly focused in cities. Conceivably, this trend to increased urban living could reverse: for instance, if there arose epidemics that were not readily preventable by vaccines or treatable by antibiotics. A more general stimulus to leave cities is high housing costs in popular urban areas. So a more dispersed pattern of habitation could lead to further growth of per capita car use, a possibility that needs to be borne in mind particularly in countries where there is space to accommodate low-density housing in sprawling suburbs.

Other problems of the transport system are more tractable than congestion, and may be facilitated by new transport technologies. Air pollution from surface transport will reduce as electric propulsion replaces the internal combustion engine. Deaths and injuries on the roads can be tackled through many means, outcomes being largely dependent on public demand and political will, with high hopes for super-safe driverless vehicles. Digital navigation helps us plan our trips and find our way, and could improve the operational efficiency of the road and rail systems. Digital platforms aid matching supply and demand, and make shared journeys more possible.

Given the scope for better outcomes, it makes sense to anticipate the consequences and plan for implementation of the new transport technologies. I outline next the main possibilities.

Innovation and investment for travel between cities

Rail travel, when efficiently managed, is speedy and reliable compared with cars on congested roads. Increasing the capacity of existing rail routes by employing digital technologies is cost-effective and publicly very acceptable. Reviving disused rail routes may be worthwhile where they still exist. However, wholly new rail routes are very costly and tend to be contentious on account of their impact on the environment and communities, while their economic benefits are difficult to forecast.

Adding physical capacity to existing inter-urban roads is popular with politicians who like to announce new schemes that they say will relieve congestion and boost the regional economy through improved connectivity between cities. Businesses also like new road capacity if funded by "free" money provided by the national government, although they would be more rigorous in their analysis if spending their own cash. Yet the outcomes tend to be disappointing. While the additional capacity initially reduces delays, this allows road users to make faster and longer trips in the time they have for travel. So the main impact of additional inter-urban road capacity is to foster commuting into cities by car from more distant locations, encouraging urban sprawl where the planning system permits development, or boosting prices of existing properties where planning consent is refused. The additional traffic from longer commutes restores congestion to what it had been, negating both the promised congestion relief and improved connectivity between cities.

More generally, research on the link between investment in transport infra-structure and economic growth is inconclusive, including the direction of cause and effect. Transport investment within cities with a dynamic economy and a growing population can unlock new housing and business development: for instance, in London's Docklands where a succession of rail projects has allowed the growth of a major new centre for business services, largely free of cars. Another example is the regeneration of Salford Quays, made accessible from the centre of Manchester by the Metrolink tram. In contrast, it is far from clear that improved links *between* cities would be a high priority for stimulating the economy in cities where growth is low.[1]

So while addition of capacity to an inter-urban road network may be warranted to accommodate population growth, it is harder to justify a major programme of investment in costly civil engineering technology to attempt to improve the performance of a mature inter-urban road network. The UK's current national road investment strategy, costing £15 billion over five years, needs careful evaluation. The objective of "a free flowing core network, with a mile a minute speeds increasingly typical" is unlikely to be achieved.[2] The proposed successor programme, worth £25 billion, requires critical scrutiny. While expenditure on asset maintenance and replacement is sensible, plans for additional capacity are questionable.

There is too much wishful thinking about the benefits of transport investment when other people's money is being spent. For publicly funded projects, cost over-runs are not uncommon and can be tolerated by public bodies that cannot become insolvent. Investment appraisal of such projects can suffer from "optimism bias". The UK Treasury recognizes "a demonstrated, systematic, tendency for project appraisers to be overly optimistic", and accordingly requires adjustments to be made to cost estimates: for example, an uplift of up to 44 per cent for standard civil engineering capital expenditure.[3] The UK National Audit Office has found that the majority of government projects have not delivered the anticipated benefits within original time and cost expectations.[4] An example is HS1, the new rail route from the Channel Tunnel to London, where passenger numbers were only a third of the level originally forecast due to unanticipated competition from low-cost airlines.[5] Such endemic over-optimism can be either unconscious or deliberate, known in the latter case as "strategic misrepresentation", a concept popularized by Bent Flyvbjerg (Flyvbjerg, Holm & Buhl 2002). This can involve estimated capital costs being adjusted downwards and usage adjusted upwards to increase the chances that the project will get funded.

As well as optimism bias, there is also a "bias to action" – a preference for doing something rather than nothing – on the part of professionals and politicians, if not spending their own money. This is well known in the financial services sector where asset managers are keen to charge high fees to manage our savings actively, switching frequently between investments, but not achieving better outcomes than passively managed tracker funds with lower charges.

More effort is needed to think through the implications of *not* making a transport investment, adopting a passive approach of keeping existing assets in good repair. The decision in the 1970s not to construct major urban motor roads in London turned out to be well judged: the city has thrived as car use has stabilized.

Julian Glover, a former policy adviser to the UK secretary of state for transport, has instanced Stoke-on-Trent, located in the Midlands and formerly dominated by the pottery industry, as the sort of place that good infrastructure is supposed to fix. But Stoke already has good transport infrastructure, which might have served to drain talent out, not draw it in. Glover argues that the sweeping belief that all infrastructure must be good, and all of it will bring a return in jobs and growth, is a fallacy.[6]

Yet there is a strong political imperative to help regions in economic decline. The virtue of improving the road system is that it is a very visible, concrete (literally and figuratively) expression of support, in place forever, unlike measures such as skills training, cultural institutions or promotional activities. On a recent trip to the interior of Spain, I was struck by evidence of depopulation: few people and cars in the villages and many "for sale" signs on properties. Equally striking was the excellent regional road network, albeit with very sparse traffic, but for that reason unlikely to make much demand on local road maintenance budgets.

Wishful thinking is not limited to the public sector. In Australia, private investors hoping to earn a return from charges to road users have funded construction of a number of toll roads. The public authority decides that a road is needed and invites bids that involve a payment to the authority for the privilege of charging users. To win a competitive bid and raise money from investors, an optimistic view may be taken of future demand. In a number of cases, traffic has fallen well short of forecast and disappointed investors have sued scheme promoters or their professional advisers.[7] Most actions have been settled out of court with no disclosure of outcome, although in one case, a prominent transport consultant paid $200 million to settle a complaint about a motorway tunnel in Brisbane where traffic turned out to be only a fifth of the forecast.[8]

As well as the difficulties involved in making good forecasts of costs and demand for transport infrastructure, major civil engineering projects are inherently expensive. It is therefore increasingly the case that the most cost-effective approach to improving both the user experience and efficiency of the road network is by means of the digital navigation technologies that I discussed in Chapter 4. Route guidance provided by private sector tech companies, often free of charge, offers road users alternatives to congested routes, with estimated time of arrival predictions that mitigate the main detriment arising from congestion – journey time uncertainty. The providers do not disclose either their methodology or performance data, although anecdotal experience suggests that journey time predictions can be reasonably good.

One well-recognized problem with digital route guidance is that traffic may be diverted to roads unsuited to the volume of traffic or to large vehicles. More generally, it is unclear whether the algorithms employed optimize use of the road network for all users, or just those equipped with the guidance. There is therefore a good case for coordination between the route guidance providers and the authorities responsible for road operation, to achieve an optimal outcome.

A bigger prize in achieving efficient operation of the road network might be accomplished by the roll-out of connected AVs, according to enthusiasts.

Shorter headways between vehicles, narrower lanes and more efficient junctions could smooth flows and increase the capacity of existing roads, while eliminating human error would reduce deaths and injuries from crashes. Road freight businesses would benefit from platoons of trucks that would save fuel through reduced air resistance and need fewer drivers. However, the practicality of this vision depends on the related issues of technical feasibility, economic benefit and public acceptability.

Geography determines the context. Feasibility and benefits of truck platoons would be greater in spacious territories, where there are long distances to be traversed and roadside locations available for formation and disassembly. Conversely, in confined geographies with dense traffic, as in Britain, feasibility and economic benefits seem insufficiently promising to justify early adoption.

Truck platoons typically involve vehicles of identical make in the charge of professional drivers. Their contribution to increasing road capacity would be fairly small. To achieve substantial capacity benefits, short headway operation would need to involve AVs of all makes and types. As I discussed in Chapter 6, this would require a safety case that reconciled the trade-off between inter-vehicle distance and resilience to failure on the part of both individual vehicles and communication between them. Moreover, occupants would need to have some incentive or requirement to travel at short headways, while manufacturers would need to identify a market for connected AVs and be willing to accept responsibility for the consequences of crashes.

It is natural for innovators to be hopeful about their inventions. Expressions of hopefulness help attract both skilled engineers and investors. Wishful thinking is to be expected. Yet the technical challenge of increasing road capacity through the general use of connected AVs seems particularly severe, such that the timing and indeed feasibility of deployment is quite unclear. It will be difficult enough to make non-connected AVs publicly acceptable on inter-urban roads.

Innovation and investment in urban transport

The new transport technologies will not revolutionize urban travel but they can improve our journey experience. Digital navigation technology is the best means we have for optimizing the use of the road network, urban as well as inter-urban, mitigating the impact on users of traffic congestion by providing estimated time of arrival and so reducing journey time uncertainty. Coordination between the tech companies and the city authorities has to be of mutual benefit. An example was prompted by delays in London's Blackwall Tunnel caused by drivers running out of fuel. Transport for London has collaborated with Waze, the route guidance app, to remind approaching drivers to have enough fuel, with 460 drivers over a period of six months rerouting to fill up.[9]

The now familiar digital route guidance apps provide information on urban travel by public transport, walking and cycling, as well as by car or taxi. These help us make unfamiliar journeys and use travel modes best suited to our needs.

Digital platforms help match demand for travel with supply, as exemplified by ride-hailing taxi services, most prominently Uber. Beyond taxis, they are being trialled for commercial operation of intermediate-sized vehicles such as minibuses. Platforms make possible dockless cycle hire, by allowing available bikes to be located and paid for using a smartphone app. And platforms make possible shared ownership of vehicles in the form of car clubs, as well as shared use of taxis. Extension of digital platforms to more than a single mode of travel is a natural step, conceptually known a Mobility-as-a-Service, where a number of trials and commercial implementations are underway.

Autonomous vehicles in urban areas have potential to extend the range of transport services by removing the cost of the driver and hence lowering fares of taxis and public transport. On the one hand, this might make taxis a more attractive alternative to buses. On the other hand, the availability of low-cost driverless vehicles could reduce the appeal of personal car ownership in urban areas, thus potentially lessening congestion. However, the feasibility and timing of the introduction of AVs into cities is very uncertain, particularly cities with historic narrow street networks.

Replacement of the internal combustion engine by electric propulsion is being driven by concerns about climate change and urban air quality. The development effort that is being brought to bear by road vehicle and battery manufacturers is impressive. There seems to be general confidence that EVs with performance and cost comparable to that of conventional vehicles will be achieved within the foreseeable future (much more confidence than for the public acceptability of AVs).

Governments are promoting EV uptake by a variety of financial incentives and tax measures. Ensuring the provision of public charging points is also important for encouraging EV use – probably the most useful action that cities can take in support of objectives to phase out sales of conventional vehicles with internal combustion engines.

As a result of these private and public initiatives, there has been a major shift in thinking about the contribution of transport to greenhouse gas emissions and climate change. Until recently transport was seen as the most problematic sector, compared with domestic and industrial energy use, where there are plentiful opportunities to reduce energy consumption and to switch to renewable sources. For transport, behavioural change aimed at reducing car dependence was seen as essential, albeit not easy to achieve. However, the prospect of electric propulsion for road vehicles has transformed the situation, although it is also a requirement that the electricity be derived from non-fossil fuel sources. (In contrast, reducing carbon emissions by aviation and shipping remains a challenge.)

Electric propulsion is also the eventual technological solution to the problem of noxious emissions from diesel and petrol engines of road vehicles. In the period until EV use becomes general, other mitigating measures would be needed, including better performance from new diesel vehicles, more rigorous testing of older vehicles and traffic management interventions that could include charges for the older, more polluting vehicles.

Taxes on petrol and diesel fuel have been an important source of revenue, both to maintain and develop the road system, and to fund wider public expenditure. The shift to electric propulsion will deprive governments of this revenue source, which may prompt the general introduction of road-user charging, already familiar in various forms such as toll roads and congestion charging in cities, notably London, Stockholm and Singapore. A road-user charging system for general use would need to recognize the type of vehicle, the category and location of the road, time of day and level of traffic congestion. The means for doing this would be similar to the apps used by ride-hailing taxis to calculate fares.

Charging for use of the road would allow devolution of revenues to local road authorities responsible for their maintenance, rather than, as is common at present, these authorities being dependent on funds from central government. This would be analogous to the ability of local authorities in Britain to retain the revenue from charges for parking and London's congestion charge, earmarked to support local transport provision.

The new transport technologies are not going to alleviate urban traffic congestion, although impacts may be mitigated: EVs lessening air pollution, digital navigation reducing journey time uncertainty. The best approach to reducing the number of people experiencing congestion is old technology exemplified by rail in all its forms, including light rail running on or near urban streets. While there seems limited scope for technological innovation, fast and reliable journey times can attract people out of their cars on congested roads.[10] Many successful cities have substantial rail systems, lessening car dependence and fostering interactions between people that contribute to economic, cultural and social success.

Transport technologies for an ageing population

Digital technologies should be of particular benefit for an ageing population. The heterogeneity of an age cohort increases as chronological age advances. While many people in their 70s, for instance, are fit and fully functional, others are less so and can benefit from support in their daily lives, including their need for mobility. What is required are "forgiving technologies" that correct our errors, simplify tasks and reduce anxieties. The exemplar is the word processor that, in contrast to historic typewriters, allows easy correction of typing errors (and which made writing this book possible) (Metz 2018c).

Task simplification is of particular benefit in later life when cognitive functions begin to decline. Ticket machines at railway stations can be challenging, given the range of options on offer; contactless card payment obviates such difficulties. Reduction in anxiety is facilitated by timely provision of relevant information, such as real-time information at bus stops, internet-based advance bus and rail timetable information to plan and book trips, and route guidance apps to help find the way. Development of motor vehicle technologies that reduce the demand on drivers will benefit older motorists, with full autonomy allowing use by all.

More generally, "inclusive design" is the preferred approach to meeting the needs of those with disabilities in later life, based on the simple idea that if we design for the young we risk excluding the old, whereas if we design our transport system and the environment at large for the old, the young would be included.[11] Where the inclusive approach is not feasible, personal needs that arise from disabilities may be met by "assistive technologies", such as motorized mobility scooters for those with walking difficulties. Personalization of digital devices will be of increasing importance. Smartphones already incorporate a number of features that enhance their accessibility to users with impairments.

Regulation of innovative technologies

The introduction of innovative technologies into a complex, extensively regulated transport system is challenging for innovators, existing operators and governments. Governments, local and national, want better outcomes for citizens, while innovators need to be rewarded for their efforts.

A perennial question concerns the roles of public and private sectors. The case for private sector transport operators is that they are more likely to be innovative through the need to be competitive, although regulation is generally required to ensure safety and protect the interests of users. A public sector transport undertaking may itself develop innovative technologies or may purchase them from private sector suppliers; it may also regulate private sector operators with innovative business models based on new technologies, such as ride-hailing taxis, but that may give rise to conflicts of interest if the innovators are in competition with the regulator as operator.

As I discussed earlier in the case of the railways, there is no generally preferred policy choice as between private or public sector transport operations. I consider now what seem to me to be the main operational and economic regulatory issues arising from the development of the new transport technologies by private sector operators. (Innovation by public sector operators may be subject to safety regulation but not normally to economic or operational regulation.)

Railways and aviation are tightly managed closed systems on which every movement requires permission of a controller who can see all such movements. High levels of capacity utilization and safety are achievable as a result. In contrast, the road network is a system open to all qualified motor vehicles and their drivers (and to walkers and cyclists, discussed below). In consequence, there is extensive regulation of the road network and its users. Vehicles are regulated for safety, fuel consumption and emissions. Drivers must demonstrate basic competence when they first learn to drive and subsequently are penalized if they breach the provisions of road traffic legislation. There are standards for road design and construction, and for signs and signals. Traditional taxis are regulated. Nevertheless, the open nature of the road system commonly results in traffic that exceeds capacity, and the result is congestion.

The question that arises is whether there are opportunities for more effective management of the road network through regulation, prompted or made feasible by the new digital technologies. I argued earlier the case for coordination between the providers of digital navigation devices and the road authorities, in the interest of optimizing use of the network for both individual drivers and collectively. Another possibility would be the general application of road-user charging, the introduction of which could arise from the wide adoption of EVs that do not use taxed oil-based fuels. As noted earlier, road authorities could set charges to cover the cost of operating and maintaining their road network, as well as contributing the revenue required by central government. Adjusting the charge to reflect the level of congestion would be one measure open to urban authorities to help manage their road networks. Higher charges for unoccupied autonomous vehicles could ensure priority for occupied vehicles. In-vehicle digital technology, similar to that of the ride-hailing app, would be used for charging and would also assist authorities in monitoring traffic flows and responding to the build-up of congestion. The experience of implementing road-user charging in London and Stockholm is encouraging in respect of public acceptability. Its use more generally could help bring demand into better balance with supply of road space, although the experience of Singapore suggests that quite high charges may be needed to have a sustained impact.

The digital platforms for ride-hailing have resulted in a major innovation in taxi hire. The popularity of Uber and other such services reflects their superior performance in meeting user requirements. However, the regulatory regime for traditional taxis does not in general fit ride-hailing providers, which is why they have been able to gate crash the market with such success. So taxi regulation requires rethinking. The traditional objectives have been: to protect users by assuring quality and reliability; to regulate fares by means of a meter; and to protect the earnings of drivers by limiting entry. However, the role of large ride-hailing businesses, with reputations to maintain, goes a long way to providing assurance to users, including prior vetting of individual drivers for character and health, and post-trip rating of driver satisfaction. The estimate of fares on the ride-hailing app prior to the trip allows the user to decide whether this is good value, even though fares may vary to reflect fluctuations in demand.

A particular feature of ride-hailing apps is the opportunity they offer for passengers to share journeys at lower cost with others going in the same direction. This increases vehicle occupancy and makes more efficient use of the road network. Another app-based service is the car clubs or shared self-drive cars, in effect self-drive ride-hailing at lower cost without a paid driver.

The entry of ride-hailing companies into the taxi market has increased competition, which would generally be regarded as offering a benefit to users, who have more choice of type and numbers of vehicles. An important question is whether network economics in the taxi market mean there is a tendency to monopoly, with the likelihood of higher fares, or whether a fairly stable competitive market would be maintained. In other regulated markets, regulators seek to promote competition to benefit consumers: in energy, telecoms, banking and financial services. Where there is a natural monopoly – for instance, the wires and pipes that supply homes with electricity and gas – charges or profits are regulated. For the taxi market, the issue is whether the main objective of regulation should be to promote competition to benefit users, or whether there are reasons why other considerations should dominate, in particular the situation of ride-hailing drivers and the impact on congestion.

Drivers were initially regarded as self-employed, part of the so-called "gig economy", without the benefits such as sick pay and holiday pay that accrue to those regularly employed. There has also been concern about the level of pay, when minimum hourly pay legislation does not apply. There have been a number of legal actions and policy reviews, in Britain and elsewhere, with as yet no settled outcomes, as I discussed in Chapter 5. A key question is whether taxi regulation should concern itself with drivers' pay and conditions, or whether this aspect should be left to be dealt with by measures that apply to the gig economy generally, in which case the ride-hailing platforms would compete among themselves and in the labour market generally for drivers.

Given that the qualifications to be a taxi driver (other than the "knowledge" in London) are not demanding, it would tend to be a sector in which the supply of drivers and vehicles would grow to meet demand, unless constrained by regulation. This prompts concern about the contribution of such growth to traffic congestion. However, as I argued earlier, congestion is largely self-regulating, which means that growth of demand for taxis would lead to reduced demand from other vehicles, particularly private cars for which the taxi is an alternative.

So it is far from clear that regulating taxi numbers to mitigate congestion would be effective. However, bringing taxis within the scope of a road-user charging regime would allow city authorities the opportunity to influence the relative proportions of different vehicle classes.

While congestion is difficult to reduce, the composition of traffic on urban roads can be influenced, both by allocation of space to bus and cycle lanes and to pedestrians, and by differential road-user charging. Urban authorities need to be able to exercise the full range of policy options to regulate and manage their complex transport systems.

Constrained futures

In developed economies, past investment in the built environment, including transport infrastructure, very substantially constrains the scope for improving how we travel. The vast bulk of our transport system is already in place and comprises long-lived assets. Indeed, road and rail routes generally have indefinite life.

This inheritance varies from city to city, from place to place. While we can add new infrastructure and buildings, for developed economies this is very much at the margin. We must make the best use of what we have, in part on account of the cost of any major rebuild, and in part because people are generally attached to their homes and neighbourhoods.

The virtue of the digital transport technologies is that they can enable us to make better use of the existing transport infrastructure in a way that can be cost-effective compared with investment in new road or rail infrastructure. The new technologies will provide cleaner and, hopefully, safer travel, with more options and fewer delays. There will be opportunities to exploit the third dimension: for instance, where improved signalling allows more frequent trains in tunnels below the surface, and as and when electric aircraft become feasible.

Nevertheless, while new technologies will be helpful in improving the travel experience, a fundamental difficulty will remain. The transport system allows us to be mobile, but at the same time gets in the way of the interactions between people that make urban living attractive. Railways have always severed communities, as do heavily trafficked roads. Proposals to push back cars in dense urban areas are usually contentious, retailers in particular being anxious about possible loss of footfall. In practice, creation of pedestrian areas in central shopping and entertainment districts generally proves successful, particularly in cities where there is good public transport as an alternative to the cars displaced.

The experience of many successful cities is that the combination of population growth but limited road capacity leads to decline in car use. London and similar large cities are thriving economically, culturally and socially, both despite declining car use and because of less road traffic interposed between people. In the twentieth century, increasing prosperity was associated with increasing car ownership and use. In the twenty-first century, increasing prosperity is linked to declining car use, at least in successful cities in developed countries. As population density increases, more local services become economically viable, access is enhanced and the need to travel beyond the locality is reduced. Walking and cycling are well suited to short trips, and public transport enters a virtuous circle with increasing patronage justifying increased service frequency. A whole range of digital technologies facilitate city living, both those that provide better travel options and others such as the dating apps for which high population density offers more new friends in the vicinity.

Beyond the cities, the car will continue to be popular where there is adequate road space for movement as well as parking, although per capita use in developed economies is unlikely to increase. The challenge faced by smaller cities and towns is whether to push back against car use, to boost the interactions between people that foster success, or to attempt to accommodate the preferences of motorists for the convenience of door-to-door travel. This challenge reflects in part a more general cleavage in society, between the urban tech-savvy young, not much interested in cars, and those for whom cars have been an important part of their lives, for daily mobility, status and the pursuit of leisure activities.

For cities in low-income countries, where car ownership is still comparatively low, the question is whether to allow ownership to grow, responding to demand of the emerging middles classes, effectively tracking the trajectory experienced by cities in developed economies where the share of car trips peaked and subsequently declined. An alternative would be to plan to avoid that peak by promoting and investing in alternatives at an early stage, reaching the same kind of outcome in the long run. The introduction of mobile phones into low-income countries made unnecessary the roll-out of land lines. The digital transport technologies may lead to fresh approaches to travel: for instance, the digital platforms for motorbike taxis mentioned in Chapter 5.

Conclusion

Let me summarize concisely the main arguments made in this book.

The average time people spend travelling has been surprisingly stable for many decades and probably for many centuries. The 24 hours of the day limits the time available for travel to about an hour a day.

The energy of fossil fuels, first coal and then oil, allowed us to travel faster, within the time constraint. We took advantage of this to travel farther, to gain access to a greater range of opportunities and choices of employment, homes and services.

As we entered the present century, the scope for yet faster travel largely ended, resulting in a cessation of growth of travel per person. This was the consequence of a tailing off of growth of household car ownership; saturation of demand for travel for many daily activities; and increased urban living and the associated traffic congestion.

The observed breaks in trend on moving into the present century reflect a behavioural transition from growth to stability of personal travel.

The main problems with the existing transport system are urban air quality, carbon emissions, deaths and injuries from crashes, and road traffic congestion, of which the last is the most intractable.

Congestion occurs in areas of high population density and high car ownership where road capacity is insufficient to meet demand for all the car trips that might be made. Some are deterred from taking their cars by the prospect of delays and make other choices: to travel by a different mode, at a different time, to a different destination, or not to travel at all. Congestion is largely self-regulating since if traffic increases, more are deterred by the increasing delays.

Conversely, congestion is difficult to mitigate. Adding road capacity reduces delays initially, which attracts drivers previously deterred, restoring congestion to what it was, hence the experience that we cannot build our way out of congestion. The same applies to measures to reduce demand: for instance, by congestion charging or the promotion of walking, cycling and public transport.

The trend to urban living increases population densities in successful cities. Road capacity cannot be increased without damaging the urban fabric, so cities invest in public transport, and the share of journey by car reaches a peak and subsequently falls. Young adult residents in particular make less use of cars. Economic, cultural and social success is associated with declining car use in such cities.

While travel per person has stabilized, population growth drives an increase in overall travel demand. The pattern of demand growth depends on where the additional people live and work. To the extent they are accommodated in new build housing on greenfield sites, the car would be the main means of travel and road investment may be needed. Accommodating population growth in existing urban areas at higher density would best be served by investment in public transport.

We have four new technologies that are beginning to make an impact on how we travel.

Electric propulsion does not change the essential characteristics of a vehicle, but does eliminate tailpipe emissions of carbon and noxious pollutants, which are a main contributor to poor urban air quality. Electric vehicles plus electricity generation from non-fossil fuel sources would largely render land transport sustainable.

Digital navigation helps us choose optimal routes for both car travel and when using public transport, walking and cycling. While tackling road traffic congestion directly is generally ineffective, the main disadvantage reported by road users is the uncertainty of journey time. Digital navigation devices that take account of prevailing congestion provide estimated journey times at the outset of the trip. This is the best means available to help mitigate the impact of congested traffic.

Digital platforms applied to travel improve the match of supply and demand, and so improve the quality of our journeys. They also facilitate sharing with others going in the same direction, which is the rationale of conventional public transport, but innovative for taxis and minibuses.

The prospects for autonomous vehicles are more uncertain than for the other technologies. They would need to be demonstrably safer than conventional vehicles. There will be little impact on the road network until they can operate in driverless mode. To the extent this proves feasible, there would be cost savings where otherwise a driver would be employed, which may make possible a wider range of public transport provision.

Generally, these new technologies seem unlikely to have much impact on the average speed of travel. They will therefore not lead to transformational or disruptive changes in how we travel. But the digital innovations will be more cost-effective than traditional civil and mechanical engineering technologies in improving the quality of our journeys. We will experience more seamless trips along optimal routing, although congestion will probably remain common in urban areas.

There are some markets where higher speed travel is, or may become, feasible: high-speed rail at present, and possibly the Hyperloop and electric urban aviation in the future. But these seem likely to be limited markets, with little impact on the average speed of travel.

In the past the important transport innovations – the railway, motorcar, aeroplane – have permitted a transformational change in access for a substantial part of the population that justified huge investment. Similarly, innovations in telecommunications and information technology that have transformed society have received enormous investment: the telephone, radio, television, internet, social media. In contrast, the new transport innovations do not offer such transformational change, which will limit investment to what users would be willing to pay for improved journey quality.

So we are in a world of incremental changes, where the authorities in charge of transport systems will need to accommodate both existing users and operators as well as innovators who wish to provide a better service. The market for travel involves both public and private providers, is highly regulated, but should accommodate useful innovations. Cities will need to manage their transport provision to achieve their economic and social objectives, taking advantage of worthwhile technological advances.

There is much wishful thinking about the benefits of investment in both innovative technologies and traditional transport technologies, particularly when funding may be attracted from investors seeking the next big tech thing or from governments wanting to show support for economically lagging regions. More analytical rigour to counter unwarranted optimism would help avoid wasted effort and expenditure.

The present challenge for transport policy – as this develops in debate involving politicians, the range of interested parties and the travelling public – is to take advantage of new technologies to achieve better means of travel for an improved quality of life. And because the transport system is for everyone – old and young, rich and poor, rural and urban – we need to balance the requirements of transport businesses with societal needs to help achieve more equitable outcomes.

Transport systems are complex, have many common features, but have developed in different path-dependent ways in different locations: countries, cities, towns and the routes between. This variety provides examples, from which we can learn, of successful investments and innovations, as well as of disappointments. This book has attempted to identify the main common features of transport systems in developed economies and has provided some illustrations of the diversity of practice. But more effort is needed to evaluate outcomes of innovations and to disseminate findings. The most fundamental transport innovation was the wheel. We can avoid its metaphorical reinvention if we are able to benefit from the experiences of others.

NOTES

CHAPTER 1

1. *National Travel Survey: England 2017. Statistical Release 26 July 2018.* London: Department for Transport. In the past, the NTS covered the whole of Great Britain, but since 2013 Scotland and Wales have taken responsibility for collecting their own travel data. Omission of Scotland and Wales has had only minimal impact on NTS average travel behaviour, which is why I refer generally to "Britain" rather than "England". The full data sets and methodology are found at www.gov.uk/government/statistics/national-travel-survey-2017.
2. Data from UN sources compiled by Kit Mitchell, presented to a meeting of the Transport Statistics Users' Group, London, 21 March 2018.
3. *Cycling Facts.* Netherlands Institute for Transport Policy Analysis. The Hague: Ministry of Infrastructure and Water Management, 2018.
4. *Bicycle Statistics from Denmark.* Cycling Embassy of Denmark, 2015.
5. *Rail Passenger Transport 2014–2016. Passenger Transport Statistics – Statistics Explained.* Luxembourg: Eurostat, 2018.
6. NTS Tables 0403, 0410; 2017.
7. *Travel in London Report 10*, Table 2.1. London: Transport for London.
8. *Reducing UK Emissions: 2018 Progress Report to Parliament*, Chapter 5: Transport. London: Committee on Climate Change, 2018.
9. *United Nations Framework Convention on Climate Change; Decisions Adopted by the Conference of the Parties*, November–December 2015.
10. *WHO Air Quality Guidelines for Particulate Matter, Ozone, Nitrogen Dioxide and Sulfur Dioxide: Global Update 2005.* Geneva: World Health Organization.
11. "Air quality: commission takes action to protect citizens from air pollution", press release, 17 May 2018. Brussels: European Commission.
12. "EPA, California Notify Volkswagen of Clean Air Act Violations / Carmaker allegedly used software that circumvents emission testing for certain air pollutants", press release, 18 September 2015. Washington, DC: Environment Protection Agency.
13. *Vehicle Emissions Testing Programme (Cm 9259).* London: Department for Transport, 2016.
14. *UK Plan for Tackling Roadside Nitrogen Dioxide Concentrations.* London: Department for Environment, Food and Rural Affairs and Department for Transport, 2017.
15. *Changes to the Low Emissions Zone (LEZ) and Expansion of the Ultra Low Emissions Zone (ULEZ): Report to the Mayor on the Consultation.* Transport for London, 2018.
16. *UK Plan for Tackling Roadside Nitrogen Dioxide Concentrations, Technical Report, July 2017.* London: Department for Environment, Food and Rural Affairs and Department for Transport. Annex J shows the reduction in economic value of health damage arising from the advice

of COMEAP set out in Annex A. My enquiries of the government's Joint Air Quality Unit elicited the confirmation that overall the updated NO_x damage costs for road transport are approximately 80 per cent lower than those used previously. This splits into roughly 60–65 per cent resulting from the revised COMEAP advice and the remainder resulting from the other updates such as new dispersion modelling and population data. A full report from COMEAP was published in August 2018, the summary of which gave an estimate of the annual mortality burden of all human-made air pollution in the UK as equivalent to 28,000 to 36,000 deaths a year.

17. *Changing Trends in Mortality in England and Wales, 1990–2017*. Newport: Office for National Statistics, 2018; Raleigh (2018).
18. *Emissions of Air Pollutants in the UK, 1970–2016: Statistical Release, 15 February 2018*. London: Department for Environment, Food and Rural Affairs.
19. "Mother is granted new inquest over daughter's death from asthma", *British Medical Journal*, published online 11 January 2019; https://www.bmj.com/content/364/bmj.1192.
20. *Ultra Low Emission Zone – Further Proposals, Integrated Impact Assessment*, Jacobs for Transport for London, 2017: Table 2.4.
21. "Cities around Paris strike a rare agreement to ban diesel cars", CityLab, 14 November 2018.
22. "German court imposes diesel ban on Berlin roads", *Financial Times*, 9 October 2018.
23. *Clean Air Strategy 2019*. London: Department for Environment, Food and Rural Affairs.
24. *Call for Evidence on Brake, Tyre and Road Surface Wear*. London: Department for Environment, Food and Rural Affairs and Department for Transport. 2018.
25. "Look! No brakes", *The Economist*, 16 February 2019.
26. *Global Status Report on Road Safety 2015*. Geneva: World Health Organization.
27. *Reported Road Casualties in Great Britain: 2016 Annual Report. Statistical Release 28 September 2017*. London: Department for Transport.
28. *Mayor's Transport Strategy*. Greater London Authority, March 2018.
29. *Obesity Statistics*, Briefing Paper 3336. London: House of Commons Library, 2018.
30. *Mayor's Transport Strategy*. Greater London Authority, March 2018.
31. Department for Transport Statistics, tables cgn0401 and 0402.
32. *INRIX Global Traffic Scorecard*. 2018.
33. "The cappuccino congestion index", CityCommentary, 2 April 2018.
34. *Local Authority Parking Finances in England*. London: RAC Foundation for Motoring, 2019.
35. "Sacred spaces", *The Economist*, 8 April 2017.
36. The discussion of congestion charging follows Metz (2018a), where references may be found.
37. *Travel in London Report 10*. Figure 6.17. Transport for London, 2017.
38. "One country, three systems", *The Economist*, 21 April 2018.
39. Sloman *et al.*, *Impact of the Local Sustainable Transport Fund: Synthesis of Evidence*. London: Department for Transport, 2018.
40. "Are these the worst ring roads in England?", BBC News Online, 5 April 2014; https://www.bbc.co.uk/news/uk-england-26036572.
41. *The Vision and Direction for London's Streets and Roads*. Roads Task Force. Transport for London, 2013.
42. "Black Death skeletons unearthed by Crossrail project", BBC News Online, 30 March 2014; https://www.bbc.co.uk/news/uk-england-london-38586525.
43. *Transport Poverty*. London: RAC Foundation, 2017.
44. *Evaluation of Concessionary Bus Travel: The Impacts of the Free Bus Pass*. London: Department for Transport, 2016.

CHAPTER 2

1. *National Travel Survey: 2017 Report*. London: Department for Transport, 2018.
2. Analysis by Kit Mitchell, in *Analyses from the National Travel Survey*. London: Department for Transport, 2018.

3. For a discussion of travel trends in the UK: *Recent Trends in Road and Rail Travel: What Do They Tell Us? On the Move 2 (1995–2014): Overview and Policy Analysis*. London: Independent Transport Commission, 2016.

4. *Summary of Travel Trends: 2017 National Household Travel Survey*. Federal Highway Administration. US Department of Transportation, 2018.

5. For reviews of travel time data, see Schafer & Victor (2000), Mokhtarian & Chen (2004), Metz (2008) and Ahmed & Stopher (2014). Various national travel surveys record average travel time, for instance the Swedish survey records 57±2 min for 2015–16 (www.trafa.se/en/travel-survey).

6. National Travel Survey Tables 0605, 0705, 9904.

7. Metz (2005), updated to 2017 using data provided by the National Travel Survey.

8. *Smart Motorway All Lane Running: M25 J23–27 Monitoring Third Year Report*. Highways England, 2018.

9. *All Lane Running*, Table 4. Report of House of Commons Transport Committee, 2016.

10. Sloman, Hopkinson & Taylor, *The Impact of Road Projects in England*. London: Campaign to Protect Rural England, 2017.

11. *Response to the DfT's Consultation on Appraisal*. London: Transport Planning Society, 2018.

12. A second or third car in a household is used less than the first car. Table NTS0701 shows the distance travelled per person per year for a household with one car in 2017 was 6,000 miles, whereas for two or more cars it was 8,500 miles.

13. Data from UN sources complied by Kit Mitchell, presented to a meeting of the Transport Statistics Users' Group, London, 21 March 2018.

14. Addition of lane-km to motorway network from Department for Transport Statistics table RDE0104. Current route length from table RDL0207. I assume an average of six lanes per route-km, and estimate an average annual increase of 0.5 per cent p.a., which is less than the 0.75 per cent p.a. growth of the UK population over the past ten years but similar to the estimate of the Office of National Statistics of the increase in the UK population of 5.5 per cent over the next ten years (*ONS UK Population Mid-Year Estimate 2017*).

15. *2018 Revision of World Urbanisation Prospects*. United Nations Department of Economic and Social Affairs.

16. *Agglomerations in the UK and the Role of Transport Policy*. London: Department for Transport, 2006.

17. "In the loop: how one railway line helped change the way Londoners commute", *The Economist*, 3 October 2013.

18. These conclusions have been disputed by Wadud & Baiert (2017); Wittwer & Gerike (2018) review the relevant literature.

19. *Understanding the Drivers of Road Travel: Current Trends in and Factors Behind Road Use*. London: Department for Transport, 2015.

20. *Latest Evidence on Factors Impacting Road Traffic Growth: An Evidence Review* (WSP and RAND Europe). London: Department for Transport, 2018.

21. An independent Commission on Travel Demand reached a similar conclusion: *All Change? The Future of Travel Demand and the Implications for Policy and Planning*. University of Leeds Institute for Transport Studies, 2018.

22. "Rus in urbe redux", *The Economist*, 30 May 2015.

23. *National Population Projections: 2016-Based Statistical Bulletin*. London: Office for National Statistics, 2017.

24. *Transport for New Homes: Project Summary and Recommendations July 2018*. London: Transport for New Homes.

25. *Roads Task Force – Technical Note 10. What is the Capacity of the Road Network for Private Motorised Traffic and How Has This Changed Over Time?* Transport for London, 2013.

26. *Travel in London: Report 11*. Table 2.3. London: Transport for London, 2018.

27. *National Travel Survey*, Table NTS9904, 2016/17.

28. Jones *et al.*, *Urban Mobility: Preparing for the Future, Learning from the Past*. CREATE Project Summary and Recommendations, 2018; http://www.create-mobility.eu.

29. *Greater Manchester Transport Strategy 2040: Evidence Base*. Figure 45. Manchester: Transport for Greater Manchester, 2017.
30. "Have US light rail systems been worth the investment?", CityLab, 10 April 2014.
31. *City Streets: Transport for a Changing Square Mile*. City of London Corporation, 2018.
32. *Connecting European Regions Using Innovative Transport. Summary Report of Sintropher Project*. London: University College, 2017.
33. Bertaud, *Cities as Labour Markets*. Paris: International Transport Forum/OECD, 2015.
34. *Commuting Trends in England, 1988–2015*. London: Department for Transport, 2016.
35. *National Travel Survey: 2017 Report*. London: Department for Transport, 2018.
36. *Retail Sales, Great Britain, March 2018. Statistical Bulletin*. London: Office for National Statistics.
37. "What in the world is causing the retail meltdown of 2017?", *The Atlantic*, 10 April 2017.
38. *Road Traffic Estimates: Great Britain 2017*. London: Department for Transport, 2018. Data sources and conflicts for van use are discussed by Le Vine, Luan & Polak, *Van Travel in Great Britain – What do we know from the National Travel Survey?* London: Independent Transport Commission, 2013.
39. *National Travel Survey*, Table NTS0201.
40. *Concessionary Travel Statistics England 2017/18*. London: Department for Transport.

CHAPTER 3

1. *The Road to Zero: Next Steps Towards Cleaner Road Transport and Delivering our Industrial Strategy*. London: Department for Transport, 2018.
2. *Reducing UK Emissions – 2018 Progress Report to Parliament*. London: Committee on Climate Change, 2018: Table 5.3.
3. See www.transportpolicy.net.
4. *Global EV Outlook 2018*. Paris: International Energy Agency.
5. *International Comparison of Light-Duty Vehicles Fuel Economy 2005–2015*. Paris: International Energy Agency, 2017.
6. *Diesel Share in New Passenger Car Registrations (Western Europe) 1990–2017*. European Automobile Manufacturers Association (ACEA).
7. For an account of EV developments: *Global EV Outlook 2018*. Paris: International Energy Agency.
8. *Battery-Powered Electric Vehicles: Market Developments and Lifecycle Emissions*. Study for the Transport and Tourism Committee, European Parliament, 2018.
9. *Electric Vehicle Outlook 2018*. Bloomberg New Energy Finance.
10. "Betting on batteries", *Financial Times*, 30 November 2018.
11. Published literature on electric motor developments is limited. There is an informative blog on the Tesla Model 3 Motor by Steve Baker on 11 March 2018 at cleantechnica.com. See also: "Let's twist again", *The Economist*, 16 September 2017.
12. "Volvo sets dates for switching off petrol engines", *Financial Times*, 6 July 2017.
13. "Electric dreams, subsidized reality", *Financial Times*, 15 June 2017.
14. "China's highly charged power play", *Financial Times*, 13 October 2017.
15. *UBS Evidence Lab Electric Car Teardown: Disruption Ahead?* UBS, 2017.
16. "A British inventor pivots to Asia", *Financial Times*, 27 October 2018.
17. For a review of charging technology: *Ultra-Low Emission Vehicle Infrastructure – What Can Be Done?* London: RAC Foundation, 2017.
18. *Plugging the Gap: An Assessment of Future Demand for Britain's Electric Vehicle Public Charging Network*. Systra, for the Committee on Climate Change, 2018.
19. See www.zapmap.com.

20. "BP to acquire the UK's largest electric vehicle charging company", BP press release, 28 June 2018.
21. *Digest of United Kingdom Energy Statistics 2017*. London: Department for Business, Energy and Industrial Strategy.
22. *Updated Energy and Emission Projections 2017*. London: Department for Business, Energy and Industrial Strategy.
23. *IEA Atlas of Energy, 2015 Data*. Paris: International Energy Agency.
24. "Forecourt thoughts: mass fast charging of electric vehicles", National Grid (undated).
25. "Future Insights Paper 5: Implications of the transition to electric vehicles". London: Office of Gas and Electricity Markets, 2018.
26. "Electric vehicle announcement and what the papers say", National Grid, 2017. Also: "Future Energy Scenarios July 2018", National Grid.
27. *Impact of Electric Vehicle and Heat Pumps Loads on Network Demand Profiles*. London: UK Power Networks, 2014.
28. "UPS vans to go all-electric in London", *Financial Times*, 20 March 2018.
29. "How China took charge of the electric bus revolution", CityLab, 8 May 2018.
30. *Electric Buses in Cities*. Bloomberg New Energy Finance, 2018.
31. "Future Energy Scenarios July 2018", National Grid.
32. *Oregon's Road User Charge: The OreGo Program Final Report*. Oregon Department of Transportation, 2017.
33. *Mission Possible*. Energy Transitions Commission, 2018.
34. *Reducing UK Emissions; 2018 Progress Report to Parliament*. London: Committee on Climate Change.
35. *The Road to Zero: Next Steps Towards Cleaner Road Transport and Delivering our Industrial Strategy*. London: Department for Transport, 2018.
36. Letter from the Chairman to the Secretary of State of 11 October 2018. London: Committee on Climate Change.
37. *Road Traffic Forecasts 2018*. London: Department for Transport.
38. *Critical Raw Materials and the Circular Economy: Background Report*. Joint Research Centre Science-for-policy report. Luxembourg: Publications Office of the European Union, 2017.
39. "Electric Vehicle and Infrastructure", Briefing paper CBP07480. London: House of Commons Library, 2018.
40. Table veh0207, *Vehicles and Drivers Statistics*. London: Department for Transport, 2017.

CHAPTER 4

1. Personal communication from Ed Parsons, Google Geospatial Technologist, 25 January 2019.
2. Personal communication from Ed Parsons, Google Geospatial Technologist, 25 January 2019.
3. "The perfect selfishness of mapping apps", CityLab, 15 March 2018.
4. Road Traffic (Driver Licensing and Information Systems) Act 1989, Driver Information Systems (Exemption) Order 1990.
5. Freedom of Information request to Department for Transport, F0016347, 31 August 2018.
6. *Red Tape Challenge – Road Transportation: Regulations and Actions Response*. London: Department for Transport, 2011.
7. "TfL joins the Waze connected citizens programme", TfL Digital Blog, 12 October 2016.
8. "How we manage London's roads". Transport for London website; https://tfl.gov.uk/corporate/about-tfl/what-we-do/roads?intcmp=2635.
9. *Surface Intelligent Transport System*. Programme and Investment Committee. Transport for London, 30 November 2016.
10. *Assessing the Value of TfL's Open Data and Digital Partnerships*. London: Deloitte, 2017.
11. *Public Attitudes to Roads in England, Wave 1*. London: Department for Transport, 2013.

12. *Road Investment Strategy: for the 2015/16 – 2019/20 Road Period.* London: Department for Transport, 2015.
13. *Draft Road Investment Strategy 2: Government Objectives.* London: Department for Transport, 2018.
14. Junction 6 on the M42 south of Birmingham, and A417 widening in the Cotswolds. Information from Highways England website; https://highwaysengland.co.uk/projects/m42-junction-6-improvement/ https://highwaysengland.co.uk/projects/a417-missing-link/.
15. *Surface Intelligent Transport System.* Programme and Investment Committee. Transport for London, 30 November 2016.
16. *Road Investment Strategy: Economic Analysis of the Investment Plan.* London: Department for Transport, 2015.

CHAPTER 5

1. Judgment of Mr Justice Ouseley, Administrative Court, *TfL vs Uber and Others,* Case number CO/1449/2015.
2. *Broadening Understanding of the Interplay Between Public Transit, Shared Mobility and Personal Automobiles: TCRP Research Report 195.* Washington, DC: Transportation Research Board, 2018.
3. *Disruptive Transportation: The Adoption, Utilization, and Impacts of Ride-Hailing in the United States.* Institute of Transportation Studies, University of California, Davis, Research Report UCD-ITS-RR-17-07 (2017).
4. *Metrorail vs. Uber: Travel Time and Cost.* Post from the District of Columbia's Office of Revenue Analysis, 11 October 2017.
5. *For-Hire Vehicle Transportation Study.* City of New York: Office of the Mayor, 2016.
6. *Unsustainable? The Growth of App-Based Ride Services and Traffic, Travel and the Future of New York City.* Brooklyn, NY: Schaller Consulting, 2017.
7. *Understanding the Recent Transit Ridership Decline in Major Cities: Service Cuts or Emerging Modes?* M. Graeler, R. Mucci and G. Erhardt, presentation at the 98th Annual Meeting of the Transport Research Board, 2019.
8. Evidence submitted by Uber to an investigation of traffic congestion in London by the London Assembly Transport Committee, 2017.
9. *Travel in London, Report 9,* section 6.9. Transport for London, 2016.
10. "BMW and Daimler team up on ride hailing and sharing", *Financial Times,* 28 March 2018.
11. *Future Roads: Public Dialogue* (Kantar Public). London: Department for Transport, 2018.
12. "The bike-share oversupply in China: huge piles of abandoned and broken bicycles", *The Atlantic,* 22 March 2018.
13. *Dockless Bike Share Code of Practice for Operators in London.* London: Transport for London, September 2017.
14. "Bike apps saddled with high labour costs", *Financial Times,* 27 December 2017.
15. "Bike-sharing firm Ofo's dramatic fall from grace a warning to China's tech investors", *South China Morning Post,* 26 December 2018.
16. *Shared Electric Bike Programme Report 2016.* Leeds: Bikeplus/Carplus.
17. *Copenhagen City of Cyclists: The Bicycle Account 2016.* City of Copenhagen.
18. *Travel in London Report 10, Table 2.3.* London: Transport for London, 2017.
19. "Investors bet on electric bike and scooter services", *Financial Times,* 11 April 2018.
20. "How I learned to stop worrying and love electric scooter", *New York Times,* 6 June 2018.
21. *Shared Mobility Device Pilot Program Administrative Regulations.* City of Santa Monica, California, 2018.
22. *Uprouted: Exploring Microtransit in the United States.* Washington DC: Eno Centre for Transportation, 2018.
23. "Uber gears up for shift from cars to bikes on short trips", *Financial Times,* 27 August 2018.
24. "Uber wants to be our one-stop transit stop", CityLab, 31 January 2019.

25. "Barcelona finds a way to control its Airbnb market", CityLab, 6 June 2018.
26. *Why People Travel: Shopping. National Travel Survey Factsheet.* London: Department for Transport, 2015.
27. *The Implications of Internet Shopping Growth on the Van Fleet and Traffic Activity.* London: RAC Foundation, 2017.
28. *Road Traffic Estimates: Great Britain 2016.* Statistical release. London: Department for Transport, 2017.
29. McAfee & Brynjolfsson (2017) discuss the development of platforms generally. Coyle (2018) considers economics and competition policy aspects.
30. "Taxi races show black cabs beat Uber on speed but not cost", *New Scientist*, 21 January 2017.
31. Len Sherman, "Why can't Uber make money?", *Forbes Magazine*, 14 December 2017.
32. Employment Tribunals Case no 2202550/2015: *Aslam and Farrer v Uber.*
33. European Court of Justice C-434/15. *Association Professional Elite Taxi v Uber Systems Spain SL.*
34. Licensing decision on Uber London Limited, 22 September 2017. Transport for London.
35. Judgment of Chief Magistrate Emma Arbuthnot, Westminster Magistrates Court. *Appeal of Uber London Limited*, 26 June 2018.
36. *Uber and the Labor Market: Uber Drivers' Compensation, Wages, and the Scale of Uber and the Gig Economy.* Washington, DC: Economic Policy Institute.
37. *Good Work: The Taylor Review of Modern Working Practices.* London. July 2017.
38. *Good Work: A Response to the Taylor Review of Modern Working Practices.* London: HM Government, February 2018.
39. "Lyft launches a legal battle over driver pay in NYC", CityLab, 1 February 2019.
40. "Bloody defeat: powerful unions in Mumbai have forced Uber and Ola into a corner", *The Economist*, 3 November 2018.
41. "Hermes couriers awarded union recognition in gig economy first", *Financial Times*, 4 February 2019.
42. *Taxi and Private Hire Vehicle Licensing: Steps Towards a Safer and More Robust System.* Report of a Task Group chaired by Professor Mohamed Abdel-Haq. London: Department for Transport, 2018.
43. "Uber and Ola jostle for space in Indian ride-hailing", *Financial Times*, 18 May 2018.
44. Data from the New York City Taxi and Limousine Commission analysed by Todd W. Schneider and posted on his blog, March 2018.
45. For the origins of Juno see S. Kolhatkar, "Juno takes on Uber", *The New Yorker*, 10 October 2016.
46. *Taxi and Private Hire Vehicle Statistics: England 2017.* London: Department for Transport, March 2019; https://toddwschneider.com/posts/taxi-uber-lyft-usage-new-york-city/.
47. See www.openbanking.org.uk.
48. "Road to IPO is fraught with doubts over value of Uber network", *Financial Times*, 19 October 2018.
49. "Uber hit with cap as New York City takes lead in crackdown", *New York Times*, 8 August 2018.
50. Evidence submitted by Uber to an inquiry by the House of Commons Transport Committee into urban traffic congestion, 2017.
51. Evidence submitted by Uber to an investigation of traffic congestion in London by the London Assembly Transport Committee, 2017.

CHAPTER 6

1. "Sensing trouble ahead", *Financial Times*, 22 February 2018.
2. *Federal Automated Vehicles Policy: Accelerating the Next Revolution in Roadway Safety.* National Highway Traffic Safety Administration. Washington, DC: US Department of Transportation, 2016.

3. *Safer Roads with Automated Vehicles?* International Transport Forum. Paris: OECD, 2018. This is an authoritative source, drawn upon in the section on AV safety.

4. *Implementing the RSS Model on NHTSA Pre-Crash Scenarios.* Mobileye. 2017.

5. *Critical Reasons for Crashes Investigated in the National Motor Vehicles Crash Causation Survey.* National Highway Traffic Safety Administration. Washington, DC: US Department of Transportation, 2015.

6. *Facts on Road Fatalities June 2015.* London: Department for Transport.

7. Automated and Electric Vehicles Act 2018.

8. *The Key Principles of Cyber Security for Connected and Automated Vehicles.* London: Department for Transport, Centre for the Protection of National Infrastructure, 2017.

9. *Automated Vehicles: A Joint Preliminary Consultation Paper.* London: Law Commission. 2018.

10. The discussion of the impact of AVs on congestion follows an open access paper (Metz 2018b) where fuller references can be found.

11. *Research on the Impacts of Connected and Autonomous Vehicles on Traffic Flow: Evidence Review.* London: Department for Transport, 2016.

12. B. Schoettle & M. Sivak, *Potential Impact of Self-Driving Vehicles on Household Vehicle Demand and Usage. Report No. UMTRI-2015-3.* Ann Arbor, MI: University of Michigan Transportation Research Institute, 2015.

13. *Quantified Parking: Comprehensive Parking Inventories for Five US Cities.* Research Institute for Housing America. Washington, DC: Mortgage Bankers Association, 2018.

14. *Shared Mobility: Innovation for Liveable Cities.* International Transport Forum. Paris: OECD, 2016. See Metz (2018b) for other simulation studies.

15. *Travel in London, Report 9.* London: Transport for London, 2016.

16. *European Truck Platooning Challenge 2016: Hypothesis and Recommendations for Future Cross-Border Field Operational Tests of Truck Platooning in Europe.* The Hague: Dutch Ministry of Infrastructure and the Environment.

17. "Quarrel breaks out over connected-car 'talk'", *Financial Times,* 14 November 2017.

18. *The Pathway to Driverless Cars: Summary Report and Action Plan.* London: Department for Transport, 2015.

19. *Industrial Strategy White Paper.* London: Department for Business, Energy and Industrial Strategy, 2017.

20. "Waymo, Jaguar Land Rover in self-driving car tie-up", *Financial Times,* 27 March 2018.

21. *Agriculture: Historical Statistics.* Briefing Paper 03339. London: House of Commons Library, 2016

22. *Managing the Transition to Driverless Road Freight Transport.* International Transport Forum. Paris: OECD.

23. "Uber's self-driving trucks hit the highway but not local roads", *New York Times,* 6 March 2018.

24. "When self-driving cars meet Florida drivers", CityLab, 4 December 2018.

CHAPTER 7

1. *London Underground World Class Capacity Programme.* Programme and Investment Committee, 3 July 2018. Transport for London.

2. *Four Lines Modernisation Update.* Programme and Investment Committee, 13 October 2017. Transport for London.

3. *Digital Railway Programme Strategic Plan, 19 January 2018.* London: Network Rail. *Rail Technology: Signalling and Traffic Management.* Seventh Report of Session 2016–17. London: House of Commons Transport Committee.

4. *Ministerial Group – Digital Railway: Recommendations on Government Policy for a Digital Railway Programme and Accelerated Development of Digital Signalling Technology.* London: Department for Transport, 2016. For a somewhat critical view, see articles by Roger Ford, a

well-informed commentator, in *Modern Railways*, April and June 2018 issues; also his evidence to the Commons Transport Committee (see endnote 3).

5. *Railway Safety Principles on Driver Controlled Operation*. London: Office of Rail and Road, 2017.

6. *Rail Franchising in the UK*. House of Commons Public Accounts Committee, 2018.

7. OECD/International Transport Forum statistics.

8. *Rail Demand Forecasting Estimation – Phase 1 Report – September 2015*. London: Department for Transport.

9. I. Williams & J. Jahanshahi, *Wider Factors Affecting the Long-Term Growth in Rail Travel*. London: Independent Transport Commission, 2018.

10. *Recent Trends in Road and Rail Travel: What Do They Tell Us? (On the Move 2 1995-2014)*. London: Independent Transport Commission, 2016.

11. *Passenger Journeys by Year – Table 12.5*. National Rail trends Data Portal. London: Office of Road and Rail.

12. *Passenger Rail Usage 2018–19 Q1 Statistical Release*. London: Office of Road and Rail.

13. Directive 2012/34/EU of the European Parliament and of the Council of 21 November 2012 establishing a single European railway area.

14. *Independent Inquiry into the Timetable Disruption in May 2018: Final Report*. London: Office of Rail and Road. 2018.

15. An illuminating note on rail forecasting was prepared by Jim Steer, founder of the consultancy of that name, for the *Commission on Travel Demand: Rail Demand Forecasting: Ten Lessons of a Lifetime, 2017*; available at: www.demand.ac.uk/commission-on-travel-demand/evidence/.

16. *Rolling Stock Perspective Fourth Edition*. London: Department for Transport, 2018.

17. *Rail Franchising in the UK. Thirty-Fifth Report of Session 2017–19*. House of Commons Committee on Public Accounts, 2018.

18. *Connecting People: A Strategic Vision for Rail*. Cm 9519. London: Department for Transport, 2017.

19. *UK Rail Industry Financial Information 2017–18*. London: Office of Rail and Road, 2019.

20. *Rail Fares Index (January 2018) Statistical Release*. London: Office of Rail and Road, 2018.

21. *Rail Infrastructure Investment*. House of Commons Transport Committee, 2018.

22. *Realising the Potential of GB Rail: Report of the Rail Value for Money Study (McNulty Report)*. London: Department for Transport, 2011.

23. "Japan's new maglev train line runs headlong into critics", *Financial Times*, 18 October 2017.

24. "Hyperloop Alpha", 2013 paper by Elon Musk, available from www.spacex.com.

25. *Hyperloop: Cutting Through the Hype*. Wokingham: TRL, 2018.

26. *Travel in London Report 10*. London: Transport for London, 2017: 49.

27. "In the loop", *The Economist*, 5 October 2013.

28. See www.boringcompany.com.

29. "Musk wins high-speed tunnel deal", *Financial Times*, 16 June 2018.

30. "The craziest thing about Elon Musk's 'Express Loop' is the price", CityLab, 15 June 2018.

31. "Second time lucky?", *The Economist*, 15 December 2018.

32. *Carbon Offsetting and Reduction Scheme for International Aviation*. Montreal: International Civil Aviation Organisation, 2016.

33. *Flying High: Shaping the Future of Drones in UK Cities*. London: NESTA, 2018.

34. "Manna from heaven", *The Economist*, 9 June 2018.

35. *Fact Sheet – Small Unmanned Aircraft Regulations (Part 107)*. Washington, DC: Federal Aviation Administration, 2018.

36. *Fast-Forwarding to a Future of On-Demand Urban Air Transport*. Uber Elevate, 2016.

37. "Flying car trailblazers try blue sky thinking", *Financial Times*, 28 April 2017; "Free as a bird", *The Economist*, 10 March 2018; "Uber takes pains to prove electric taxi service will fly", *Financial Times*, 11 May 2018.

38. *eVTOL Vehicle Requirements and Missions*. Uber Elevate, 2018.

39. "Reinventing the aircraft", *Financial Times*, 19 September 2018.

40. UK National Travel Survey, Table NTS 0313. 2017.
41. UK National Travel Survey, Table NTS 0103. 2017.
42. *Travel in London Report 10*, Table 2.1. London: Transport for London, 2017.
43. *Transport Statistics Great Britain*, Table BUS0110. London: Department for Transport, 2017.
44. *Road Investment Strategy for the 2015/16 – 2019/20 Road Period*, Map p. 34. London: Department for Transport, 2015.
45. An example is the M60 orbital motorway data. *Manchester North-West Quadrant Study*, Figs. 10 and 23. London: Department for Transport, 2016.
46. *Post Opening Project Evaluation of Major Schemes: Meta-analysis 2013: Main Report.* Fig. 4–18. Highways Agency.
47. My critique of orthodox transport investment appraisal is at Metz (2017). Mackie, Batley & Worsley (2018) have defended the conventional approach.
48. *Appraisal and Modelling Strategy: Informing Future Investment Decisions (Consultation).* London: Department for Transport, 2018.
49. *Land Value Capture: Final Report.* Transport for London, 2017.
50. *National Infrastructure Assessment.* London: National Infrastructure Commission, 2018.
51. *Partnering for Prosperity: A New Deal for the Cambridge–Milton Keynes–Oxford Arc.* London: National Infrastructure Commission, 2017.

CHAPTER 8

1. I. Docherty & D. Waite, *Evidence Review – Infrastructure.* Productivity Insights Network, 2018; available at www.productivityinsightsnetwork.co.uk.
2. *Road Investment Strategy: For the 2015/16 – 2019/20 Road Period.* London: Department for Transport, 2015.
3. *Green Book Supplementary Guidance: Optimism Bias.* London: HM Treasury, 2013.
4. *Over-Optimism in Government Projects.* London: National Audit Office, 2013.
5. *The Completion and Sale of High Speed 1.* London: National Audit Office, 2012.
6. J. Glover, "Infrastructure alone is unlikely to solve all economic ills", *Financial Times*, 25 August 2017.
7. R. Bain, "Ethics and advocacy in forecasting revisited – consultants in the dock". *Local Transport Today*, 4 September 2015; available at www.robbain.com/LTT680 Rob Bain.pdf.
8. "AECOM unit pays $201 million to settle Australian toll-road lawsuit", *Wall Street Journal*, 21 September 2015.
9. "TfL works with Waze and Eurotunnel to prevent Blackwall Tunnel closures", Transport for London press release, 8 December 2017.
10. The UK Department for Transport issued a *Call for Evidence* on the opportunities for new Light Rail Systems in February 2019.
11. The inclusive approach is recognised in the UK Department for Transport's 2018 policy paper: *The Inclusive Transport Strategy: Achieving Equal Access for Disabled People.*

REFERENCES

Aguiar, M. *et al*. 2018. "Leisure luxuries and the labor supply of young men". Working paper, Department of Economics, Princeton University.

Aguilera, A., C. Guillot & A. Rallet 2012. "Mobile ICTs and physical mobility: review and research agenda". *Transportation Research Part A* 46 (4): 664–72.

Ahmed, A. & P. Stopher 2014. "Seventy minutes plus or minus 10 – a review of travel time budget studies". *Transportation Reviews* 34 (5): 607–25.

Allen, J. *et al*. 2018. "Understanding the impact of e-commerce on last mile light goods vehicle activity in urban areas: the case of London". *Transportation Research Part D* 61 (B): 325–38.

Anciaes, P. & P. Jones 2018. "Estimating preferences for different types of pedestrian crossing facilities". *Transportation Research Part F* 52: 222–37.

Awad, E. *et al*. 2018. "The moral machine experiment". *Nature* 563: 59–64.

Banister, D. 2018. *Inequality in Transport*. Marcham: Alexandrine Press.

Barrios, J., Y. Hochberg & L. Yi 2018. "The cost of convenience: ridesharing and traffic fatalities". *Chicago Booth Research Paper No. 27*.

Bastian, A., M. Borjesson, & J. Eliasson 2016. "Explaining 'peak car' with economic variables". *Transportation Research Part A* 88: 236–58.

Begg, D. 2016. *The Impact of Congestion on Bus Passengers*. London: Greener Journeys.

Berger, T. *et al*. 2018. "Uber happy? Work and well–being in the 'gig economy'". *Working Paper*, Oxford Martin School, October.

Beuse, M., S. Schmidt & V. Wood 2018. "A 'technology-smart-battery strategy for Europe'". *Science* 361: 1075–7.

Bloodworth, J. 2018. *Hired: Six Months Undercover in Low-Wage Britain*. London: Atlantic.

Bocarejo, J. *et al*. 2014. "An innovative transit system and its impact on low income users: the case of the Metrocable in Medellin". *Journal of Transport Geography* 39: 49–61.

Bonnefon, J., A. Shariff & I. Rahwan 2016. "The social dilemma of autonomous vehicles". *Science* 352 (6293): 1573–6.

Boquet, Y. 2017. "The renaissance of tramways and urban redevelopment in France". *Miscellanea Geographica: Regional Studies on Development* 21 (1): 5–18.

Brett, A. & B. Menzies 2014. "Cambridgeshire guided busway, UK: an analysis of usage". *Proceedings of the Institution of Civil Engineers – Transport* 176 (3): 124–33.

Broughton, N. & B. Richards 2016. *Tough Gig: Low Paid Self-Employment in London and the UK*. London: Social Market Foundation.

Buehler, R., J. Pucher & O. Dummler 2018. "Verkersverbund: the evolution and spread of fully integrated public transport in Germany, Austria and Switzerland". *International Journal of Sustainable Transportation* DOI: 10.1080/15568318.2018.1431821.

Cairns, S., C. Hass-Klau & P. Goodwin 1998. *Traffic Impact of Highway Capacity Reductions: Assessment of the Evidence*. London: Landor.

Camerer, C. *et al*. 1996. "Labour supply of New York City cabdrivers: one day at a time". *Quarterly Journal of Economics* 112 (2): 407–41.

Champion, T. 2014. "People in cities: the numbers". Future of Cities Working Paper. London: Government Office for Science.

Chatterjee, K. *et al.* 2018. *Young People's Travel – What's Changed and Why?* Review and Analysis. Report to Department for Transport. Bristol: University of the West of England.

Christie, N. 2018. "Is Vision Zero important for promoting health?" *Journal of Transport and Health* 9: 5–6.

Coyle, D. 2018. "Practical competition policy implications of digital platforms". *Working Paper 01/2018*. Cambridge: Bennett Institute for Public Policy.

Cramer, J. & A. Krueger 2016. "Disruptive change in the taxi business: the case of Uber". *American Economic Review* 106 (5): 177–82.

Cwerner, S. 2006. "Vertical flight and urban mobilities: the promise and reality of helicopter travel". *Mobilities* 1 (1): 191–215.

Delbosc, A. & P. Mokhtarian 2018. "Face to Facebook: the relationship between social media and social travel". *Transport Policy* 68: 20–27.

Dienel, H. & R. Vahrenkamp 2018. "For a social history of shared taxi services: some notes". *Journal of Transport History* 39 (1): 7–11.

Dudley, G., D. Banister & T. Schwanen 2017. "The rise of Uber and regulating the disruptive innovator". *The Political Quarterly* 88 (3): 492–9.

Dunne, M. 2018. "The dark horse: will China win the electric, automated and shared mobility race?". In *Three Revolutions: Steering Automatic, Shared and Electric Vehicles to a Better Future*, D. Sperling (ed.). Washington, DC: Island Press.

Emmerson, G. 2014. "Maximising the use of the road network in London". In *Moving Cities: The Future of Urban Travel*, S. Glaister & E. Box (eds). London: RAC Foundation.

Farber, H. 2015. "Why you can't find a taxi in the rain and other labor supply lessons from cab drivers". *Quarterly Journal of Economics* 130 (4): 1975–2016.

Ferbrache, F. & R. Knowles 2016. "Generating opportunities for city sustainability through investments in light rail systems". *Journal of Transport Geography* 54: 369–72.

Flyvbjerg, B., M. Holm & S. Buhl 2002. "Underestimating costs in public works projects: error or lie?" *Journal of the American Planning Association* 68 (3): 279–95.

Fraade-Blanar, L. *et al.* 2018. *Measuring Automated Vehicle Safety: Forging a Framework*. Santa Monica, CA: RAND Corporation.

Gao, Y. & P. Newman 2018. "Beijing's peak car transition: hope for emerging cities in the 1.5C agenda". *Urban Planning* 3 (2): 82–93.

Givoni, M. & D. Banister 2013. *Moving Towards Low Carbon Mobility*. Cheltenham: Edward Elgar.

Goodwin, P. 2012. "Peak travel, peak car and the future of mobility". Discussion Paper 2012–13. International Transport Forum. Paris: OECD.

Goodwin, P. & K. Van Dender 2013. "'Peak car' – themes and issues". *Transport Reviews* 33 (3): 243–54. This editorial introduces articles in a special issue devoted to peak car.

Graham, A. & D. Metz 2019. "Limits to growth". In *Air Transport – A Tourism Perspective*, A. Graham & F. Dobruszkes (eds). London: Elsevier.

Greaves, S. & T. Stanley 2018. "Policy for a sustainable future". In *Handbook on Transport and Urban Planning in the Developed World*, M. Bliemer, C. Mulley & C. Moutou (eds): 202–30. Cheltenham: Edward Elgar.

Hall, P. 1994. "Squaring the circle: can we resolve the Clarkian paradox?" *Environment and Planning B; Planning and Design* 21: S79–S94.

Hall, J., C. Palsson & J. Price 2018. "Is Uber a substitute or complement for public transit?". *Journal of Urban Economics* 108: 36–50.

Harding, S., M. Kandlikar & S. Gulati 2016. "Taxi apps, regulation and the market for taxi journeys". *Transportation Research Part A* 88: 15–25.

Harper, D. *et al.* 2016. "Estimating potential increases in travel with autonomous vehicles for the non-driving, elderly and people with travel-restrictive medical conditions". *Transportation Research Part C* 72: 1–9.

Headicar, P. 2009. *Transport Policy and Planning in Great Britain*. London: Routledge.

Headicar, P. 2013. "The changing spatial distribution of the population in England". *Transport Reviews* 33 (3): 310–24.

Headicar, P. & G. Stokes 2016. *On the Move 2: Making Sense of Travel Trends in England 1995–2014*. Technical Report. London: Independent Transport Commission.

Herrmann, A., W. Brenner & R. Stadler 2018. *Autonomous Driving: How the Driverless Revolution Will Change the World*. Bingley: Emerald.

Holgate, S. & H. Stokes-Lampard 2017. "Air pollution – a wicked problem". *British Medical Journal* 357: j2814.

Ingvardson, J. & O. Nielsen 2017. "Effect of new bus and rail rapid transit systems: an international review". *Transport Reviews* 38 (1): 96–116.

Jones, K. *et al*. 2017. *The Electric Battery*. Santa Barbara, CA: Praeger.

Lay, M. 1992. *Ways of the World*. New Brunswick, NJ: Rutgers University Press.

Leeder, D. 2017. "Why London needs a new bus strategy", *Transport Times*, March: 22–4.

Ligterink, N. 2017. "Real-world vehicle emissions". Discussion Paper 2017–06. Paris: International Transport Forum.

Lipson, H. & M. Kurman 2016. *Driverless: Intelligent Cars and the Road Ahead*. Cambridge, MA: MIT Press.

Little, A.D. 2018 "Future of Batteries: Winner takes all?" Luxembourg: Arthur D.Little.

Mackett, R. 2014. "Has the policy of concessionary bus travel in Britain been successful?". *Case Studies on Transport Policy* 2 (2): 81–8.

Mackie, P., R. Batley & T. Worsley 2018. "Valuing transport investments based on time savings – a response to David Metz". *Case Studies on Transport Policy* 6 (4): 638–41.

Marsden, G. & I. Docherty 2013. "Insights on disruptions as opportunities for transport policy change". *Transportation Research Part A* 51: 46–55.

McAfee, A. & E. Brynjolfsson 2017. *Machine, Platform, Crowd*. New York: Norton.

Melia, S. 2015. *Urban Transport Without the Hot Air*. Cambridge: UIT Cambridge.

Mervis, J. 2017. "Are we going too fast on driverless cars?". *Science* 358: 1370–4.

Metz, D. 2005. "Journey quality as the focus of transport policy". *Transport Policy* 12 (4): 353–9.

Metz, D. 2008. "The myth of travel time saving". *Transport Reviews* 28 (3): 321–36.

Metz, D. 2010. "Saturation of demand for daily travel". *Transport Reviews* 30 (5): 659–74.

Metz, D. 2013a. "Peak car and beyond: the fourth era of travel". *Transport Reviews* 33 (3): 255–70.

Metz, D. 2013b. "Mobility, access and choice: a new source of evidence". *Journal of Transport and Land Use* 6 (2): 1–4.

Metz, D. 2014. *Peak Car: the Future of Travel*. London: Landor LINKS.

Metz, D. 2015. "Peak car in the big city: reducing London's greenhouse gas emissions". *Case Studies on Transport Policy* 3 (4): 367–71.

Metz, D. 2016. "Changing demographics". In *Handbook on Transport and Urban Planning in the Developed World*, M. Bliemer, C. Mulley & C. Moutou (eds), 69–81. Cheltenham: Edward Elgar.

Metz, D. 2017. "Valuing transport investments based on travel time saving: inconsistency with United Kingdom policy objectives". *Case Studies on Transport Policy* 5, 716–27.

Metz, D. 2018a. "Tackling urban traffic congestion: the experience of London, Stockholm and Singapore". *Case Studies on Transport Policy* 6: 494–8.

Metz, D. 2018b. "Developing policy for urban autonomous vehicles: impact on congestion". *Urban Science* 2: 33.

Metz, D. 2018c. "Future transport technologies for an ageing society". In *Transport, Travel and Later Life*, C. Musselwhite (ed.). Bingley: Emerald.

Millard-Ball, A. & L. Schipper 2011. "Are we reaching peak travel? Trends in passenger numbers in eight industrialised countries". *Transport Reviews* 31 (3): 357–78.

Mills, G. & P. White 2018. "Evaluating the long-term impacts of bus-based park and ride". *Research in Transportation Economics* 69: 536–43.

Mitchell, K. 2018. "Are older people safe drivers on the roads, testing and training?". In *Transport, Travel and Later Life*, C. Musselwhite (ed.). Bingley: Emerald.

Mokhtarian, P. & C. Chen 2004. "TTB or not TTB, that is the question: a review of the empirical literature on travel time (and money) budgets". *Transportation Research Part A* 38(9–10): 643–75.

Mokhtarian, P., I. Salomon & M. Singer 2015. "What moves us? An interdisciplinary exploration of the reasons for travelling". *Transport Reviews* 35 (3): 250–74.

Mudway, I. *et al.* 2018. "Impact of London's low emission zone on air quality and children's respiratory health: a sequential annual cross-sectional study". *The Lancet Public Health*. November.

Musselwhite, C. (ed.) 2018. *Transport, Travel and Later Life*. Bingley: Emerald.

Nedelkoska, L. & G. Quintini 2018. *Automation, Skills Use and Training*. OECD social, employment and migration working papers, no. 202. Paris: OECD.

Newman, P. & J. Kenworthy 2007. "Greening urban transportation". In *State of the World 2007: Our Urban Future*. Worldwatch Institute. London: Earthscan.

Newman, P. & J. Kenworthy 2011. "'Peak car use': understanding the demise of automobile dependence". *World Transport Policy and Practice* 17 (2): 31–9.

Newman, P. & J. Kenworthy 2015. *The End of Automobile Dependence*. Washington, DC: Island Press.

Newman, P., J. Kenworthy & G. Glazebrook 2013. "Peak car use and the rise of global rail: why this is happening and what it means for large and small cities". *Journal of Transportation Technologies* 3: 272–87.

Pierce, G. & D. Shoup 2013. "SFpark: pricing parking by demand". *Access* 43: 20–28.

Polzin, S. & D. Sperling 2018. "Upgrading transit for the twenty-first century". In *Three Revolutions: Steering Automatic, Shared and Electric Vehicles to a Better Future*, D. Sperling (ed.). Washington, DC: Island Press.

Raleigh, V. 2018. "Stalling life expectancy in the UK". *British Medical Journal* 362: k4050.

Raulff, U. 2017. *Farewell to the Horse: The Final Century of Our Relationship*. London: Allen Lane.

Rayle, L. *et al.* 2016. "Just a better taxi? A survey-based comparison of taxis, transit and ridesourcing services in San Francisco". *Transport Policy* 45: 168–78.

Rincon-Garcia, N., B. Waterson & T. Cherrett 2017. "Requirements from vehicle routing software: perspectives from literature, developers and the freight industry". *Transport Reviews* 38: 117–38.

Schafer, A. & D. Victor 2000. "The future mobility of the world population". *Transportation Research Part A* 34 (3): 171–205.

Schwieterman, J., M. Livingston & S. Van Der Slot 2018. *Partnerships in Transit: A Review of Partnerships between Transport Network Companies and Public Agencies in the United States*. Chaddick Institute for Metropolitan Development, De Paul University, Chicago.

Shladover, S. 2018. "Connected and automated vehicle systems: introduction and overview". *Journal of Intelligent Transportation Systems* 22 (3): 190–200.

Service, R. 2018a. "Lithium-sulfur batteries poised for a leap". *Science* 359: 1080–81.

Service, R. 2018b. "Liquid sunshine". *Science* 361: 120–3.

Shaheen, S. 2018. "Shared mobility: the potential of ridehailing and pooling". In *Three Revolutions: Steering Automatic, Shared and Electric Vehicles to a Better Future*, D. Sperling (ed.). Washington, DC: Island Press.

Shoup, D. 2018. *Parking and the City*. New York: Routledge.

Sivak, M. & B. Schoettle 2017. *Mortality from Road Crashes in 183 Countries: Comparison with Leading Causes of Death*. Report SWT-2017-14. Ann Arbor, MI: University of Michigan Sustainable Worldwide Transportation.

Sivak, M. 2018. *Has Motorisation in the US Peaked? Part 10. Vehicle Ownership and Distance Driven, 1984–2016*. Report SWT 2018-2. Ann Arbor, MI: University of Michigan Sustainable Worldwide Transportation.

Small, K. 2012. "Valuing travel time". *Economics of Transportation* 1(1–2): 2–14.

Smith, R. *et al.* 2017. "Impact of London's road traffic air and noise pollution on birth weight: retrospective population based cohort study". *British Medical Journal* 359: j5299.

Sperling, D. 2018a. "Electric vehicles: approaching the tipping point". In *Three Revolutions: Steering Automatic, Shared and Electric Vehicles to a Better Future*, D. Sperling (ed.). Washington, DC: Island Press.

Sperling, D. 2018b. "Pooling is the answer". In *Three Revolutions: Steering Automatic, Shared and Electric Vehicles to a Better Future*, D. Sperling (ed.). Washington, DC: Island Press.

Stapleton, L., S. Sorrell & T. Schwanen 2017. "Peak car and increasing rebound: a closer look at car travel trends in Great Britain". *Transportation Research Part D* 53: 217–33.

Steg, L. 2005. "Car use: lust and must. Instrumental, symbolic and affective motives for car use". *Transportation Research Part A* 39(2–3): 147–62.

Stokes, G. 2013. "The prospects for future levels of car access and use". *Transport Reviews*, 33 (3): 360–75.

Stopher, P., A. Ahmed & W. Liu 2017. "Travel time budgets: new evidence from multi-year, multi-day data". *Transportation* 44 (5): 1069–82.

Thaler, R. 2018. "Nudge, not sludge". *Science* 361: 431.

Turcheniuk, K. *et al.* 2018. "Ten years left to redesign lithium-ion batteries". *Nature* 559: 467–70.

van Vuren, T. *et al.* 2012. "Managed motorways: modelling and monitoring their effectiveness". *Transportation Research Record* 2278: 85–94.

Verma, S. 2014. "Customer technology: the ticket to greater mobility". In *Moving Cities: The Future of Urban Travel*, S. Glaister & E. Box (eds). London: RAC Foundation.

Wadud, Z. & M. Baiert, 2017. "Explaining 'peak car' with economic variables a comment". *Transportation Research Part A* 95: 381–5.

Watkins, K. *et al.* 2011. "Where is my bus? Impact of mobile real-time information on the perceived and actual waiting times of transit riders". *Transportation Research Part A* 45(8): 839–48.

Wolmar, C. 2018. *Driverless Cars: On a Road to Nowhere*. London: London Publishing Partnership.

Woodard, D. *et al.* 2017. "Predicting travel time reliability using mobile phone GPS data". *Transportation Research Part C* 75: 30–44.

Xu, Y. & M. Gonzalez 2017. "Collective benefits in traffic during mega events via the use of information technologies". *Journal of the Royal Society Interface* 14: 20161041.

INDEX